THE SURROGATE MOTHER

"Science is not the highest value. We must consider the implicit danger to man's right to life of discoveries in the field of artificial insemination, birth and fertility control, and genetic engineering."
—*Pope John Paul II*
speaking to an audience of Italian physicians, October 27, 1980

"Science cannot stop while ethics catch up."
—*Elvin Stackman*
speaking as President of the American Association for Advancement of Science, January 9, 1950

The Surrogate Mother

by
NOEL P. KEANE
with
DENNIS L. BREO

New York **EVEREST HOUSE** *Publishers*

Library of Congress Cataloging in Publication Data:
Keane, Noel P., 1938–
   The surrogate mother.

   Includes index.
   1. Surrogate mothers. I. Breo, Dennis L., 1942–
II. Title.
HQ759.5.K4   1981   306.8   81-5495
ISBN: 0-89696-113-3   AACR2

dedication from Noel P. Keane

to some of the most important people in my life
MY WIFE, KATHY
who has been supportive in *most* of my endeavors
over the past fifteen years
MY SONS, CHRISTOPHER and DOUGLAS
who bring a tremendous amount of joy to me
and MARTHA
probably the best secretary in the world,
who has been a tremendous asset to me

dedication from Dennis L. Breo

TO MY SON, DAVID
who came to the world in the usual way
and who has been a constant delight

CONTENTS

ACKNOWLEDGMENTS

MOSTLY, our debt is to the adoptive parents and surrogate mothers, who willingly bared their souls so that others might know what they have gone through to have children and why they have done it. This book is their story, told to help others like them.

We want to thank Jerry Gross, our Everest House editor, and his assistant, Mike Cantalupo, for helping guide and shape the book and keeping the text on target. And our literary agents, Gayle Benderoff and Deborah Geltman, for having the foresight and persistence to get the project off the ground.

Special thanks to Martha Makridakis, who manages the law office, typed most of the interview transcripts and manuscript, and helps make order of this often-confusing business of the surrogate mother. Also, thanks to Nancy Malinowski who helped type the transcripts and manuscript.

Noel P. Keane
Dennis L. Breo

AUTHORS' NOTE

THE NAMES, places, and scenes of some of the people in this book have been changed, but these are true stories. What you read in these pages is what happened to the first people who made the surrogate mother not something out of science fiction but as real as a baby's yell. We hope it helps others, who may find themselves in the same situations.

INTRODUCTION
"Noel, you're onto something really big."

BEFORE the celebrity and the cause, there were simply people who needed help.

A woman sat across from my desk and cried. That's how it started, my strange career as the legal champion of "surrogate mothers," a revolutionary new source of hope for infertile couples.

The woman had been everywhere and tried everything, but nothing had changed. She was now thirty-eight, her husband thirty-six, and still, the experts told her, they could not have children. She cried and he squirmed, and they asked for help in curing their infertility.

Incredibly, though, they not only asked for help, but they also had an idea, an idea that at the time I thought very weird.

We'll call them Tom and Jane. They had been married eleven years, and they were living a life of agony. This was their last chance for happiness. They asked me this question:

"Can you help us find a very rare woman? A woman who will legally agree—perhaps for a fee, perhaps for medical expenses only—to be artificially inseminated with Tom's sperm, conceive and carry a child, give birth, and surrender the child for adoption?"

I did not believe it possible then, but I tried. We did find such a woman and today, Tom and Jane have a life enriched by Tommy Jr., their adopted child born to surrogate mother Carol.

At that time, we had never heard of the term "surrogate mother." The news media would later force that phrase upon us. We found Carol through a classified newspaper ad asking for a "female donor for test-tube baby." We placed a newspaper ad because that was the way it had been done in the past. It was the only precedent we had ever heard about, a precedent that occurred in, where else but, California.

That was five years ago. Today, that "weird" idea is the basis of a powerful new option that may replace adoption as the major hope for the infertile: the surrogate mother.

Surrogate parenting means finding a woman who will legally contract with a married couple to be artificially inseminated with the husband's sperm, conceive and carry a child, give birth, and surrender custody for adoption. Exactly what Tom and Jane and Carol did years ago to bring Tommy, Jr. into the world.

By the end of 1981, there will be about a hundred children born to surrogate mothers and adopted by others. Ordinary people, extraordinary births, brave new children. These are children who are truly wanted.

This book represents the first comprehensive look at surrogate parenting, its promise and potential perils. It fully discusses the dimensions of the controversy and outlines recommendation for state regulation of the phenomenon.

But, before we get into the issues, I want to share with you those early memories.

Jane was in pain, enormous pain. "People argue about abortion," she said, "but millions of people can't have children and nobody cares. I mean it's something many twelve-year-olds can do, right, and yet there are so many like me who can't get pregnant. And nobody really knows why. Whenever I see a pregnant woman in the street, I think of running her down with my car. It seems so unfair."

Once, perhaps, she might have adopted. But the pill and abortion have changed that. There are very few babies to adopt. The only way Tom was about to have a baby, it seemed, was if he divorced Jane and found a new partner. Yet when you looked at Tom and Jane and saw how they loved each other, you knew this was not what they wanted.

Their struggle to conceive a child had shaken their marriage to its foundation, but the marriage held. Jane's confidence in her sexuality and self-image had been undermined. They thought they would never realize their dream of having a baby, but a rare woman—surrogate mother Carol—made it come true.

The ability to help people like Tom and Jane is what sustains me when the going gets rough—when the people in my parish tell me, "What you're doing is immoral," or when the editorial writers scoff, "Rent-a-womb."

Says Jane today: "Carol has become one of my closest friends. It's not that we see each other that much, but she will always know that if she needs something, we will be there." Says Carol: "There's a friendship there, a bond that will never be broken." Says Tom: "I would not have thought there was such a woman out there. What she did for us is the deepest gift anyone can ever give."

Carol carried Tom's baby for Tom and Jane out of love. She was not paid a fee and she never entered into a legal contract. Neither was necessary. Their experience started what has become a movement. Some things have changed from that time, though. Now most people pay fees and almost all sign contracts. The basic elements of the surrogate mother situation, however, remain the same.

Despair. One of every six American couples is infertile. That's roughly twenty million Americans unable to bring a child into the world. And those who want children but cannot have them are often desperate. There are thousands of people out there like Tom and Jane; the question they ask is whether there are other people out there to help them like Carol helped Tom and Jane. My answer is yes.

Weirdness. The first time you hear about surrogate mothers, it sounds weird, way out, and strange. But the more you think about it, the more you realize that it has to be the only answer for certain people who cannot have children.

Hope. The surrogate mother option offers hope where once there was only aching desperation. It is no longer a curiosity. It is, in fact, becoming somewhat common. As I said, there will be by the end of 1981 about a hundred children born to surrogate mothers and adopted by others. These births represent my clients and those of Richard Levin, M.D., a Kentucky physician who started Surrogate Parenting Associates, Inc. three years after I began work in this new field with Tom and Jane.

Controversy. Along the way, of course, surrogate parenting has been followed intensely by the news media and, as a result, has stirred a storm of controversy—legal, medical, religious and moral. As the attorney who represented the first people to pursue surrogate parenting, I have found myself in the thick of that controversy, which can only increase in the years ahead.

But as we proceed with the story, try to understand why I got started in this new field of law. Because it is really very simple. Desperate people came to me in pain with their problems and I decided to try to help.

Our potential clients are the 15 percent of the population who cannot have children. Those who want to take life can turn to abortion. Those unfortunate people who want to create life yet cannot do not have such a simple solution. The waiting list to adopt is often seven years or more, and even then there is no guarantee that a child will be available. Surrogate mothers provide another source of children for the infertile.

Many infertile couples, it is true, have decided they can live quite well without children. And with many of these couples, the problem is male infertility, for which there is a simple solution—

artificial insemination (AI). But for *most* of these couples, the problem is a barren woman who desperately wants to have children, for herself and for her mate.

So they sit in my law office and they ask about this thing they've heard about called "surrogate mothers." For these couples, every day is one long ache of emptiness. They express their disappointment in many ways, but they do not want to accept it. They cling to their dream. And they ask for help to make that dream come true—their dream of having a baby. They ask if surrogate motherhood can possibly be *their* solution? Am I, one even asked, her savior?

At the time I first heard this request, I had never even done as much as an adoption. Today, I find myself the expert in what is a virgin legal frontier. There is not one law on surrogate mothers. Period. Those of us who started this movement five years ago are exploring a frontier where no one has ever ventured before. In this book, you will hear the pioneers, speaking in their own voices and describing a journey that has been both pleasure and pain. They are telling their stories in the hope that others like them will be helped. That is the purpose of this book.

Surrogate parenting is an idea whose time is coming, not only for infertile married couples but also for single men and women who want to have children without romantic entanglements.

There is a simple reason why people prefer finding a surrogate mother to adopting: the child will bear the genetic imprint of the man. Thus, couples composed of an infertile woman and a fertile man can, through AI and a surrogate mother, have a biological connection, just as couples with an infertile man can, through AI, have a biological connection through the fertile woman. People want this blood tie.

For those married couples who want children but cannot have them, there is now new hope. Surrogate mothers will become as accepted and as common a solution for the barren wife as sperm banks have become a solution for the sterile husband in the past.

Beyond that, of course, is the dramatic option the surrogate mother offers to single men who want children without marriage. It will do for single men what artificial insemination now does for single women. In the most controversial of this type of case, we anticipate requests from gay men who want to raise children.

Although our greatest demand comes from couples whose infertility is due to the woman and from single men, the requests for surrogate mothers covers the entire range of possibilities.

For example, I have been sought out both by barren single women and by fertile single women. Those single women who are barren see surrogate motherhood as their only hope. And some single women who can have children choose not to for a variety of reasons: some because their religious beliefs will not let them be pregnant and unwed; others because a pregnancy would interfere with their career plans. These women see the surrogate mother as their best option.

Obviously, there is a demand for the surrogate mother. But how about the supply? Why would a woman want to become a surrogate mother? There are many reasons.

Money, of course, is one. We are paying many of our surrogate mothers $10,000, which we think is a reasonable fee for the time and hardship of pregnancy. In Michigan, however, where I practice law, the payment of a fee to a surrogate mother is currently illegal if there is to be an adoption. So most of my cases so far have involved volunteer surrogate mothers, women who have done it simply for medical expenses. The exceptions have been single men, who, of course, are already the child's father and therefore do not need to adopt.

Like Michigan, most states have laws barring a fee. This is to prevent "black-market babies," a horror holdover from earlier days when most adoption laws were written. An exception, however, is Kentucky, whose laws do not encourage the payment of a fee to a surrogate mother but do not prohibit it. So for those of my clients who wish to pay a fee or who can only find a surrogate mother by paying, we have a procedure to meet Kentucky residency requirements, which may or may not be required for the adoption. And, of course, Dr. Levin's clinic for surrogate parents is located in Kentucky, a circumstance that also allows his clients to pay a fee.

Recently, Kentucky Attorney General Steven L. Beshear issued an advisory opinion holding that paid surrogate parenting is illegal in Kentucky, as well. This opinion, which is not binding, will be tested in Franklin County (Kentucky) Circuit Court and will probably take years. In the meantime, we are proceeding as usual with the payment of a fee to surrogate mothers. In the handbook section on surrogate parenting, I will explain in detail why the existing Kentucky law allows a fee to be paid and how adoptive parents must proceed.

Money, however, is not the only reason. Women are volunteering to be surrogate mothers—without a fee—for all the reasons women want to have babies. Among my early clients, one did it out of sincere love for a friend, another as a private protest against abortion, a third to have the experience of giving birth.

With surrogate mothers, we are talking about giving life. Those who want to deny life can practice contraception or obtain an abortion. Previously, barren couples and single people have had few places to turn. Now, for the first time, the childless have the opportunity of hiring a surrogate mother.

Current procedures can vary widely. Adoptive couples can pay anywhere from $30,000 to bare medical expenses. They can either contract with a surrogate mother in strict anonymity or they can make her almost another member of the family. The artificial insemination can be performed by a physician, by the surrogate, or, as has happened in several of my cases, by the adoptive mother. It is really up to the people involved. Every case I have worked with has been unique to the people involved.

Today we are moving toward institutionalizing the procedures, toward implementing a process that will assure the optimal well-being of everyone involved. I am trying to achieve this protection as soon as possible, consistent with proper safeguards. The ultimate answers, of course, will be found in litigation and legislation.

In the future, surrogate parenting should be regulated by the state. Programs can be administered through existing adoption agencies.

We are years away, but it is coming. There are three major procedures that must first be established:

- ✓ Allow the payment of a reasonable fee to the surrogate mother for her services.
- ✓ Create binding agreements between surrogate mothers and adoptive couples that will stand up in court.
- ✓ Establish screening procedures that will assure the medical and psychiatric health of the people, their competance to carry out the contract, and their ability to give the child a proper home.

Let's look at each one a little more carefully.

Payment of a fee will assure an ample supply of surrogate mothers, though most of those with whom I have worked so far preferred not to be paid anything but medical expenses. I have filed a lawsuit in Wayne County (Michigan) to make the payment of a fee to surrogate mothers legal and plan to pursue this landmark litigation all the way to the U.S. Supreme Court, if necessary.

Let me explain what we are after with our lawsuit:

The Michigan adoption laws are in two basic parts, both designed to discourage "baby-selling." One part disallows direct adoption unless the adopting parties are related within the third degree of consanguinity, which would bring the blood relationship down through cousins. This law means that all adoptions in Michigan must go through social agencies. Private adoptions are outlawed unless there is a blood relationship. This rule was enacted five years ago—right before I became involved with surrogate mothers—to prevent people from going out and "making their own deals" to adopt children born to others.

However, up until five years ago, direct (private) adoptions were allowed in Michigan. This is why the second part of the Michigan adoption law has been on the books for years. The second part prohibits the payment of anything but medical expenses to a woman whose baby is being placed for adoption. Its purpose is to prohibit any undue influence on her.

The surrogate-mother arrangement has to work within the context of this Michigan law, which is similar to laws in many other states.

The first part of the law is met because, as a result of employing artificial insemination, the husband of the adoptive couple is already the father. This blood relationship qualifies the couple for direct adoption; all that remains is for the wife to adopt. This procedure takes only months, not the many years required for an agency adoption.

The second part of the law, I believe, should not apply to the surrogate-mother arrangement. Critics say the adoptive parents are "buying half a baby," but I argue that the constitutional right to privacy overrides any state interest in preventing the legal payment of a fee from people who want to adopt through AI and the use of a surrogate mother.

Binding agreements will assure that the people seeking children will know that if they enter into an agreement and if their surrogate mother becomes pregnant, they will get their child but that, at the same time, they are bound to accept and adequately care for the child, even if the child is retarded or deformed. This will require legislation and state regulation, which is the long-term goal for surrogate parenting. In the meantime, the big fear is that the surrogate mother can at any time and for any reason change her mind and keep the child. Legally, she could probably do this and perhaps even compel the father to pay child support. If this eventuality ever comes up—and I represent one case where it very well might—it will have to be settled in court and then codified into legislation.

Screening protocols will assure that both people seeking children and the surrogate mothers are competent, healthy, and otherwise acting in the best interests of the children they will be creating. Certainly, the surrogate mothers should be screened medically and psychiatrically to determine that their motivation is positive and their medical condition healthy. Those applying for children should consent to home studies to assure that they can afford and are fit to raise a child. In the past, I have, for legal reasons, used my office as a clearing house, done the preliminary screening, and then allowed the people seeking children and those wishing to be surrogate mothers to choose each other. Some people prefer total anonymity between applicant and surrogate, but on balance most people want to know the people with whom they are about to become so intimately involved quite well. In our early work, we had some cases that read like soap operas. The screening process simply broke down and some people were allowed to be surrogate mothers who upon hindsight might better have been rejected. For the future, we will need screening safeguards that will assure safety within the limits of human nature.

When these three major goals are accomplished, you can anticipate a rush to surrogate motherhood. Already thousands of couples have besieged my office with requests to enter surrogate parenting. There are those, though, who do not like the idea of surrogate mothers one bit.

One is Pope John Paul II. In a major speech last year to Italian physicians, the Pontiff warned of ethical dangers posed by artificial insemination, birth and fertility controls, and genetic experimentation. He attacked the harmful effects of progress "that cares more for itself than for man whom it must serve," and warned, "Scientific progress cannot pretend to place itself in a sort of neutral ground."

Now, I am Catholic, my wife, Kathy, is Catholic, and our two sons, Chris and Doug, are Catholic. We go to a Catholic church and our children go to a Catholic school. Ironically, my parish is named Our Lady of the Divine Child. And most of the people you will meet in these pages, the first surrogate mothers and adoptive parents, are Catholic.

My reaction to the Pope is well represented in a recent *New York Times* editorial responding to some of the Pontiff's other concerns.

"For a million years," the editorial writer noted, "mankind has progressed by learning to master nature in one aspect or another. Are we now to draw a line and say, 'No farther'?"

The emergence of the surrogate mother is coinciding with what well may become a revolution in child-rearing. Children are being conceived in clinics. Surrogate parenting is an important part of this emerging revolution, along with test-tube fertilizations, embryo-transfer procedures, improved methods of artificial insemination, and sperm-splitting and sex-selection. More importantly, there is a trend toward single parenthood by choice, not circumstances. This includes the millions of homosexual male and female Americans.

It will not happen overnight. In 1978, there were 3.5 million births in the United States and almost all were under traditional circumstances. As I will describe later in detail, three of those births were to surrogate mothers obtained by clients of mine. Certainly, a modest beginning.

Also in 1978 there was the birth of the first test-tube child, Baby Louise. She was conceived in a Petri dish by doctors who took the mother's egg, mixed it with the father's sperm, produced an embryo, implanted it in the mother's womb, and, nine months later, delivered a baby girl. But in the past three years, Baby Louise has been joined in the exclusive *in vitro,* or test-tube fertilization, club, by only three others—Baby Candace in Australia, another child in England, and an unconfirmed birth in India. This country's first test-tube clinic opened March 1, 1980 (for married couples only and with strict requirements) in Norfolk, Virginia, but there still have been no pregnancies. Scientists know they can make life in a dish, but they admit they do not know why it works in some cases and not in others. In their first seventy-nine attempts, the British physicians succeeded only twice.

The most uncertain of the new reproductive technology is artificial embryonation—the transferring of a fertilized egg from one woman to another. At the Reproductive and Fertility Clinic in Chicago, Drs. Randolph and Richard Seed attempted the flushing of the womb with a catheter to recover a fertilized egg from donors who are artificially inseminated with sperm from men whose wives are barren. The physicians working in the field have recovered just a handful of eggs—only one of which was fertilized—and they are not yet ready to attempt a transfer.

The simplest of all the alternative forms of conception remains artificial insemination, which requires only a woman, a syringe, and some sperm. The procedure, begun eighty years ago and for years the focal point of intense controversy and opposition on moral grounds, is today an accepted medical procedure. Each year, it produces 20,000 babies who would not otherwise be born.

In a controversial form of artifical insemination, some scientists are now perfecting methods to split the male sperm to obtain an abundance of male-carrying Y chromosomes. Such sperm, enhanced to 92 percent male-carrying chromosomes, has been up to 90 percent successful in producing a boy. Some people prefer to have a son, usually couples who already have daughters. But again, only a few pioneers—including my clients—have as yet experimented with these sex-selection procedures.

Recently, I have been approached by several single men and women who want children without having to get married or become romantically involved with the opposite sex. In one case, we are seeking a surrogate mother for a single man, and plan to have the man's sperm split in a laboratory procedure to enhance the male-carrying Y chromosomes, artificially inseminate the surrogate mother, and produce a most controversial pregnancy. Single women are coming to me and asking if can they not only be artificially inseminated but is there some way to preselect the male donor to assure "prize" sperm? On the horizon, it appears, are requests from gay people to find surrogates by whom they can have children.

I have been approached by all kinds of childless people who are willing—desperate, usually—to attempt any or all of these new fertility procedures. For the present, however, most of my work is with infertile married couples. I tell them that their most promising prospect is the surrogate mother method.

Now I know that surrogate motherhood is the last taboo in the fertility field. I have chosen to break this taboo because of a very strong and straightforward bias. I believe that children fulfill one's self in a way that nothing else can ever equal. My two sons have united Kathy and I in a joint responsibility to provide them with a good home and a good life. I would never have had the imagination to think of a surrogate mother on my own, but knowing what I do now and knowing how important to me my children are, I know exactly what I would do if fate had left Kathy and I childless: look for a surrogate mother immediately. And since I believe so strongly in children myself, I feel that any qualified couple or individual who wants a child should be able to have one, as long as they are not breaking a law or harming anyone else.

From the start, the experts tried to warn us off. The attorneys wouldn't help because there were no case laws; the doctors wouldn't help because there was no malpractice insurance; the sociologists wouldn't help because there were no bureaucratic guidelines. I have never been bound by expert advice. I once had a high school counselor who urged me to learn a trade because, as he put it, "You simply are not college material." Thank God I never listened to him.

I tend to have a very independent turn of mind and have never been afraid to take on controversial or unpopular causes—if I believe in them. I believe in surrogate motherhood because I know there are thousands of people who want it and need it, including the surrogate mothers. I intend to help them. That's how I got into this and that's why I'm staying.

As I said, in 1978 there were 3.5 million births in America. Three of the 3.5 million were decidedly unique. These were the first three children born to surrogate mothers who were acting as agents of adoptive couples. I represented these nine people and am proud to say that we produced three beautiful babies—two boys and a girl—three proud sets of parents, and two proud surrogate mothers. Unfortunately, we also had one surrogate mother who turned out to be less than ideal, but we had a happy ending anway. I will tell you about them in this book.

In subsequent years, I would find surrogate parenting a startling new aspect of my law practice, one that has become increasingly popular and complicated. The news media followed our every move, and I will also describe in detail the twists and turns I had to take to pursue my cause.

But it is the early memories that stay in my heart and mind. If you have not been there, if you have not wanted children or had no problem in having your own, then you cannot presume to know what drives these childless people.

Understand this need, for this book is my legal brief on behalf of a controversial cause to make surrogate motherhood a common reality in the years ahead. I think it will replace adoption.

It was only years later before I would first get a glimmer of the magnitude of surrogate parenting. It happened while I was visiting with (now retired) Judge James Lincoln of the Wayne County (Michigan) Juvenile Adoption Court. I was simply a maverick attorney trying to learn on the job about a strange new area of law practice. I picked Judge Lincoln's brains about this "thing" called surrogate motherhood.

"Noel," he told me. "You know, I'm going to be retiring soon, but I have to tell you that only once or twice in my entire legal career have I had the feeling that I was involved in something very, very big. It has to do with being in a certain place in a certain time. I think this surrogate motherhood thing you're working on is going to have an impact you cannot today even begin to imagine.

"You're onto something really big."

But now let me tell you more about Jane, the woman who sat across from my desk and cried.

THE SURROGATE MOTHER

·1·

"Is our malpractice insurance paid up? I'm about to do something different!"

SHEER coincidence. That's how it started. Tom and Jane came to me in September 1976 with their unusual request. They wanted to have a child by artificially inseminating another woman with Tom's sperm. How would they go about it?

They were desperate. I was confused. But somehow we made it happen.

Tom and Jane are from a small Michigan town, and Tom's sister is a friend of my sister Maureen. By the fall of 1976, Tom was thirty-six and Jane thirty-eight and they were beginning to despair of realizing their lifelong dream—having a baby.

Tom, a Moslem from Lebanon and the oldest boy in a family of ten, had met Jane, a soft-spoken "Army brat" and only child, while serving at a military post in the Deep South. Tom came from a culture where children are highly prized as a symbol of manhood, and Jane had wanted children "ever since I was a little girl and used to play with dolls." But fate decreed otherwise. Two tubal pregnancies had ravaged Jane's Fallopian tubes and doctors had told her she would never have a baby. Adoption agencies held out little hope—the wait was at least seven years.

My sister Maureen owns a candy store in Detroit's Renaissance Center, and one day Tom's sister Betty stopped by to chat. In the course of a routine conversation, she casually referred to "poor Tom and Jane" and how Tom "has this harebrained idea of finding another woman to carry a child for them. But he doesn't have the slightest idea of how to go about it. He seems to think he'll need an attorney. What a long shot!"

Maureen responded, "Well, you know, my brother Noel is an attorney here in Dearborn. Maybe Tom and Jane should look him up. I'm sure he'll talk to you, anyway."

And so began my involvement with surrogate mothers.

I spent an hour with Tom and Jane that first time, but the uniqueness of what they were after hit me in the first five minutes or so. As they described their infertility problem, I thought to myself: "I don't know what the hell you are talking about and I don't know how in the hell I am ever going to be able to help you."

But I didn't say that to them. I listened very patiently to what was a sad story. Tom is a handsome man, with dark curly hair and strong features. His manner is quiet and solid, the strong silent type. Jane is a very open and friendly person with light brown hair and brown eyes that sparkle with love and warmth. In many ways, they are your Everyday Happily Married Couple. Only one thing was missing: a child.

They were married in 1965 and by 1971 Jane had received the bad news. She told me, "Before we were married, an ovarian cyst ruptured on one side so I only had the one ovary. Now, I could conceive but I just couldn't seem to get the egg down where it belonged. Twice, I had tubal pregnancies and after the second one things became dangerous. My Fallopian tube was getting shorter and shorter.

"In the meantime, I began talking to a local adoption agency just in case. I knew that Tom was reluctant, but he seemed to be going along and we had interviews with the social worker and talked a great deal about it and I thought everything was going fine. In fact, by 1971, we were only about a year away from the home study and getting our baby through adoption. To me, it seemed like it was adoption or nothing and I was all for it. But when the day came to say 'go' or 'no go,' Tom said 'no.' I was shattered.

"Tom told me that having children was not all that important to him, that he was content to live our lives out without them. But I wasn't ready to let go. I decided I would go back to my doctor one more time and find out if there were any hope at all for me to carry a child. I made up my mind that this would be the final word on it. Well, the doctor performed minor surgery, made a tiny incision and inserted a periscope, and checked me out. His conclusion: 'Give up.'

"Frantic with unhappiness, I persuaded Tom to talk to the adoption agencies again. But having backed out once, we now faced a seven-year wait or so. Then came a long period of my trying to mentally adjust to not having any children. I had given up. Tom was still dead set against adoption.

"It was a very, very difficult time for me. In my opinion, it's really the only trial our marriage has ever had. It was just a shattering thing to me. For years we would have these deep discussions and every time I would bring up adoption, Tom would counter with this crazy idea about finding someone else to be artificially inseminated. I thought it was just an excuse, that every time I would say 'adoption,' he would dig up this bone. It was driving me crazy. So I decided to call his bluff. I told him, 'Look, let's either do it or quit talking about it.' It was like going to the doctor to find out if I could possibly have children. One way or the other, I had to know.

"That's why we're here."

I turned to Tom, who had been looking on with somewhat of a pained expression.

"Maybe it's egotistical," Tom said, "but I want my own child.

Adoption leaves me cold. I guess for some women, as long as they have a child, it's fine. But for me, it's like if I see my child do something, I need to know that he's really mine. Like I say, maybe it's egotistical.

"I've had this idea for a long time. Jane and I met while I was in the service and the Vietnam War was on. I knew that a lot of our people were getting killed over there and it seemed like a simple enough idea to help somebody out. I never really thought it out too well, but it seemed that, say, if a woman had a couple of children and her husband was killed in the war, and, say, she needed a few extra dollars for the family, well, then maybe she could help somebody out who couldn't have children. The Lord intended women to have children and I thought maybe one would want to do what came naturally and maybe help somebody else out while helping herself and her family. I knew that artificial insemination was an approved procedure and I thought maybe this was our answer. Like I say, it's just a fly-by-night idea I had.

"But the more I thought about it, the more I began to think, why not? But I didn't know how to go about it. I talked to a friend of mine who's a doctor and he said, sure, technically it can be done. I talked to another friend who's an attorney and he said, sure, it's fine. If you can find a woman who'd agree to it. My idea was to do it anonymously. I mean I didn't want to know her or her us. That's why I was talking to an attorney. If I didn't want anonymity, I wouldn't need an attorney. I could just go out and look for a woman."

Jane cut in, "We need somebody to find our mother for us. That's the whole problem. The idea has been his from the start and it seems impossible, but I want to settle it one way or another."

Then Jane recalled, "A few months ago, I was working part-time for Kelly Girls and I had taken an assignment with a law firm. Well, after I got to know the attorney fairly well, I decided to try Tom's idea out on him. It had been stewing within me for a while. So one day I asked him if I could talk with him when he wasn't busy and a few days later I told him what Tom wanted to try to do. He said he'd think about it and he set up an appointment for Tom and me a few weeks later.

"We came in after hours and as I listened to what he had dreamed up, I could only think of one word, 'Unreal.' He wanted to have Tom's sperm frozen, take it over to Lebanon, find a surrogate, have her inseminated, come back, and then, when it was time for birth, go back to Lebanon, pick up the child, and bring him or her back to us in Michigan. He had been to Lebanon before and really liked it. He said he would do this for us for $15,000 or so. Of course, he would have to stay over there a month or two each time to make sure things worked out. We told him as politely as possible we just didn't have that kind of money."

Tom added, "He just wanted a vacation in Lebanon. Period."

We all looked at each other in silence. I had no idea what to tell these people. Jane was crying, Tom was uncomfortable. I certainly didn't want to try to get their hopes up, but I wanted to let them know I cared. They were good people—that was obvious—and they sincerely wanted a child.

I stared out my window at the Detroit skyline and down below to where an artificial pond dominated the center of our office complex. A young boy wrestling with a fishing pole reminded me that it was Saturday and I had to leave to watch my son's football game. I told them the only thing I could: "I will look into the situation and get back to you."

During the conversation, the words "surrogate mother" never came up. Tom and Jane had the concept, but they didn't use the phrase. I routinely dictated for the files, "Tom and Jane have requested legal help in having a baby by finding a woman who will agree to be artificially inseminated with Tom's sperm and to surrender the child for adoption."

Months flew by and I was busy with other things, but the idea was always in the back of my mind. I couldn't help but muse over the ironies in the American outlook on children. Half the people will do anything to have children and the other half will do anything not to have to have them. Mother Nature, unfortunately, has quite often bestowed fertility on the wrong half.

Each month, millions of American women faithfully take their oral contraceptives—"The Pill"—to prevent unwanted pregnancies. More than one million American men have had vasectomies, a virtually irreversible procedure, to accomplish the same thing. There are 5.5 million American women who have been sterilized by any number of methods. Planned Parenthood groups lobby to assure that facilities—and funds—are available for legal abortions.

At the same time, millions of women and their mates head off each month for fertility clinics, where they will laboriously try medications, surgery, and meticulous procedures to try to outwit nature. Millions will go to adoption agencies, where they will usually be told they must wait five to seven years—or longer—to be considered for a child, and even then there is no guarantee that the child they want will be there. Pro-life groups lobby vigorously to make abortion illegal or, failing that, to make sure it is not paid for by public funds.

I knew people who represented all these extremes and I knew that having a baby stirs up people's strongest emotions. But I had never heard anyone suggest what Tom and Jane had in mind, and I still had absolutely no idea what, if anything, I could do about it.

One day, I had spent an afternoon browsing through the law library and I found nothing in Michigan law that would prevent such a scenario from happening. Or, to be more accurate, I found nothing in the law that even remotely applied to their suggestion. There were simply no laws about it.

The law was no help, but the newspapers were. Right after Thanksgiving, Tom and Jane returned from visiting their folks— hers down South and his in Michigan—and found a surprise: a wire service story published in the *Detroit Free Press* under the headline, CALIFORNIA FATHER IS PROUD OF HIS TEST-TUBE BABY. My wife Kathy, who manages a beauty salon in the Dearborn Tower office building where I have my office, and with whom I share all my work problems, had brought the same article to my attention.

With the terse style typical of the wire services, the first paragraph read; "A man who advertised last year for a 'test-tube' mother to bear his child through artificial insemination is now the proud father of a baby girl."

The man had advertised in the *San Francisco Chronicle* and after his daughter had been born and given to him, he in gratitude to the paper agreed to talk to a *Chronicle* reporter on the condition that he and the mother remain anonymous. That story, as subsequently picked up by the wire services, said the man was the last of his family line and that he wanted a child—his child—to carry on the family name. But his wife was barren. The story went on:

"He chose artificial insemination because he said it would be immoral for him to have a sexual relationship outside of marriage to father a child. He also ruled out adoption because he wanted a child that was biologically his."

Stunned at the eerie parallels to what Tom and Jane had been suggesting, I read on to learn that the California man had paid $7,000 to the mother and another $3,000 in legal and medical expenses. He had selected the mother from among 160 responses to a tiny classified ad. They had poured in from eighteen states, Canada, England, New Zealand, Australia, Kenya, and even one from Bangladesh.

The mother had been chosen in December 1975, and the man took a sample of his sperm to the office of a San Francisco-area physician. He left, the mother arrived, and she was inseminated with the sperm. "It took the first time," the man told the newspaper. The story continued, "The baby, a five-pound, six-ounce girl with red hair and blue eyes was born September 6th (1976). Minor medical problems cropped up at first, but she is at home now and doing well."

By God, I thought, this baby was born three weeks before Tom and Jane first came to my office.

One other section of the story caught my attention. "The couple won't reveal their names," it said, "because the idea of a test-tube birth exists in a 'sort of legal vacuum.' The man's lawyer could find no legal precedent for such a procedure. 'It isn't bizarre when you think about it,' the lawyer said. 'It is exactly equivalent to artificial insemination of women by anonymous donors, a standard practice when a husband has an insufficient sperm count.' "

The legal void had been bridged by a lawyer, the insemination had been performed by a physician. How about the people themselves, I wondered. Did things all work out for them?

The news story answered those questions, too: "The man said his wife was 'a bit dubious' at first, but she loves that baby now like it was her own." He described the mother as an "an angel in human form, taking pity on a forlorn and helpless man." The natural mother told her boss and co-workers what she was doing. Her boss at first reacted with, "That kind of thing isn't going on in my office," as though there were sexual pleasure involved, the man's lawyer said. He changed his mind when the mother argued that she was doing something morally positive. As for the father, "he still thinks about having a son, too. 'I can't afford it right now', he said, 'but I may try again.' "

The story stirred only minor interest in the Detroit area, but There were three of us who read it with near disbelief: Tom, Jane and myself. Within a few weeks, Tom and Jane were back in my office. Tom told me he felt like a "a prophet without honor."

I showed him another news clipping that had subsequently come to my attention. It was a description of the same event, as reported in a trade newspaper, *The Obstetrics/Gynecology News*.

This story was based on an interview with the physician who performed the insemintion, Harris F. Simonds, M.D. of San Rafael, California. Its headline was my first encounter with a phrase I would come to know like my middle name. The headline read, 'SURROGATE MOTHER' IS RECRUITED BY AD FOR ARTIFICIAL INSEMINATION.

The story began, "Artificial insemination of a 'surrogate mother,' possibly the first such procedure ever performed, has resulted in the woman's pregnancy. . . ."

This is a medical newspaper directed to physicians specializing in obstetrics and gynecology and Dr. Simonds, an obstetrician, quickly summed up the event: "The technical phase," he said, "depositing the sperm at the right time was simple. The ethical, legal, and logistic aspects of the problem were more complicated."

The story included a reproduction of the classified ad that had run April 14–15, 1975, and that produced a pregnant surrogate mother by the end of the year. It was the *San Francisco Chronicle*'s Want Ads #30—Personals—and it ran right above #31—Business Notices, which was a call to "unmarried adults to join the Singles Hobby Society." The seven-line ad in agate type read, "Childless husband with infertile wife wants test-tube baby. English or Northwestern European background. Indicate fee and age. All answers confidential. Write this paper. Ad No. 16297."

We learned that the father-to-be, "Mr. X," was overwhelmed by the response to his plea. Over a period of years, he had asked dozens of medical specialists, including physicians in Denmark and Sweden, for help in selecting and artificially inseminating a surrogate mother and they had all told him it was "quite impossible." And now this. "Mr. X" concluded, "I truthfully didn't dream that such a reservoir of willingness to help a stranger in need, at one's own expense, could be found in the world. From that standpoint alone, it has been a wonderful and enlightening experience for me."

We learned that Dr. Simonds had proceeded carefully and patiently before performing the insemination. He first required an interview with "Mr. X" and found "his reasons for wanting the baby were valid. I then talked with other physicians. Nobody was worried about ethics; they warned about legal aspects. I requested a letter from Mrs. X's physician confirming she was infertile. I then agreed to help select the final candidate. Mr. X did not place the ad until he had my word that I would help in the selection process and perform the insemination. Based upon information submitted and telephone interviews, Mr. X narrowed the original 160 offers down to two candidates and I scheduled appointments for final interviews. The first one never showed up, but the second one was 'perfect.' She was fertile, healthy, the appropriate appearance, and a good age for childbirth. She appeared sensitive, intelligent, and psychologically able to give up the baby to Mr. and Mrs. X. She was engaged to a man who had had a vasectomy and she wanted the experience of having a baby. We decided to proceed, and determined the woman's ovulation time and arranged an appointment for insemination. The first appointment was cancelled by the woman because she was having 'second thoughts.' A second appointment was subsequently made and she was inseminated. Mr. X. had been advised by his attorney and it was his own intention not to be introduced to the woman who would carry his child. So I had to usher one in the front door and the other through the back door and be careful not to use the name of either party while working with the other. It was a hectic morning.

"I performed the insemination because there are enough unwanted children and children of poor genetic background in the world. I didn't see anything wrong with bringing one into the world who will be loved by parents who are prepared to provide a good home."

We learned that "Mr. X" 's attorney had drawn up a contract for the surrogate mother, that money for her had been placed in escrow, and that all that was required legally for the insemination was consent from the surrogate mother.

Line by line, the three of us, Tom and Jane and I, pored over the two stories and pondered the possibilities. What did it all mean? Would what worked in California play in Michigan? Should we proceed the same way? Did I really want to get involved?

We didn't decide anything that day. I told Tom and Jane I would have to think about it some more. They understood.

We were now in the midst of the Christmas holiday, and this

traditionally has been one of the happiest times of the year for our family. I still hadn't decided what to do about Tom and Jane's problem. Reaching a decision would require making some bedrock determinations about my own values.

I knew the church would be opposed. Now, in many ways, I'm a pretty old-fashioned guy. I'm probably one of the few people in the world with a tape collection of every song ever recorded by Bing Crosby and I still love to listen to them. My two sons are enrolled in a Catholic school and I wanted to keep them there.

But at the same time, I've never been one to bow to expert advice. I also tend to have a very independent turn of mind. That's because I had a strong father who wanted me to be a tradesman, as he had been, and I finally had to break away from him. I have never been afraid to take on controversial or unpopular causes and work hard for them if I believe in them. That comes from ten years of holding down jobs while going to college and law school. They used to call me "Mr. Red Eyes" at the Dearborn Police Department, where I worked the midnight booking shift while attending Eastern Michigan University by day and Henry Ford Junior College at night.

I was slowly building toward a decision. Since I believe so strongly in children myself, I thought, why should any qualified couple who want a child not be able to have one, as long as they are not breaking a law or harming anyone else? It seemed to me that wanting a child to love and care for is the farthest thing from evil, and that anyone who can say this is bad or wrong really does not understand the whole concept of love.

Tom and Jane were good people and I wanted to help them, if I could. After all, that was one reason why I got into law. So that I could help everyday people with everyday problems. I was just a poor kid from East Dearborn who had gotten a few breaks and was starting to make something of himself. Why not try to help somebody else?

I had never done as much as an adoption, but if they can do it in California, I thought, what the hell, we can do it here. The

California story presented a precedent. The man had advertised for a surrogate mother and he had paid her a fee. That was the way it had been done. That night, as Kathy and I were shopping for Christmas presents, I made up my mind. "Kathy", I said, "I'm going to try to find a woman to carry a baby for Tom and Jane. I don't know how it's going to work out, but we're going to go for it."

The next morning, I walked into the office and sat down for coffee with my partner, Charles V. Fellrath. Now, Chuck and I get along fine, but we are a real contrast in temperament and tradition. I'm the son of Irish immigrants who grew up in gritty circumstances. Chuck is from the other side of town—wealthy family, influential friends, the country club life. But he didn't bat an eyelash when I told him:

"Chuck, is our malpractice insurance paid up? I'm about to do something different!"

·2·
"Call us. We've already done it!"

EARLY the next year, I tried to place the ad. Tom and Jane and I sat down and worked on the wording. None of us really felt comfortable yet with the term "surrogate mother"; that was a phrase the news media would later make popular. We decided to follow the format of the California ad that had been published in the *San Francisco Chronicle.* After several attempts, we finally agreed on this:

> "Childless husband with infertile wife wants female donor for test-tube baby. Caucasian background, indicate fee and age. All answers confidential, make responses to Box 43, 1129 E. Parklane Towers, 1 Parklane, Dearborn MI 48126."

I called in my office manager, Martha Makridakis, and said, "Well, here it is. Here's what we're going to ask for. Now let's see if we can get it published."

My law career up to then had been general practice in the truest sense of the word, and Martha was used to working on some of the strange cases that seemed to find their way to my desk. But this was breaking new ground.

"Where should we try?" she asked.

"Well, "I replied, "Let's go with the biggest papers. Send it to the *Detroit News* and the *Detroit Free Press.*"

It didn't work. The rejection letters were abrupt and curt. Neither the *News* nor the *Free Press* could publish such an advertisement, they informed me.

That left the college newspapers. I selected three—the Wayne State University *South End Newspaper*, the Eastern Michigan University *Eastern Echo*, and the University of Michigan *Michigan Daily*.

The campus papers were considerably more tolerant. On January 19, 1977, the Wayne State University Department of Advertising Sales sent me a routine form indicating the ad had been accepted. The Eastern Michigan University and University of Michigan papers soon followed suit. The classified ad ran for two weeks in the three campus papers.

The billing invoices arrived first. The Wayne State bill asked $20.50 for "Personal ad—'Childless husband' (31 words) ran January 21, 1977—February 3, 1977 (8 days), #821." Eastern Michigan and University of Michigan also billed me for about $20 each. "OK, Martha," I said, "let's put these vouchers in a separate file. We're about to start a new part of the business."

Then I heard from a reporter. "I read with interest your classified ad in the personal ad section of *The Michigan Daily*, the University of Michigan's student newspaper," began the letter from Bill Dalton, a reporter from the *Ann Arbor News*. The letter, addressed simply, "Dear Sir," went on to suggest:

"Naturally, your story would be a very valuable human interest feature story that undoubtedly might be picked up by wire services throughout the nation. I could guarantee the story would be handled in a very sensitive manner, exploring whatever areas you would feel comfortable discussing. Of course, we would also guarantee complete confidentiality, with no names used, if you do desire. Your story may help others in similar situations. Please let me know as soon as possible if you are interested in an interview at your convenience. Or, if you will wish to discuss possibilities further, simply call me and feel free to remain anonymous. Thank you."

The letter included Dalton's business card. He was listed as the newspaper's "Dimensions" reporter. The phone number—994-6861.

I was confronted with my second dilemma in this puzzling new area. My first quandary had been whether or not to represent Tom and Jane. I now had a second choice to make. Should we involve the news media?

I was pretty naïve about how the news business works, but it certainly seemed that this story would be of considerable human interest. But Tom and Jane were and are both terribly private people, and I knew they wanted a child, not notoriety. We would have to have another discussion.

They were against it. "I want everything to be anonymous," said Tom. "I couldn't possibly talk about something so private to a reporter," said Jane.

I told them they were wrong, that they had no choice. "It seems to me," I said, "that if you really want to find a woman to carry your child, you're going to need all the publicity, all the visibility you can get. You're asking for help. You need people to hear you. I have reservations, but I recommend we go public."

Tom and Jane are both soft-spoken and quiet and they could do nothing but sit and stare at each other. They had not counted on controversy and publicity intruding into their quiet, orderly lives. This time, they would have to get back to me.

The call came the next morning. Speaking in her soft Southern drawl, Jane said, "OK, Mr. Keane, we'll do it. We don't want to, but if you think it will help us get a baby, we'll do it."

My fingers actually shook as I dialed the reporter's number. Publicity was not something I had counted on, either. I can be as much of a ham as the next guy and I would later come to enjoy news interviews, but this first time was something else. Still, I thought it was something we had to do if we were going to proceed with our search.

Tom and Jane come to my office for the interview. Dalton brought along a photographer from the Associated Press. The photographer and his intimidating equipment flustered Tom and Jane. A story, yes, but not, my heavens, their picture splattered across the country. This was my first contact with the news business in action and I got a crash course in the art and wiles of those who gather and report news.

A photograph, the news team argued, would add immediacy, human interest, impact to the story. It would guarantee bigger play. It was essential.

We compromised. All right, I said, you can photograph me talking to Tom and Jane, but they can be shown only in silhouette and only from the back. They must not be identifiable. All right?

It was all right. That's the way it appeared the next morning on the front page of the *Ann Arbor News*—Tom and Jane in silhouette staring into the face of Noel Keane, who sat at his desk across from them, hands folded and resting atop a pile of legal papers. I was dressed in a vest and necktie and wearing wire-rimmed glasses, and my friends would later tease me that I looked very professorial. The story was everything we were told it would be—sensitive, straightforward, with Tom and Jane's privacy assured.

The first paragraph stated the quest: "After two early miscarriages during eleven years of marriage, a childless Detroit-area couple are still determined to have the baby they know they could never have together. They're willing to pay someone to have the child for them."

Jane had been very worried about talking to a reporter, but once she began, her essential honesty took over. Jane revealed her true feelings and it would be her comments that carried the story. She said that not having children "has been the biggest disappointment in my life,"and asked, "How can there by anything wrong when all you want to do is have a baby to love?" She confided that her closest friend had offered to have the child for her, but that she didn't think it would work with someone so close. The story concluded by emphasizing that Tom and Jane never considered breaking up their marriage because of their inability to have child together. Tom said, "My wife is more important than a baby." Jane added, "As much as Tom wants a baby—his own baby—and since he can't have one with me, this is the last resort. If this doesn't work, we'll give it up."

We were now public with our weird idea—AP took it across the country—and we awaited the outcome.

It would not take long. A few days later, Martha came into my office and dumped a pile of letters on the desk. "Well, Noel," she said, "I guess somebody's out there listening."

And so they were. More than 200 letters came rolling in. Almost all were from young white women willing to accept artificial insemination and bear a child for Tom and Jane. Some said they were responding to the classified ad, others to the newspaper story. Some mentioned both. They all wanted a fee and they asked from $200 to $10,000.

Slowly, I sifted through the outpouring. The motives were amazing. One, who said she wanted to be a Good Samaritan, described herself as "white, 23, blonde, green-eyed, slow to anger, strong-willed." Another was a medical student who asked that her tuition be paid for a year. A third was a twenty-nine-year-old mother of two who wanted to bear another child, but could not afford to keep it. The most unusual letter came from a man who volunteered his girlfriend.

Now I'm no psychiatrist, but I had agreed to do some of the early screening for Tom and Jane. I got it into my head that it would be better to have a single woman carry the child because she would have no previous maternal feelings about children and, therefore, might be better able psychologically to give birth and then give up the child. I also made a note to myself to call a physician friend who worked at the University of Michigan Hospital in Ann Arbor. I knew that we would have to proceed cautiously and would need medical and psychiatric screening of all surrogates.

As I waded through this paperwork, Martha brought in three telephone messages. Guess who wanted to talk to me? First, reporters from the *Detroit Free Press* and the *Detroit News*, the papers that had refused our ad, and second, another couple from Michigan who wanted to do the very same thing that Tom and Jane were doing.

I began to panic. Was I getting in over my head? I had to remind myself that I was an attorney and that this was a legal matter. The first step, obviously, was to get some legal advice. I knew absolutely zero as to where I was heading and what problems would be waiting for me. For that matter, neither did anyone else. As I had told the reporters, there were no legal precedents in this area. I had no one to talk to about surrogate parenting. Up to then, I had confided my legal dilemma only to Kathy and Martha, and, wonderful women though they are, neither had the slightest idea as to what I could—or should—do.

I dictated three letters. One, to Michigan Attorney General Frank Kelley, advised him of my plans and asked for his opinion, as the State's top legal officer, as to the legality of what we were about to do. Another, to Wayne County Juvenile Probate Chief Judge James Lincoln, asked for guidance and assistance. The third, to a University of Michigan physician, sought his assistance in performing the medical screening and the actual insemination. That left me with the requests from the Detroit papers and the new couple. I called Tom and Jane to sound them out on further publicity. At first, Tom's attitude was, "Ah, let them bug off. They wouldn't take our ad, why should we give them our story?" But Jane's view prevailed, "Honey, we crossed that bridge when we talked to Bill Dalton. Noel's a Detroit attorney and we live near here. We have to talk to the hometown paper." She told me, "Noel, set up the interview." I called the reporter, Susan Brown, and scheduled an interview for the next day. I then told Martha to call the new couple, whom we'll call Bill and Bridget, and set up an appointment. I was going to proceed full steam ahead until told otherwise.

The results were mixed.

Susan Brown wrote a nice story. I am intrigued at how different reporters will find different ways to describe the same set of facts and she gave us a new description—"host mother"—to report what Tom and Jane were seeking. The lead read: "Tom and Jane are looking for a mother for their baby." The *Free Press* closed its story the same way the *Ann Arbor News* had, quoting Jane as asking, "How can there by anything wrong with wanting to love a baby?"

The new couple, Bill and Bridget, turned out to be immensely likeable. But their situation was as desperate as Tom and Jane's. In fact, even more desperate. Bill and Bridget were truly dead-ended.

Bridget was seven years older than Bill and had three children from a previous marriage. Her teenage daughter and son lived with them. Bill, an ex-Marine who wore big tattoos on his arms but his heart on his sleeve, wanted his own child. In the early years of their marriage, Bridget could have conceived, but Bill had a low sperm count. While Bill spent years working with a local fertility clinic trying to get his sperm count up, their luck ran out. Bridget was forced to have a hysterectomy. By now, Bridget was forty-five and Bill thirty-eight, and their chances of having a child together seemed impossible. Because she was over forty and had already had a fifteen-year-old daughter living at home, she was, according to agency procedures in Michigan, virtually unqualified to adopt. Bill thought his only choices were to divorce Bridget and marry someone else—a circumstance he could not bear—or to do without his own child.

Then he said, "I picked up the paper one day and read about your efforts to find a woman to carry a child for Tom and Jane. It seemed like a miracle, like you are meant to be the answer to our prayers."

I was not so sure, but I told Bill and Bridget what I had told Tom and Jane, that I would think about it and get back to them. Bill was bursting with hope and excitement and I didn't want to let him down hard. "There are," I warned, "legal questions and medical questions that need to be answered. The answers to those questions will determine what I can or cannot do for you."

Those answers were coming in. Some were disappointing, Frank Kelley, the Michigan Attorney General, refused to render an opinion to a private individual. The question posed, he said, would have to come from a state law-enforcement agency.

The physician I knew sent regrets, but emphasized that malpractice fears would preclude him from getting involved. His boss is one of the nation's leading medical figures in the fertility field—he is a past president of several national organizations—and the boss had made it quite clear that neither the department nor any of its members were to involve themselves in anything so new and so unproven.

But there was one bright spot. Mrs. Margaret Pfieffer, a lady whom I would come to know and love, called me from Judge Lincoln's office and said the judge would be glad to discuss this unusual matter at length with me.

On February 9th, I spent four hours with Judge Lincoln and, for the first time, poured out my own anxieties, doubts, and frustrations. These were good people, I told the judge, and I wanted to help them. Basically, all they wanted to do was find a way around their infertility and have a child that they could raise and love. I didn't see anything wrong with that. And, apparently, there were a lot of women who were willing—for a fee—to be artificially inseminated and carry a child. I didn't see anything wrong with that, either. But was it legal? Would the surrogate mother actually be able to give up the baby? What if she didn't? What were the medico-legal implications? What would other attorneys and judges think? I had to know.

Judge Lincoln was then nearing the end of a long and distinguished career and he had seen many perplexing legal problems, particularly those involving children. But this, he conceded, was different. He would have to get back to me.

The answer came in the form of a March 2, 1977, memorandum from the judge to me and it was to become a focal point, a legal foundation for everything I would do in the future.

I had put in writing two crucial questions to the judge.

The first was: "A married couple suitable for adoptive parents wish to adopt a child. The wife cannot have a child. The husband would artificially inseminate an unrelated woman. Would the child born as a result of this relationship be considered as related to the adopting parents, so that the adopting parents could file with the court for adoption without going through an adoption agency?"

The second was: "Could the adopting parents pay the woman for having the child or consenting to its adoption?"

If the answer were "no" to both, I knew that I didn't have a prayer of helping Tom and Jane and Bill and Bridget.

Judge Lincoln's answer to the first question was short and sweet. It was "yes." The judge wrote: "After considerable study and consultation, I would hold that it makes no difference what means is used in impregnating the woman. The father is the person who produced the sperm that impregnated the woman. He could even be held liable for child support."

This was the green light. Had the judge said no, there could not have been a private adoption, and we would have been involved in something akin to baby-selling, in dealing with what could be interpreted as black-market babies. And, of course, I would have had nothing to do with that. My efforts would have ended right there.

But now we could proceed with the arrangement with the intent of having the infertile couple adopt the baby born to a surrogate mother

However, his answer to the second question assured that we would have difficulty accomplishing our goal.

A fee, the judge emphasized, definitely was out of the

question—and outside the law. The judge's answer read, "No, with emphasis. The law clearly forbids it."

So that was that. We could not pay a fee. But I had also posed a third and less important question: "Could the adopting parents pay the expenses of the pregnancy and delivery—medical, hospital, doctor, transportation to hospital, and attorney fees?"

The judge answered "yes," with reservations. He wrote: "The law permits payment of reasonable expenses, and it has been the custom of all Michigan Probate Courts to allow the payment of such expenditures. I, personally, would not be concerned with permitting payment of reasonable costs and transportation to a hospital and so on. I do not care about the manner of transportation, as long as the expense was actually incurred. Of course, I would not approve of giving a car, or anything similar. That would be regarded as paying the woman. Likewise, I would not permit the payment of lost wages."

The judge closed his memorandum with this caveat:

"I will probably not be the judge who handles this adoption. The petition cannot be filed until after the child is born. This will be early in 1978. The judge who handles this case will make all the rulings to determine what expenditures to approve or disapprove. All that I can do is give my opinion on all of these matters. My opinion is not binding on the judge who will hear the petition. I appreciate the fact that Mr. Keane wishes to clear all matters for his client prior to proceeding and I wish I were in a position to give him something other than what I would do if I were handling the case."

So I was on my own, but at least I knew I would not be breaking the law. The problem appeared to be in finding a needle in a haystack—a woman who would become a surrogate mother simply for humanitarian reasons and not for the payment of a fee

I made three requests of Martha. "Xerox Judge Lincoln's opinion about twenty times or so—this is our road map. Add Margaret Pfieffer's name to our Rolodex—we're going to be calling on her quite a bit. Send this letter out to all our potential surrogate mothers and tell them we cannot pay a fee. Then, ask if they're still interested."

I added, "Tell them that if they're still interested to give me a call."

The letters went out but the calls never came back. The supply of surrogates dried up as quickly as they had sprung. Almost all of the early responses, it appeared, were motivated by one word. Money.

I was back to Square One with Tom and Jane. I put Bill and Bridget on hold. By now, the wire service stories about Tom and Jane had trickled down into every section of the country and daily my phone was ringing with calls from women who wanted to be surrogate mothers for a fee. The calls might just as well not have come in. There would be no fee. Would there then be a surrogate mother?

I called Tom and Jane back for another conference and explained to them the roadblocks we were up against.

"I have gone just about as far I can go within the law," I said. "We cannot pay a fee and that means it is going to be very difficult to find a woman who will do this for you.

"Furthermore, the woman we find should be single. Michigan does not have direct adoption unless one of the adopting parents is related. Now, since the child will be conceived with Tom's sperm, Tom will be considered the father and we will pass that legal test.

"But under Michigan law, if a child is born to a married woman, then legally the child is presumed to be from that couple. That means that we need a single woman so that we would not have to overcome the legal presumption applying to chidren born to a married couple.

"So that's where we are. Trying to find a single woman who will do this for you strictly on its merits. It's not going to be easy. Do you want to continue?"

I knew what their answer would be—proceed. I had been collecting piles of letters from potential surrogate mothers and separating them by whether or not they required a fee. The fee pile was a mountain; the free pile was an anthill. I told Tom and Jane I would go through the list of possibilities and advise them how to proceed.

By now, I was having third and fourth doubts about the whole thing. The attorney general had not told me that what I was doing was illegal, but he had not said it was legal, either. Judge Lincoln had said the concept was theoretically possible but he had ruled out the practical means—payment of a fee. Also, his opinion was only advisory, not binding upon whoever might replace him.

Plus I was getting some nasty letters, too. People telling me that what I was trying to do is immoral.

A lady in my parish came up to me one day, told me off in no uncertain terms, and stomped off.

One letterwriter said: "It is a pity that older children, children in sibling groups, minority children, and handicapped children are suffering a slow emotional death because no one cares enough to give them a home. Too many childless couples have forgotten that adoptions originated to provide families for homeless children, not babies for childless couples."

Another wrote: "The motives for wanting a baby have to be seriously questioned if a couple is willing to go outside their marriage. Doesn't a child have a right to be conceived by two people who love each other instead of by some cold, clinical method? And imagine being told that your natural mother had no maternal feelings for you! Sad that some people think that it is their inalienable right to have a child!"

Some of my wife's beauty parlor customers were also quietly expressing a concern or two.

The experts, of course, wanted nothing to do with it. The doctors wouldn't help. Malpractice fears. Lawyers had no advice. No case laws. The social workers were used to the traditional advice—adopt.

Could all these people be right, I wondered? Was I wrong?

God knows, my background was such that I never would have chosen to get involved in something that would focus attention on me. As a kid, I was bashful and shy. My father's drunken forays against my mother and brothers and sister had convinced me at an early age that if I ever had a family I would never subject them to abuse. Yet I wondered, would all this notoriety hurt my own family?

I decided that I must run the risk. I had made a commitment to Tom and Jane and Bill and Bridget and I would see it through as far as law allowed.

But first, I wanted the opinions of two women.

In times of doubt, my best adviser has always been my wife Kathy. I put it to her straight. Will this new work of mine embarrass you? Will it hurt Chris and Doug? Will we be thrown out of the church?

Kathy quickly cut through my concern. "Noel," she said, "if you believe in it and if it's not illegal, then I'm with you one hundred percent. Period."

My office manager, Martha Makridakis, had been with me from the start on this adventure, and I have always valued her judgment. She is the mother of two beautiful children and a woman of eminent good sense and strong opinions. "Martha," I asked, "is this the kind of business we should be in?"

Martha has always been one of my biggest fans and I was secretly afraid that she might have become a little upset with this surrogate motherhood controversy. She took a few days to think about it and one morning walked in and handed me an envelope. She had written down her feelings and after reading them I was never to look back.

"I personally feel that no one can sit in judgment of another unless there has been an evil crime committed against God and society.

Does the mother tucking her little ones in bed at night and kissing away the hurts of the day know the loneliness of the woman who yearns with all her heart to be able to do this but who is by a quirk of a nature denied the gift?

Does the parent who has not known the tragedy of losing a child to sudden death know the pain and anguish of the parent who has? Does the person running the marathon and experiencing the pain of aching feet know the heartache of the young man confined to a wheelchair? Does the woman flaunting her femininity and svelte body know the grief of the mastectomy victim?

I think not, and I also think that those who have children and those who can have children but choose not to cannot comprehend the aching pain of those who yearn for children but are told they cannot have them.

One can hardly blame another for wanting a child."

Thank you, Martha. I would proceed.

With painstaking care, I went through my correspondence and selected all the letters from potential surrogate mothers who had not explicitly specified a fee. The list of names, addresses, and biographical information took up six sheets of my yellow legal pad, but I knew that many of the prospects were doubtful.

Many of the older, mature women whose reasons for volunteering to carry a child sounded so genuine were married. This meant that adoption procedures would be complicated. We would have to overcome the strong legal presumption that a child born to a married woman is hers and her husband's and no one else's.

Many of the younger single women seemed vague in their motivation. They didn't quite seem to have their heads screwed on straight.

I went down the list and called the potential surrogate mothers to assess their ability to do this unusual thing. Mostly, I was trying to determine if each woman were truly competent to carry out such an agreement and then give up the child.

It required some Solomon-like decisions, and I have to admit I wasn't fully up to the task. How can you tell from a phone conversation whether or not a woman has character, strength, and genercsity of spirit? You cannot, but I had no trouble eliminating half the list out of hand. These people hadn't said they wanted a fee, but it turned out they did.

When Tom and Jane came to my office a few days later, I had a list of about thirty names for them. "But," I told them, "there are probably only three or four who are real possibilities. If you want to continue, we will draw up a legal agreement between you two and myself. There is one condition, though. You are going to have to get directly involved and talk to these women. You are going to have to choose your surrogate mother."

Jane turned white. She and Tom wanted to stay out of it. They wanted anonymity.

"It's either that," I said, "or forget it. I've gone as far as I can go. I cannot make the choice for you."

Tom cut in, "OK, OK, we've come this far, we're not going to quit now. We will talk to the women ourselves."

On March 23, 1977, the first legal agreement relating to surrogate motherhood was drawn up between myself and Tom and Jane. It stipulated:

> We, Tom and Jane, hereby make the following declaration. That we have retained Noel P. Keane to represent us in an attempt to secure a surrogate mother to deliver a child by means of artificial insemination. It is our understanding that we are not assured that a surrogate mother will be found. That if a surrogate is found and is, in fact, inseminated, there is not assurance she will give up the child. That we are not permitted to pay money or anything of value to this surrogate mother other than costs and fees approved by the court. That because of the very nature of this action, we agree to hold Noel P. Keane free and harmless in the event we are not successful in receiving a child.

That was the agreement. Before they signed, I pressed home the point, "Do you fully understand that we may go through all this trouble and the surrogate mother may keep the child? That you, Tom, may have to pay child support to this surrogate mother?"

They didn't like to hear these types of questions, but it could be no other way. "We have come this far," Tom said. "We will take the risks."

We signed the agreement and Tom and Jane gave me a retainer of $1,000. I had been working on the surrogate-motherhood concept for six months and I had just earned my first dollar.

We adjourned to the conference room and began to go through the names on the legal pad. Tom and Jane did most of the talking, and I tried to stay out of it as much as possible. I told them what I knew about each of the women, but tried to let them make the decision. After three hours or so, we were down to three names. I suggested cutting that down to two.

One of the volunteers, whom we'll call Carol, was divorced with three sons. She lived in Michigan and Tom and Jane thought she might work out. "I would recommend against her," I said. "She's had three children and established a love bond with them. I really doubt that she could carry your child and give it up. It sounds like her maternal instincts are too strong."

Tom pointed out the obvious, "Well, Noel, we really aren't in any position of being extremely choosy. It's not like we have the whole world to pick from."

I replied, "All right. Suit yourself. Let me know what happens."

Meanwhile, Bill and Bridget were still calling me for help. I had decided to defer action on their request until we had a better idea of how Tom and Jane were going to do. But Bill was desperate. I hate to see a grown man cry, particularly an ex-Marine with arms so massive that the huge tattoo of a Navy anchor is swallowed up by his bicep. "But, Bill," I said, "there just aren't any volunteers now who don't appear to want a fee. I know of only a few possibilities and Tom and Jane are trying them. We're just going to have to wait and see what happens."

Both Tom and Jane and Bill and Bridget are working-class

people and neither couple could easily afford the fee of $10,000 we had been prepared to pay—if found to be a legal possibility—for a surrogate mother. But they had been determined to mortgage their homes, if necessary, to make the payment. Now the financial demands were eased but there seemed no way to find the right woman. Bill made the suggestion:

"Noel, you know I heard about you through the newspapers. If it weren't for their stories, I never would have even known about this thing. Maybe that's true of a lot of women. They might be willing to do this, but they simply aren't aware of it. Would it help if we told our problem to the newspapers?"

Several radio and television stations had previously called me to see if I would come on a talk show with Tom and Jane. I had refused because I knew that Tom and Jane wanted to stay out of the limelight as much as possible. But this seemed our only hope.

"All right," I said, "If you'll agree to discuss your search in public, we'll try it. It may not work, but we'll try it."

Bill and Bridget also gave me a $1,000 retainer. Their $1,000 and the $1,000 from Tom and Jane would represent the entire earnings I would make from surrogate motherhood in the next two years. I didn't want to take money because I wasn't sure I had anything to offer.

One of the local radio talk shows said they would be delighted to hear from Bill and Bridget and within a week there we were in the radio sation waiting to go on.

It was a soft rock station and our portion of the programming was intended mainly to satisfy Federal Communications Commission requirements for public service news. The station news manager briefed us over coffee before we went on and Bill and Bridget were very nervous. The news manager, an attractive young woman with a friendly but brisk manner, was frankly amazed by the whole thing.

"What is it you want to do again?" she asked. Bill mumbled, "Noel, you tell her. You're the expert."

The show, though, went off smoothly. Bill and Bridget got

over their stagefright and came across candid and open. They wanted a child and hoped someone out there listening might be able to help them have one.

It was a call-in show, but most of the calls were unhelpful. People opposed to the whole thing, people wondering what in the world was wrong with us.

I was beginning to tire of the whole thing. There was only so much to be said, only so much to be done. If it wasn't in the cards, then so be it.

Bill and Bridget dropped me off at the office about noon.

Martha was heading off for lunch, but she had a message. She had listened to the radio show, too, and had been disappointed by some of the calls.

"The best call, though," she said, "wasn't to the radio station. It came to me. Here, take a look at this."

Slowly it sank in as I read the telephone message:

"Call us. We've already done it!"

ˌ3ˌ
"I can give her the best gift. A baby."

THEY were to become world famous, but at our first encounter they simply wanted to share their secret.

Debbie, Sue, and George (the only real names of clients used in this book) had, incredibly, already done what for months now Tom and Jane and Bill and Bridget and I had been groping toward.

Sue, twenty-four, a virgin, had been artificially inseminated by her best friend, Debbie, twenty-five, with the sperm of Debbie's husband, George, twenty-eight. Debbie had a hysterectomy and despaired of her lifelong dream, having a baby, until Sue was "hit like a bolt of lightning with the idea. Why, I can do it for her!"

It was late spring of 1977, and by chance Debbie, Sue, and George listened to the radio show on which I pleaded for a surrogate mother for Bill and Bridget. Sue was already pregnant and living with Debbie and George. These three ordinary, Catholic young people from Detroit were filled with joy at the extraordinary thing they had done. Their only regret was that they did not think they could tell anybody else. The voices of three strangers on the radio changed all that.

They tried to call in to the radio station, but their call never made it. There were too many complaints being aired, apparently, to let this call through. So they called my office and left a message.

It was the first thing I did that morning. I called Debbie at her suburban Detroit home. She was brisk and cheerful. "We've already done it and we can't wait to tell you about it."

I made an appointment for the following afternoon and these three surrogate-mother pioneers came in together.

Their story is at once so simple and so striking that it should be shared widely. Basically, the trio resourcefully worked out their own solution to a problem others had written off.

I had been working for eight months now in this area and there was little light at the end of the tunnel. As they unfolded their story to me that first day, I could only shake my head. And, I must admit, laugh from time to time. Who would have believed this?

"All I ever wanted from life," begins Debbie, "was to get married and have children. That was my dream and I never stopped believing in it. Until this past January."

Debbie is an animated woman, with short-cropped hair and a solid, stocky build. As she talks, her hands gesture, her feet tap, and her mind races. She, clearly, is the dominant one in the group. But, Sue and George will emphasize, they like it that way. It is, they say, a loving, nurturing thing.

"I'm a fighter," Debbie resumes, "always have been. I'm the fourth of six children and it always seemed to me that the oldest daughter, Lynn, was the apple of my parents' eyes. Nothing I could ever do was good enough. So I grew up fighting for what I believed in.

"But last January all the fight went out of me. That's when the doctors did the hysterectomy. Before, I knew my chances were limited, maybe fifty-fifty at best. But I knew God would find a way. Then, this. I thought my life was over. I wanted to die."

Sue is an intense, shy woman with a slender figure and striking blue eyes. Attractive but retiring. You hardly knew she's there. But now she speaks up:

"It was terrible that night last January. I drove Debbie to the hospital. We had to go thirty miles through one of the worst snowstorms ever to hit Detroit. Debbie was in terrible pain with severe stomach cramps and bleeding. I didn't think things could ever get any worse, but they did.

"Three days later, the doctors went in for 'exploratory surgery.' They later told Debbie they 'had to take everything out because it had deteriorated with infection.' "

Debbie adds, " 'Everything?' I asked them. 'Everything,' they replied.

"My husband, George, my mother, and my sister, Lynn, were at my bedside, looking very serious. I asked them all to leave. I wanted to be alone. That's the way I felt. Totally alone. If your chances of having children are one in a hundred, you can hope. Mine were zero in a hundred. Zero. I could not understand it."

George has been sitting silently. He is a handsome man, with thick, prematurely graying hair and a manner of quiet geniality. He says, "I told Debbie that I married her because I loved her, not because I wanted to have children. I was perfectly content to live our lives out just the way we were. I have eight other brothers and sisters and they can worry about carrying on the family line. But Debbie was really down in the dumps. We've been married for six years and this was the biggest problem we've ever had."

How could they possibly have hit upon this idea, I wondered. "Tell me," I asked, "how did this pregnancy come about?"

Debbie begins the narrative. "We were home in bed, George and I, reading our books. I was reading a book about a Korean girl named Kim who had been adopted by American parents. I don't know how many books I've read about adoption. After my hysterectomy, it seemed like the only hope. Some hope. Seven years is the wait, they told me. Minimum. Then, there was no guarantee. The whole procedure was insulting, really. They acted like they were doing us a big favor just talking to us. I called every adoption agency in the area. Korean, Hungarian, Jewish. They all said, 'Go to your own religious denomination." So I went to the Wayne County Catholic Social Services, and they said, 'Here's the application. Fill it out and call us in seven years.'

"They were very curt about it. There were 2,000 applicants on their list and we were at the bottom. What was the use?"

George cuts in, "You know what bothers me? You cannot pay a surrogate mother to have a baby; it's against the law. But you can pay Social Services. It's different, of course. They don't discuss money, but they expect a donation, usually 10 percent of your annual gross income. If you make $20,000, they get $2,000. Tell me, isn't that a 'black-market baby?' "

Interesting question, I thought.

Debbie continues, "Anyway, there we are reading in bed. I was really starting to go crackers. I had always worked for insurance companies and banks and I just couldn't see spending the rest of my life worrying if someone's house is insured against tornadoes or if somebody is going to get a home mortgage. There's got to be more.

"I can remember it like it was last night. We were about to turn off the lights. I took one last look at the faces of Kim. She had grown from a frightened child to a laughing little girl. The words of her mother stuck with me: 'Kim, I never carried you under my heart, but I have always carried you in my heart.' In my heart, there was only an ache.

"The phone rang.

"Now, we were living then in a small trailer and it was almost midnight and the ringing of that phone sounded like a fire alarm. I jumped to my feet and felt something soft. It was Rascal. He's only a pup, a gift from George to cheer me up and now his yelp is drowning out the telephone. 'God,' I thought, 'I can't do anything right.'

"Nobody else would call that late. I knew it had to be Sue."

Sue picks up the story. "I work nights at a bank processing loans. Debbie was on my mind. She had been on my mind quite a bit lately. You see, she's the first real friend I've ever had. The day

I met Debbie about a year ago was the day my life began. She has made it possible for me to trust people again.

"I had a very bad childhood. Both my parents were drinkers. We were on welfare and my parents and I and my two younger brothers were living in a three-room coldwater flat that was always dark and dirty and dingy. That's all we'd ever known. We three children thought everybody lived that way. One night, my father came home and bashed a carton of milk over my mother's head. Another time, he stuck a butcher knife in my stomach. Not hard, but it drew blood. He kept yelling at me, 'How would you like to have a knife stuck in your stomach?' When I was twelve, my aunt showed up one day with the police. We hadn't eaten for days. When you're not used to it, you don't miss it. We were sent to live with my seventy-two-year-old grandmother. Our living conditions improved, but we remained social outcasts. My grandmother told me not to go near boys.

"I grew up never trusting people. That's why I used to have thirty cats or so. Animals are something you can trust.

"When I met Debbie, I was near rock-bottom. I was drinking heavily, I was in debt, and I was depressed. She turned me around, made me care again. I had maybe three hand-me-down dresses from the 1960s; she gave me some of her clothes. I drank for entertainment; she taught me how to play cards and enjoy other things. I had no concept of money; she taught me how to balance my checkbook, pay off my debts. Mostly, she convinced me that I had something to offer.

"I'll never forget one day last summer. I was really down and my brother, Adam, suggested we go fishing. I asked Debbie to come along. I know fishing is not one of Debbie's main things, but she said sure. She came along to comfort me. Now, it was about three A.M. or so when we reached this little lake my brother liked. He fished, but Debbie and I sat down on the shoreline and talked and talked. I poured my heart out. Everything. My parents, the drinking, the poverty, the shame, the fear. I had never told anybody any of this before. It was like my eyes opened for the first time. I had been keeping it inside and it was killing me. Debbie just listened and I talked. The next thing we knew the sun was rising.

"My life has never been the same since and Debbie and I became almost inseparable. I knew how desperately she wanted a baby and I always used to pray that she would have a baby. When I heard about Debbie's hysterectomy, I think it hurt me almost as much as it did her. And the change in her! She seemed to have lost her spirit, her spunk. It was almost as if we were trading places. I was becoming happy and Debbie was becoming depressed.

"So, about a month ago, I was sitting at work on my break and stirring a cup of coffee. Debbie works days at an office right across the street from me and I always pop in on her on my way to work. This day, she seemed unusually down.

"I thought of everything that Debbie had done for me and I wished that I could do something in return. She is really sort of a mother to me, the mother I had always needed and never really had. 'What have I done for her?' I thought. 'Oh, sure, once or twice, I bought over some fried chicken dinners so she wouldn't have to cook. That was about it.'

"The idea just hit me. It's very simple, really. 'Why, I can have a baby for her!' I thought.

"Now, I'm a virgin. A lot of men show an interest in me, but maybe it's because of my grandmother's upbringing or the fact that I don't like to dance or whatever, but I've never been in bed with a man. I knew I would have to have a man to have a baby, but the idea seemed so simple and so pure that I didn't want to clutter it up with details. There were two men I knew would have sex with me, but I didn't want to dwell too long on the possibilities. One, Floyd, who I really like and who I knew he wouldn't pressure me, would agree with the idea, and would have sex only during my fertile time. The other man, Bill, is divorced and I'm not sure I could have sex with him more than once, but I knew that if I were pregnant he would be glad to forget about me. Both Floyd and Bill are good-looking—blonde hair, blue eyes, trim builds. I've never paid much attention to my appearance, but I guess I look OK. I thought the baby would look just fine for Debbie and George.

"Just like that, I went to a pay phone and called Debbie. I told her, 'Now, Debbie, don't say anything until you've heard me out because you may change your mind later. I want to have a baby for you. It's really very simple. . . .'"

"It seemed like a cruel joke or something," Debbie recalls. "Except I knew that Sue isn't cruel. I told her, 'No, no. No way. Look, Sue, I'll call you tomorrow.' She replied, 'Well, just think about it, will you? We don't have to decide right away. The offer stands.'"

Debbie continues: "Now, when George is asleep, he's usually asleep for the duration. But Rascal had woke him up. We had a strange conversation and George came up with the magic idea. The conversation went like this:

'Was that Sue?'

'Yes.'

'What does she want?'

'Oh, nothing, really. She just called to say she wants to have a baby for us.'

'Unbelievable. Is she crazy? My God, what would people think? And, pray tell, has she given any thought as to how she might go about having a baby? You tell me she's still a virgin.'

'Oh, I'm sure she didn't think about it at all. It's just a crackpot idea. She was trying to cheer me up.'

'Well, that's out of the question. We can't even consider having Sue sacrifice herself for us in that way. She'd have to find a man to make love with her and there's no way we're going to have that on our consciences. The only way we have a child like that is if I'm the father. My sperm. Maybe artificial insemination or something.'

'That's it, George. Of course, why not by artificial insemination? But what will our families think? You don't really think we could do it, do you?'

'Well, look at it this way. You can have that baby you want in nine months, not seven years.'

'Are you serious, George? Do you really think it will work?'

'I don't know, Debbie. Let's talk about it tomorrow.'

'But can we tell Sue that it's OK, that we want to try it?'

'OK.'

George was asleep, but Debbie's mind was flying. The conversation had taken maybe five minutes, but the implications stretched to infinity. How do we do it? How do we find a doctor? How do we tell our parents and friends? What do we name the baby?

"She called me back," Sue said, and "gave me their answer: 'Sue, George and I discussed it and the answer is yes. But, Sue, only if George is the father through artificial insemination. Sue, we've got a lot to talk about so why don't you come on over here when you get off work.' "

Debbie and Sue described for me that first night and the ensuing weeks as they calmly and quietly executed their wild idea. What struck me was the singlemindedness of their purpose and the simplicity of the procedures.

I looked at them very carefully. They were very much alike, the three of them. Really nothing more than three middle-class, white, Catholic young people trying to make their way. They even looked alike in many ways: that well-scrubbed look peculiar to so many Polish children brought up by God-fearing parents. George was Polish-German, Debbie Polish-Canadian, and Sue Polish-Lithuanian. I could understand how they quickly decided one point was nonnegotiable.

"Sue," Debbie said, "You must be absolutely sure about having our child because once the child is conceived there will be no stopping the growth. None of us believe in abortion."

There would be no turning back.

The only other alternative, Debbie told Sue, was this. "If you change your mind about keeping the baby, then the baby will be yours."

Within days of their midnight conversation Sue was pregnant with Debbie and George's baby. It was surprisingly easy. But how did they do it?

Debbie says, "When Sue came over, I made a pot of coffee. Now, when I make a pot of coffee, I expect it to be drunk, all of it. We stayed up all night on coffee, working out the details. Over the years, I've collected quite a medical library to understand my pelvic infections and learn about adoptions and so on. I picked up one of my medical books, turned to 'Artificial Insemination,' and read to Sue:

ARTIFICIAL INSEMINATION. *Mechanical introduction of semen into the vagina or uterus to induce pregnancy. If successful, conception, pregnancy, and childbirth occur in a perfectly normal way. The first recorded attempt at human artificial insemination was performed by the famous English surgeon, John Hunter, in 1799. . . . There are no exact figures on the number of children (popularly called "test-tube babies") conceived by artificial insemination, but the numbers run into the thousands and some of these children have themselves become parents of one or more offspring.*

Debbie continued, "Sue and I decided there was going to be at least one more 'test-tube' baby. Ours."

Sue interrupts, "It was all starting to seem so simple. Debbie and I figured that my fertile date would be April 26th—only a week away. My period had started five days before. We had to move fast and the first thing was to find a doctor to do the insemination. We went to George's family doctor. He was the first person we told our story to and it was very awkward, but somehow the three of us got the idea across of what we were about. Were we surprised at the doctor's reaction! He thought it was fantastic. He and his wife could not have children and he said, 'I wish there was someone to do this for us.' He said he couldn't perform the insemination, but he would try to find a doctor at the University of Michigan who would. A few days later, he called back and said there was only one doctor who would do it. We called this man and he was on vacation. We were getting anxious. All the other doctors said no. Too many legal problems. The insemination had to be done in a matter of days, or we would have to wait another month."

Debbie: "Like I said, I have quite a medical library. I had been reading everything I could about conception, birth, and artificial insemination. One day, I realized that all the information we needed was right there in my *Reader's Digest Family Health Guide*. It had a clear, precise description of exactly how artifical insemination was done. Now, the book intended to tell women what to expect during the procedure, but we decided we could do it ourselves. I mean, girls get pregnant in the back seats of cars all the time, and I figured that if we took precautions and performed the insemination under sterile conditions, everything would be OK.

"Then, everything started to turn into a comedy. The house where Sue was renting was sold, so we decided the easiest thing would be for her to move into the trailer with us. We were definitely going to do it April 26th. Let me tell you about getting the equipment to do it. We had a sterile glass, but we needed the syringe. George and I went to see his family that day, so we stopped at a drugstore near his house to buy the syringe. Guess who greeted us from behind the counter? George's sister, Beth. We had no idea she worked there. I said to George, 'Go talk to Beth and keep her busy. I'll talk to the druggist.' I went to the backroom and told the druggist, 'I need a syringe.' He looked at me and said, 'Aren't you married to Beth's brother?' I replied, 'Yes, but I need a syringe. A syringe with a needle that comes off and I'd like it to be glass.' He kept looking at me strangely and I thought, 'Oh, brother. How am I going to get him off the subject of my being married to Beth's brother?' I didn't want him to think I was going to use the syringe for anything illegal, so I kept saying, '*Do you sell them without a needle?*' He finally got the syringe I wanted and explained, 'Look, with this syringe, you just throw the needle away, OK?' Then, he looked at me like I was nuts. Maybe I was, I thought! I bought two syringes, just to be sure."

Sue: "I had been taking my temperature every day, because it was supposed to rise on the day the egg was released. On April 25th, I was shaking the thermometer and it fell in the sink and broke. It was late at night and I didn't have a car to go get another one. The excitement and pressure was getting to me and the breaking of the thermometer seemed like a bad omen. I thought the whole world had fallen in. I called Debbie and she said not to worry, we would do it on the 26th anyway. The next day she picked me up right after she got off work—I had taken the night off—and we drove to their house. I don't think we said a word to each other all the way. We were too keyed up."

George: "I got home that night about 6 P.M. and Debbie and I went straight into the bedroom. I had decided we would just start like we were going to make love and when the time came, I would ejaculate into the syringe. That's what I thought at first, that I would just fill the syringe. Debbie pointed out, 'George, the syringe is only *this* big, and you think you're going to make it in there, right?' I said, 'Sure, no problem. Do you have two syringes?' Debbie set me straight. 'George, you only need one syringe. There's not a lot of semen when it's ejaculated. It just seems like a lot. Use the glass, and we'll fill the syringe from there.' Yes, Debbie, I said."

Debbie: "George and I started to make love, but we had never been interrupted before. It seemed so strange to us and we were so hyper that it couldn't have taken more than a few minutes for George to come. He had abstained for five days before and we were both used to the honeymoon pace of lovemaking. George filled the glass."

Sue: "When they came out of the bedroom, they were both grinning. I grinned, too. Debbie said, 'OK, Sue, now it's your turn.' "

Debbie: "We had agreed that Sue would do the actual insemination herself. Sue and I went in the other bedroom and I said, 'Here's my robe. Get comfortable while I fill the syringe. Then I'll leave.'

Sue: "Debbie could tell that I had been thinking about her helping me. I was scared to do it, because I thought something might go wrong with the baby."

Debbie: "I asked Sue, 'Do you want me to do it?' She said yes with the biggest sigh I'd ever heard. I told her it was going to be painful, and that we would both probably sweat to death. She said she understood, so I told her, 'OK, get comfortable.' To me, it was just like being at the gynecologist's office. I was very nervous because I didn't want to hurt Sue. For all I knew, Sue's hymen was still intact because not only was she a virgin but she had never even used a tampon before. When Sue told me that, I thought, 'Oh, God, now it's going to hurt for sure and she's going to bleed.' As it happened, I never broke her hymen that night. I simply pushed against it and the semen shot right through the hymen. I never got into her vagina. Her hymen was broken later, when the gynecologist first examined her. He explained that, naturally, if blood can come out during menstruation, something can go in."

Sue: "The doctor later explained that the hymen only partially closes the entrance of the vaginal passage. It's like a web, full of perforations. Apparently, the semen shot right through the hymen, which afterwards helped keep the sperm in. As for me, I knew I was pregnant that first moment. I was."

Debbie: "George wanted to do it again the next day, just to make sure. I told him, 'If it's meant to be, it's already happened.' "

Sue: "That's how I felt. If it was God's will, then it was done. I felt like it was done. In fact, we all went out that night to a restaurant to celebrate."

"My God," I thought, "that's about as close to an immaculate conception as you can come." I asked, "Was that it? Did you become pregnant just on one attempt?"

Debbie: "We hit the bull's eye the very first time."

Sue: "Now all we had to do was wait. For a while, it seemed

like everything was falling down around us. George had to have an emergency appendectomy. The trailer burned down and we had to move into first, a motel, and then, the home of Debbie's aunt and uncle, who were on vacation. About the time, I was supposed to start my period, I felt like I was going to but I didn't. We couldn't be absolutely sure, though, because it might have been a false pregnancy. We made an appointment with the doctor. He did the tests and gave me a pelvic exam. I think I'd rather do anything than have a pelvic exam. Now, all we had to do was wait for the tests. We called almost every day. First, the tests weren't back yet. Then, the tests were back, but the doctor wasn't in and only he could give the results. The next day, I called again. Debbie and George were standing right beside me. The nurse said the doctor wasn't in, but she would give me the results anyway. I'll never forget the flat tone of her voice. 'They are positive,' she said. I just said quietly, 'Oh, really,' then hung up quick. I was afraid she might change her opinion. Debbie and Sue just stared at me. I took my time about telling them, played it out a little bit. 'Well,' I said, 'it looks like you have a pregnant lady on your hands!' "

George: "Debbie and I hugged each other and then Debbie and I hugged Sue. It all seemed unbelievable."

Of course, there were other questions to be answered. What to tell friends and parents? And, later, the child?

Debbie: "My parents will be supportive. My mother has a theory that if you never talk about anything, it will go away. So I know she'll accept it and act as if nothing out of the ordinary happened. And Dad is a great big teddy bear of a man. If it's good for me, it's good for him. George's parents are going to be tough. You know, his father is more Catholic than the Pope. Now, if we adopted a Korean child or a Black child, he would think it was just superneat. Because it would make him look great that his son did such a noble thing. But this may embarrass him."

George: "Debbie is right, but I'm hoping that I can talk to my mother about it, and she will bring Dad around."

Sue: "My brother Adam, I know, will support me no matter what I do. And Mike, I no longer value his opinions anymore, anyway. Ever since he said all those nasty things to me because I was seeing so much of Debbie, saying that Debbie was running my life and there must be something strange going on between us. I just lost interest in him as a person if he can be that far off on who I am and what kind of a person I am."

Debbie: "My brothers and sisters and George's brothers and sisters will stand by us, no matter what. It's just his father we're worried about."

I cut in, "What do you tell the child down the road?"

Debbie: "The truth. We tell her that George is the father and that her mother loved her very much, but gave her to us. It's up to Sue to tell her she's the mother, if she so chooses.

"You say her," I said, "do you think it will be a girl?"

Sue: "Debbie and I both know it will be a girl. I read somewhere that the male-carrying sperm are the faster swimmers, but the female tend to penetrate further. This pregnancy required a sperm that had to go the distance. A female sperm."

Debbie: "We already have the name. Elizabeth Anne. George's sister, Anne, is going to be the godmother and Sue's middle name is Elizabeth. I want the baby to have part of Sue's name. Besides, George likes the name Elizabeth."

Sue: "Elizabeth Anne sounds great to me."

Debbie: "Of course, we'll love a boy, too. His name will be Vincent Gregory. I like the name Vincent and George likes Gregory."

We had been talking for hours now. Sue was getting over shyness and starting to talk at will.

"It just happened," Sue said. "I'd been bothered for weeks, trying to think of a way to get Debbie out of her misery. And then it came to me. There I was, a perfectly normal, healthy woman able to have children. Why not? I couldn't think of a reason not to. And I didn't think past that point. How? When? It just didn't matter. I called Debbie.

"And, you know, that phone call was probably the first real decision I ever made on my own."

Debbie summed things up. "Sue has Blue Cross at work and the insurance will cover hospitalization and delivery. George and I will pay for everything else. The doctor told us that prenatal and postnatal costs would be about $225.

"Can you imagine that. For $225, you can realize a dream that you never believed possible!"

I figured that was the cue, the link to Tom and Jane and Bill and Bridget. It was now summer and they were still trying to find surrogate mothers who would help them realize their dreams. Certainly, the case of Debbie, Sue, and George would open their eyes.

Debbie said, "You know, Noel, hearing you on the radio seemed like a godsend. Our only regret has been not being able to tell anybody how happy we are. We feel like we have to walk on eggs all the time.

"Everything is going so fine, it's almost scary. Our new doctor is just perfect. We told him our story and he said, 'Fine, I'm not about to try to psych you out. I'm sure that all you're interested in is a normal, healthy baby. That's all I'm interested in. A normal birth. Working together, we'll make it happen.' Now, our only other concern is what do we do after the baby is born. We want the adoption to go as smoothly as everything else. At first, we thought George and I would tell our families and friends that we adopted the baby through an agency. Sue would tell the people at work the child was stillborn. But now, we're so proud that we want to tell those close to us exactly what happened. But we want everything to be perfect legally. We want the adoption to be letter-perfect."

George had not been saying much up to now, but he asked the question: "Noel, we want you to be our lawyer. Will you?"

The question did not surprise me. Debbie, Sue, and George would need a lawyer, though they had certainly done just fine by themselves up to now. They were seated across from my desk and

I was staring out the window at the building beyond. Absent-mindedly, I noticed that my ficus plant was reviving. It had been dying on the vine and Martha's ministrations and those of the other women in the office were of no avail. I had repotted it myself, brought it back to life. I was proud of that. Strange, I thought, what achievements our lives may bring. Noel Keane, apprentice printer and young rowdy, now a tender of ficus plants and attorney to surrogate parents.

"Of course," I said. "I will be your attorney."

It was Saturday afternoon, and I was due at one of Chris's baseball games. We traded home phone numbers and agreed to stay in touch. Then I stopped downstairs at my wife's beauty salon. "Kathy," I said, "I know you hear a lot of stories from the women down here. But you're never going to hear one like the story I just listened to. I'll give you the details."

I was now representing three couples in this crazy new field. It all seemed unreal. I decided to check up on Tom and Jane and Bill and Bridget. They had never met each other, and now I was thinking that perhaps not only should they meet but that the four of them should also meet their latest comrades in arms—Debbie, Sue, and George. In the next few days, I called Jane and Bridget. For some reason, I always found it easier to work with the women.

Jane was happy, as always. "Noel, we've found the woman," she said. "We could have looked the world over and I don't think we could have found a better surrogate mother than the one we've found right in our own backyard. She's Carol, the woman you thought wouldn't work out. She's absolutely perfect, but we're having trouble connecting on the artificial insemination. She isn't pregnant yet."

I told Jane to stick with it, that I knew it could be done. "You're not going to believe this, Jane," I said, "but I'm now representing three people who have already done it. The surrogate mother is three months pregnant. And I want you to meet them."

Bridget was not as happy. "Noel," she said, "We've been

talking to a lot of women, but they just seem to be playing with us. It's really frustrating. I think Bill is about to go crazy.

"One woman sounded real sincere and we figured her fertile day and everything was set. The night before the insemination, she backed out. Said her mother was against it. Another woman said she would do it, but demanded $10,000. A third was ready to go, but there was one condition. She wanted two children. She would keep the first and give us the second. That sounded too risky. Then, a fourth one we were really excited about, pulled the rug out from under us at the last moment. She said the doctor told her she had a heart murmur, that it would be unwise to carry a baby. We think she's lying, but what can you do?

"It's so hard, to get your hopes built up and then have them crash back down. Our only hope now appears to be a girl from the South, from Georgia. We'd like to have someone from around here, but there doesn't seem to be such a person."

I told Bridget, too, to stick with it, that we had a precedent right in our own backyard, three people who had just up and did it. The out-of-state connection sounded like legal trouble, but I told Bridget to come in and talk about it.

The next day, I called Debbie and said, "Debbie, this is your lawyer. Would you like to meet some people who would very much like to be in your shoes?"

"Of course. Just set a time."

Saturdays were my time for the surrogate-motherhood business. It was becoming an office joke. Noel's strange Saturday clientele. But these people didn't have a lot of money and Tom and Jane and Bill and Bridget all lived quite a distance from Detroit. Getting to my office was a major sacrifice for them, and Saturday was the only day they could usually do it. Plus, I was usually busy in court during the week.

Unusual clients were not new to me. Only recently, I had represented a female impersonator who had been in an auto accident and had injured her breasts. The breasts were silicone implants and she was suing the other driver—who was at fault—for disfiguring injuries. The judge was having trouble following my arguments when we went to a bench trial. "Your Honor," I requested, "may we have a private moment in chambers so I can explain to you and defense counsel the nature of these injuries?" The judge agreed, and I proceeded to explain my client's unusual predicament. I'll never forget his words: "Mr. Keane, do you represent a circus?"

A circus, indeed. What would the judge think now, I wondered? I did not worry about it.

The following Saturday, I met with my fellow pioneers. Tom and Jane and Bill and Bridget and Debbie, Sue, and George. It was July and the city was sweltering. My ficus plant was standing tall, but the air conditioning broke down. We were all a bit nervous and ill at ease anyway. The humidity was now making it a fiasco. I did what I always do when trouble strikes—run to Kathy.

"Well, Noel," she said, as her beauticians and customers looked on in amusement, "there's a room at the back of the shop you can use, I guess." It was the laundry room/storage area for the beauty shop, but it was cool.

That's where the first meeting of the surrogate-motherhood alumnae—and alumni—society was held. In a laundry room.

Jane asked the obvious question. "Sue," she said, "how did you ever get the idea, how did you ever make up your mind to do this?"

Sue said, "It was easy, really. You know, I process checks for a living. Now, that's not affecting anybody really. This is affecting a lot of lives. I did it for friendship. I decided:

" 'I can give her the best gift. A baby.' "

·4·
"I got not one but two cigars!"

THAT summer of 1977, we stood in a laundry room, a confused, somewhat scared little group about to embark on a brave new adventure. By the following summer, our ranks would have increased by three. Those three were the first children born to surrogate mothers and surrendered to other couples for adoption.

Tom and Jane would have Tom, Jr., a strapping lad delivered by surrogate mother Carol. Debbie and George would have Elizabeth Anne, a beautiful girl delivered by surrogate mother Sue. Bill and Bridget would have Bill, Jr., a handsome boy delivered by surrogate mother Diane.

As their stories unfolded, the funniest thing happened. We became celebrities of sorts, myself and Debbie, Sue, and George, who decided to go public with their story. Tom and Jane and Bill and Bridget preferred to stay out of the limelight, but the publicity helped their dreams come true.

The year would take me from incredible highs to incredible lows.

Debbie, Sue, and George would proceed with their plans as if surrogate parenting were the simplest, most natural thing in the world. Along the way, they would tell their story to the world and become lightning rods for the coming storm of controversy.

Tom and Jane would find a surrogate mother, Carol, who was so wonderful that the two women were to become lifelong friends. Their story is truly a love story.

Bill and Bridget, however, were not so fortunate. Their surrogate mother, Diane, would eventually deliver Bill, Jr., but along the way she would severely test not only our patience but our belief in the possibilities of the entire concept.

Let me tell you their stories.

Several days after our laundry-room summit conference, Debbie invited Bill and Bridget to her home for more talk. They brought along the young Georgia woman, Dawn, who had heard them on the radio show and who said she wanted to be a surrogate mother.

Bill recalls, "We all started talking at once. The privacy of a home really opens up the communication lines. Dawn seemed so open and honest. She said she would have a baby for Bridget and myself for two reasons. First, she wanted to have the experience of childbirth again, because when she had her first baby she was only sixteen and never really appreciated what was happening to her body. And second, she wanted to know the pleasure of making other people as happy as she was with her son.

"George and Susan were pretty quiet, but Debbie couldn't stop talking. She explained how she had artificially inseminated Sue with George's sperm and how we could do the same thing with Dawn. This was good news because we had been unable to find a doctor to help us. When we left their home, we were all pretty excited."

It was not to last long. Within days, Dawn had a different idea for Bill and Bridget. She wanted $10,000. That was the end of that, because I had made it perfectly clear to Bill and Bridget, as I had to Tom and Jane, that no money or anything of value was to be paid to a surrogate mother other than costs and fees approved by the court.

Tom and Jane, meanwhile, were trying to get their surrogate mother, Carol, pregnant. It wasn't easy.

They, like all the others, were forced to wing it without any real medical help. Ironically, I had told Tom and Jane not to use Carol, figuring that her three sons by previous marriages meant she had too great a love bond to children to ever carry one and then give it up. Carol was to prove me wrong, however.

"Noel," Jane told me, "Carol was our last chance. We took her name right off your legal pad, and we knew that if she didn't work out, we were out of luck.

"Our first conversation went very well, but it was obvious that her initial interest had been due to the fee we had once thought we could pay. Carol wanted to help make a better life for her three sons. She was disappointed that there could be no money but said she would call back.

"The second call, she said she would do it without a fee but she wanted to check with her parents first. I figured that meant no go. Our only other real possibility had been a lady from Alabama, who finally backed out when her parents objected. This woman and her husband had six children, but she had once had an abortion. Her guilt was such that she thought having a baby for someone else would make up for the child she had killed. Her husband was all for it. But she was an only child and her mother said, 'Hey, this would be our grandchild, regardless of who the father is, and you cannot just give it away.' So that was the end of that. Now, we were afraid that Carol might decide the same thing.

"Well, when Carol called for the third time, I was out visiting a friend. Tom took the call, and said he would go find me. He brought me home and we waited for Carol's return call. I was about to climb the walls, I was so nervous. Carol called again and with her first words my heart began to sink. 'My parents say no,' she began. 'That this will be their grandchild and I cannot give a grandchild away. But I am going to do it anyway.' I'll never forget the feeling when Carol said she would do it. The hair stood up on my arms. I had goosebumps. She had met her parents' objections head on and decided to do it, anyway. She explained that although she had always wanted to think her parents really cared about her and were close to her, she knew deep in her heart that they were not. This was something she wanted to do and she decided her parents' opposition was not enough to stop her. We made an appointment to meet with her.

"That first meeting was in a Big Boy restaurant, and we hit it off from the start. She was about my age and coloring and Tom and I could tell immediately that she was sincere about wanting to do this wonderful thing for us."

Carol told me, "I wanted that first meeting to be at a restaurant because we weren't ready yet to start meeting at houses. I hadn't told my boys yet what I was up to. My sons, Tim, fourteen, Chuck, thirteen, and David, seven, are all pretty good guys and I wanted to make sure that Tom and Jane deserved something like this before I put my boys through it. The minute I met them, I knew this was the right thing to do.

"I could just tell that Tom and Jane were very much in love. I guess, to be perfectly honest, I felt that Tom was the kind of husband and father I had always wanted but never found. My taste seems to run to romantic men. You know, real charmers but still little boys at heart. None of them really wanted the responsibility of being a husband and a father. That's why they left. I'm pretty proud of the job I've done raising my boys and I've become pretty independent, but I still admire a happy marriage. Tom and Jane have a happy marriage. You can tell that by looking at them. Jane and I were to become very close, but I never would have done it if I hadn't believed in Tom. He was the husband and father my boys had never known. Jane is wonderful, but to my mind you can't have Jane without Tom.

"I decided to be a surrogate mother for Tom and Jane after about five minutes in that Big Boy restaurant.

"That night, I told my boys. They were in bed and I woke them. I started real slow and just sort of felt them out. Finally, Tim said very nonchalantly, 'Go ahead, Ma.' I told them what good parents Tom and Jane would be, and, from the start, we agreed we would call it Tom and Jane's baby, never Mother's baby.

"I knew my family would give me trouble. Let's face it, most people are negative to this type of thing. Now, Dad's seventy-one and Mom's sixty-six, and they've been Catholics all their lives. Dad went to his priest and the priest said that this was wrong. Dad didn't give me a lot of details, he just said, 'Carol, it's wrong. That's our grandchild you'll be giving away.' They both know I'm not religious anymore, but I guess they figured the Church would scare me. My brother said the same thing, that this was his niece or nephew that I would be carrying for someone else. That really hurt. I thought my brother would support me. I feel badly that my family is not on my side, but I figure I have my own life to lead and nobody else can tell me how to do it.

"Why would I want to carry a baby for someone else? I guess pregnancy was always one of the happiest times of my life. There was a period, between the time Tim and Chuck had been born and the time David was born, when I just couldn't get pregnant. I remember how miserable I felt, so I can really sympathize with someone like Jane who tries so hard to get pregnant and fails. But I guess it was just as well I didn't get pregnant that third time with my first husband. He later had a nervous breakdown and had to be hospitalized. He would come home and threaten me and the boys with a baseball bat. He really flipped out, became schizophrenic. We were terrified. I had to divorce him and start a new life. Then, I met Jimmy, who I suppose is the real love of my life. He and I ran off to Florida once while I was in high school. Now this was a strict Catholic school and at the time it was a pretty racy thing to do. But Jimmy always had a sense of adventure that I loved. He's a real good carpenter and I ended up falling in love with him again after my divorce. That's how I ended up with my son David. But Jimmy just isn't cut out for the home life. He knows it and I know it. I love him, but I cannot live with him. So here I am with three boys and a job as a waitress. But we're making ends meet. My guys are turning out fine. I'm sure that one day I'm going to meet the right man—a man like Tom—and that one day I'm going to find the right job. I've been studying business courses to become an executive secretary, but for now I'm going to have this baby for Tom and Jane. I can't exactly explain why, but this I know—it feels right."

Tom begins to explain the difficulty in impregnating Carol.

"When we started," he said, "there was this doctor at the University of Michigan, a pretty big name, who had agreed to do the insemination if we could find a surrogate. Well, when the story hit the papers and all, he began to worry about malpractice. He talked to me three or four times on the phone, but the bottom line was he wouldn't do it.

"What happened next is a bit of classic advice. Never listen to a friend when you need an expert. A friend of mine was having trouble getting his wife pregnant and he had been going to a fertility clinic. I figured I would ask him for advice. Now apparently his problem was a low sperm count and his doctor had recommended that he have sex only every third day or so of his wife's fertile period. He told me that the sperm needed two to three days to mature in the woman's body if it were to become potent. Well, that sounded good to me, so we decided we would try to inseminate Carol only every third day during her fertile period.

"Another complicating factor is that Carol's period ranges widely, anywhere from twenty-eight to fifty days. So we never knew what was going on. Whether the high and low temperatures really meant anything and whether she was on a thirty-day cycle or a sixty-day cycle. When you figure that the target zone for sperm to meet the egg can be as little as five minutes, you know what we were up against. Basically, Jane would take Carol's temperature every morning and the minute it got up in the high zone and stayed there, we would try to inseminate her.

"It was becoming a real drag. I work afternoons as a skilled craftsman at an auto plant, and Jane would pick me up at midnight. We would drive across town to see Carol, who would have had to wait up for us all this time and explain to her children what she was doing and all. We would visit for a while and then I would go in the bathroom and masturbate into a glass jar. Carol would then inseminate herself. Carol had to work the next morning, her three sons were sleeping, and yet, there she was at two in the morning trying to get pregnant with my sperm.

"This went on for two months. Jane and I were worried we would lose Carol. We had no reason to believe that her motivation was as strong as ours. Finally, I began to think that maybe it was my fault, that my sperm count was low. I made an appointment with a fertility expert, a physician from India. He tested me and said my sperm count was perfectly normal. 'Tell me what you are doing', he said. Well, I didn't tell him about the surrogate-motherhood part of it, but I had the charts and temperatures and everything and I told him how we were making attempts two or three times during the fertile period. The doctor laughed. 'What's the matter?,' he said. 'Don't you like sex?' I explained, 'Well, it's not that. But, you see, we have to give time for the sperm to mature.' He laughed even louder. 'The sperm,' the doctor said, 'will take care of itself. It will mature right now, just like this. Don't worry about the sperm. You can do it three or four times a day.' Well, so much for the advice from my friend. Jane and I started to go out to Carol's house every night during her fertile period. And, wouldn't you know it, she got pregnant right away."

Carol's pregnancy would turn out to be one of the happiest moments in Jane's life. She can hardly discuss Carol without getting choked up, but as she tells how she happened to find out Carol was pregnant, Jane makes no attempt to turn back the tears.

"I will never forget that day," Jane says. "It even sounds a little silly. A friend of ours had a private plane and he had been after us to go for a ride. We had set a date for a Saturday, but then Carol set an appointment the same day for a pregnancy test. Tom and I both thought Carol would become pregnant, now that we no longer had to worry about the sperm 'maturing.' We didn't know whether or not to take the plane ride. Finally, I told Tom, 'Look, the results may not even be in by the time the ride is over. Why don't you go ahead and go up and I'll stay at home just in case.'

"Now, we had a prearranged signal. We have a pool in our backyard and Tom could locate the house by the pool. I told him to fly over the house and if Carol were pregnant, I would wave my hands. Well, sure enough, Carol called me to tell me she was pregnant. When I saw Tom's little plane flying over the house, I jumped up and down and waved and waved. I didn't have any idea if he could tell if he could see me waving.

Tom cuts in, "I could see Jane and I thought she was waving, but it was so far away I couldn't be sure. I had to hear it for myself."

Jane: "About an hour later, Tom was coming up the walk. He looked anxious. I couldn't wait to tell him. 'Honey, the answer is yes. Yes, yes, yes. Carol is pregnant.' "

Tom: "I couldn't believe it. We had tried so hard and so long to get Carol pregnant and nothing seemed to work. And now it had happened. She was pregnant. I thought, 'Hey, we did it. We're going to have a baby.' "

Jane: "A lot of things were racing through my mind. I wanted to put Carol under a glass bowl. You know, don't do this, don't do that. Are you eating right? Are you drinking enough? Are you taking your vitamins? All the things I would do if I were pregnant. I made her some maternity clothes, brought her flowers, took her out to eat. We have become very close."

Carol: "We've had some good times. I'll take the boys over to Tom and Jane's and we'll lounge around the pool, broil some steaks. My boys really love that."

I sat there and looked at Carol, who was now obviously pregnant, and reflected back on that day almost a year earlier when she was little more than a hope in Tom and Jane's eyes. Jane had been crying a year ago and she was crying now, but they were tears of joy. Whenever I would have doubts about surrogate motherhood, I would summon up that visual slide of Tom, Jane, and Carol sitting in my office and telling me how happy they were. It kept me going.

About this time there came a phone call from Chicago that was destined to put surrogate motherhood on the front page. Or, more precisely, on the popular Phil Donahue television show, which is syndicated out of Chicago. Donahue's programming people had been noticing the Detroit publicity about Tom and Jane and Bill and Bridget, and wanted to know if either or both couples would appear on the show.

Knowing how private they are, I thought it highly unlikely that either couple would appear on national television.

But we now had two surrogate-mothers-to-be who were pregnant—Carol and Sue.

Carol wanted no part of television. "I'm doing this for Tom and Jane," she said. "Period. This summer, while I was trying to get pregnant, it was hot and muggy and hard. We went two months without any luck and by the third month I was thinking, 'If it doesn't take this month, I don't know what I'm going to do.' I cannot tell you how relieved I was when we finally hit during the third month. I'm happy for Tom and Jane and I'm happy for myself. My boys accepted it. That's enough for me. I don't have to tell the world."

Sue surprised me. Knowing how shy she is I had assumed she would want no part of going on a live talk show with a studio audience monitoring her every word. But I felt obligated to make the request. "Sue," I said, "Phil Donahue wants to know if you'll fly down to Chicago the end of August and be his guest. What do you think?"

Her reply was quick. "Sure, but only if Debbie and George will come with me."

The soon-to-be-famous trio agreed to do the show. One reason for their decision had happened a few nights before. A co-worker in whom Sue had confided her secret wanted to know, "Are you selling your baby?" Stunned, Sue responded: "I'm placing my baby up for adoption and George and Debbie are adopting it."

Enraged that anyone would think Sue would sell a baby, the three decided that maybe it was time to set the record straight to the world. They agreed to an August 29th taping. Then it hit Debbie: "My God, now we'll have to tell our families or they're going to find out on TV."

Debbie recalls, "I was pretty sure my parents would not condemn us, but I worried about how George's parents would react." George thought, "We'll have to present it just right. Now, my father thinks he's a great liberal, but he's not. Once he hears that we've come up with this idea to have our white baby, he'll think it's terrible. Had we adopted a Black child, he would have thought it was the greatest thing in the world. We'd go to heaven. We'd be at the right hand of the Pope, or whatever. But this? Forget it."

Debbie continues, "We told my parents right away, about Sue's pregnancy and the TV show. My mother said that she understood all that we had told her and that we should wait for my father to get home from work. He worked nights and wouldn't be home until two A.M.. So we sat around and killed time and everyone was kind of stiff. Finally, Dad came in and began to tell us a story about something that had happened at work. I interrupted to tell him our story. Everything. And that we were going on TV in a week. He replied, 'You people are adults and know what you are doing.' Then, he calmly resumed his story about the guy at work. My mother was a little upset, but she would never let us know it.

"Then, we went to see George's Aunt Lucey and Uncle Gene. We had always been close to them and they had an adopted son. We thought they would give us some pointers in telling the rest of the family. They were both very happy for us, and said they wished they could have had a child the same way. Uncle Gene said that what we did was our business and if other people didn't like it, well, it wasn't their lives. Aunt Lucey gave us tips on how to tell our baby about adoption. Next, we told my Uncle Don and

Aunt Lucky. They accepted it and gave Sue the biggest hug and kiss that I have ever seen."

George was not as fortunate with his family. "My father," he said, "would simply not accept it. In fact, he would not believe it. He told me to my face that he didn't believe it was artificial insemination, that he thought there was something sexual between Sue and me. If he were not my father, I would have hit him. Instead, I just walked out of the house. What can you do when your father says he doesn't believe you in something as important as this? On the other hand, my brother was coming back from Arizona to get married and when my parents told him what we said we had done, he told them, 'I know that whatever George did, it was the right thing.' That made me feel good. But I knew that going to my brother's wedding would be a big strain on all of us."

The families were told, but not that there was to be a television appearance.

The flight to Chicago for the Donahue show was in itself an experience. It was the first time Debbie and Sue had ever been on an airplane.

I appeared on the show with the trio, my first of several such appearances to discuss surrogate motherhood. Since the topic is so controversial, I have thought from the start that it is best to cooperate with the news media. That way you are not hiding anything. Everything is out in the open. People can judge for themselves.

Donahue, of course, has built his popularity around daytime talk shows that promote women's causes. The women love him and nearly 90 percent of his always-packed audiences are women. They were packed to the rafters for this show and they were not disappointed.

In their own styles, Debbie, Sue, and George told their story with confidence and dignity. Debbie, as usual, did most of the talking, but Sue came across as very believable in wanting to give a gift to her friend and George left no doubts that he was mighty pleased at the thought of being a father.

I could only state the obvious. There were no laws in this area. If Sue changed her mind, it would be her baby and George might have to pay child support. If Debbie and George backed out, it would be Sue's baby. No fee could be paid. The entire risk was based on one word—trust.

The audience and the call-in viewers had their doubts, that was clear. Most of the people seemed to think, "What if this happens. . . . . What if that happens?" Legally, of course, there were no answers, only educated guesses. Many people were put off that Debbie performed the insemination herself. Debbie replied, "I feel honored to be the one who helped make conception of our child possible."

We were all satisfied with the way the show went, but as George would observe, "I'm not sure it really sunk in to these people about how happy we are. That we're about to have a baby. They seemed to be all hung up on everything that could go wrong and at how unusual it is."

By now, I was turning my mind to the legal challenges ahead for my three clients.

I had recently received a call from a potential surrogate from Tennessee named Diane, who said she was willing to carry a child for Bill and Bridget. She sounded sincere, but I knew that an out-of-state surrogate would present special problems to custody transfer and adoption.

While Bill and Bridget's legal problems were in finding and contracting with a surrogate mother, Tom, Jane, and Carol and Debbie, Sue, and George presented a happier legal problem. How to arrange for hospital privileges for the adoptive couples and how to accomplish the adoptions of their children born to surrogate mothers?

There was one startling fact. Neither couple thought it necessary to have a legal contract with their surrogate mother. "We trust Carol," said Tom and Jane; "We trust Sue," said Debbie and George. I told them that a contract might facilitate other things, but they were adamant. They had come this far on trust and they would go the distance on trust. Knowing their stories so far, I could not really argue with them. For that matter, I have never had a contract with Debbie, Sue, and George. My legal fees to them are absolutely zero.

The big thing on everybody's mind was getting Carol and Sue through their pregnancies as comfortably as possible and having two healthy babies. My work would come after those happy events.

I kept in touch and was pleased to learn that everything was proceeding for both threesomes smoothly.

Debbie would share with me her diary entries. "On October 4th," she wrote, "I heard my baby's heartbeat for the first time. It was so exciting to know she was really there. I couldn't contain myself in the doctor's office. I couldn't wait to tell George. We ran out and bought a stethoscope so that George could hear the heartbeat also, but the instrument wasn't strong enough. I told George that from now on he would come with us to the doctor's office.

Debbie, Sue, and George started out having a little trouble with doctors. It was very important to Debbie that she be allowed in the delivery room and be allowed to feed the baby the first time. In effect, she also wanted "father's privileges." Her first doctor would not allow this. Beyond that, a psychiatrist to whom the three had been referred for an optional consultation, had trouble believing and understanding what the three had wrought. After several hours of talking in circles, Debbie finally decided, "Well, we can all do without this. The man simply cannot believe what we have done. Why should we talk to him?"

I suggested to the three that they first pick a hospital and then select an obstetrician on that staff. If the doctor agrees to your situation, I suggested, then I'm sure you can be part of the birth. That's what happened. Dr. Keith Curtis of Dearborn's Oakwood Hospital accepted their case, saying, "Look, I'm not going to try to analyze what you've done. All I want to do is deliver a healthy baby."

Sue was having a very easy pregnancy, though she was always very tired.

From Debbie's diary, I learned that a housewarming party (George and Debbie bought a small house to replace their trailer which had burned and Sue moved in with them) was a big success, with the meeting between a pregnant Sue and the relatives of Debbie and George going well. "My family," Debbie wrote, "treated Sue just as if she were family. They asked her how it felt to be big as a house. George's family was courteous to Sue, but nothing more. Of all the gifts, by far the most precious was from my parents. It was a photo album. As I unwrapped it, I thought what in the world is this, but when I saw my wedding album I couldn't stop crying. George and I lost our album in the fire and here my mother was giving us hers. It was the happiest moment in my life so far. I could never thank her enough."

An even bigger treat was a surprise baby shower that a hugely pregnant Sue gave for her best friend Debbie. "Can you imagine my surprise," Debbie wrote, "when I saw all these wonderful people? The only disappointment was that George's mother didn't show. I felt like telling her never to set foot in my house again and that I would never set foot in hers. I was very upset that she would choose to snub a shower for her granddaughter or grandson."

On January 26, 1978, at four A.M., Sue woke up Debbie with screams brought on by her labor contractions. The night before she had done the same thing and Debbie rushed her to the hospital. But it had been a false alarm. This time, it was the real thing. Debbie's diary has the story:

"I thought how ironic it was. We were having another terrible snowstorm, the worst I had seen since the day Sue drove me to the hospital for an emergency hysterectomy that I thought meant the end of my dream to have a baby. Now, here I was driving Sue to the hospital to fulfill the dream.

"The driving conditions were brutal, but there was no way I was not going to get Sue to the hospital. We made it, and the first thing I did was to call George at work and tell him, 'If you want to see the birth of your child, you had better get here quickly.' He was working the midnight shift, but had made arrangements to leave early if necessary. George arrived in record time, and, together, we sat with Sue for about thirty minutes. She was in such pain that we begged the nurse to let her lie down. They put her in a labor room and said that only one of us could be with her. We could not switch off. George told me to go ahead and stay with her. Dr. Curtis was there, and he told us he had some appointments, but that he would be back at the hospital as soon as possible. Sue was put on the fetal monitor, which would light up every time she was about to have a contraction. For two hours, I sat and held her hand to help her through the pain. Then, I took a cigarette break to talk to George. Suddenly, it hit me: Here I was having a cigarette while Sue was having my baby. I rushed back into the labor room in time to catch another contraction. She was having a very difficult time, and there was nothing I could do for her except put cold washcloths on her lips and forehead. Not once did she cry. Then came a crazy scene. Sue likes to work crossword puzzles, so I had brought some with me. So there we sat, as Sue alternately contracted with labor pains, tried to calmly work a crossword, and dozed off.

"It was now three P.M., eleven hours after Sue woke up in pain, and our doctor had still not returned. He was in emergency surgery. I could see the pain in Sue's face every time she had a contraction. We both were crying openly now, me because she was going through such pain for me and Sue because she thought she was upsetting me by being in pain. When Dr. Curtis arrived at four P.M., I went out to see George, who was sleeping. It was then I realized Michigan was having its all-time worst snowstorm. And my baby was about to be born on this day. George said he wanted to see Sue, and I said fine. I knew one of the labor room nurses from high school, and I was pretty sure she would let George take my place in the labor room. Some fifteen minutes later, George returned white as a sheet and said, 'Sue is in great pain. She's having dry heaves from the medication.' I went in to help her, and was astonished when Dr. Curtis told me, 'She's only dilated one centimeter and she has nine more to go before the baby can be born.' I didn't have the heart to tell Sue, though she looked at me with pleading eyes.

"Then, the doctor told me that Sue was exhausted and he was going to shut down labor induction, let her rest through the night, and start up in the morning. I was shocked. How could Sue possibly go through all of this again the next day? I went out to tell George, and he was almost in tears. We both begged the doctor not to prolong this. He said he would monitor the baby's heartbeat and decide what to do. After a half hour, he said she was through with labor for the day and he would give her a shot to rest. George went home to sleep and I decided to stay with Sue through the night.

"About ten minutes after George left, the doctor took the fetal-heartbeat monitor off Sue's stomach and inserted it through the vagina onto the baby's head. Sue has always hated pelvic exams, and this was probably the most painful moment in her life. She screamed so loud that I had to leave the room. I didn't want her to see me upset because that would only have upset her more.

"Dr. Curtis was worried. For the next fifteen minutes, he noted that the baby's heartbeat was almost 200 a minute. Normal is only 128-150. Dr. Curtis called me aside and said, 'We cannot wait any longer. We are going to do a Caesarian.'

"I was overjoyed. Sue would not have to face any more pain. When I told her, her face lit up with relief. I stayed with her until they wheeled her off to surgery. 'Sue,' I said, 'everything will be OK. We love you and when you come back, we'll be right here.'

"I rushed to the phone to call George, but there was no answer. I panicked. Then, I remembered. The snow, stupid. It's going to take him some time to get home. Fortunately, we only lived a few minutes from the hospital. When George finally answered, all I could say was, "They're doing a C-section right now. By the time you get here, you'll be a father!' He said, 'I'll be there.'

"I sat in the waiting room, blankly looking at a TV screen. All I could think was, 'Within the hour, you'll be a mother.' I was crying when George walked in. I couldn't believe that he had driven through a snowstorm and beaten his child to the hospital. "By eight P.M., George and I were both so anxious that we just walked over to the labor area and waited. Suddenly, the doctor that assisted in the delivery came walking down the hall. He had a big smile. 'She is doing fine, and the baby is beautiful,' he said. He started to add, 'It is a . . .' when I screamed out. 'No, don't tell us the sex. That is for Susan to do.'

"About five minutes later, they wheeled Sue down the corridor on a stretcher. She was crying. I just looked at her and said:

" 'Well?'

"She said, 'Didn't they tell you, yet?'

" 'No, we are waiting for you to tell us.'

"Sue said softly, 'I give you a girl.'

"I was still crying when Dr. Curtis came around the corner and said, 'Here she is.'

"I couldn't believe my eyes. She was beautiful and wonderful. All I could do was hug Susan, hug George, and thank God.

"I looked at my daughter very carefully and said, 'Elizabeth Anne, I could never carry you under my heart, but I have always carried you in my heart. I love you, Elizabeth Anne.' "

Three months later, Carol would deliver a boy, Tom, Jr., for Tom and Jane.

Carol calls it "an easy pregnancy, one of my easiest. Oh, I was throwing up the first few months, but all I had to do was stop smoking. That's how I know I'm pregnant. When I can't stand cigarettes. I kept getting bigger and bigger. I knew it was going to be a boy, a big boy. The only problem I had was going to my guys' basketball games. I mean I was showing pretty big, and some of my sons' friends know that I am not married. But nothing was ever said. It was just in my mind."

Jane picks up, "Carol was two weeks late and Tom and I were both worried. She's had three children, so, obviously she knows the ropes. Now, Carol is just the kindest person you'll ever meet.

She lived quite a distance from us and though we wanted to take her to the hospital, she didn't want to bring us out for nothing. Here she was about to have our baby, but she didn't want to inconvenience us. Finally she called. 'Jane,' she said, 'I think my water bag's broken. I'm not sure, but, maybe you want to come over just in case.'

"I said, 'We'll be there. It was nine P.M. and Tom and I jumped in the car. Now, Tom was trying to be super calm or something, but he was just ambling along like we were out for a Sunday drive. I said, 'Honey, we have a one hour drive ahead of us to get to Carol. Maybe if you step on the gas, we can make it in forty-five minutes.' When we finally pulled up in front of her house, a neighbor was getting ready to take her to the hospital. We put her in the front seat of our car, and I got in the back. She was having a hard time, and I rolled down the windows to let the cold air hit her. We were all nervous, but at least Tom had found out where the gas pedal was."

Carol: "I was about to get in my neighbor's car when Tom and Jane pulled up. So, I got in the car with them and told the neighbor, 'Please take good care of my boys. I'll be back.'

"All I can remember about the hospital is the pain. I had decided that for once in my life I was going to have a natural birth. Jane and I went through the classes together. It all seemed pretty easy during the pregnancy, but when the moment of truth came I thought I was going to die from the pain. My back was killing me."

Jane: "Tom and I had driven the route from Carol's house to the hospital several times in advance because we wanted to be ready. This was a strange part of town to us. We made it to the hospital, got Carol admitted, and were standing around waiting. I found the nurse and said, 'Do you know that she and I went to natural childbirth class together? That I'm supposed to be in the delivery room with her?' Well, the nurse was pretty vague about the whole thing. I started to panic. 'She's not on top of this,' I thought. 'I'm going to miss the whole shot.'

"But no, luck was with us. The nurse came back and said, 'We're ready for you now. Just put on this outfit.' I went into the delivery room, where Carol was already strapped down on the table, and laid my head down next to hers. We both were looking at a big mirror to watch the baby be born."

Tom: "I guess I should have gone into the delivery room, too. I know Jane wanted me to. But I was trying to make it as easy as possible for the surrogate mother. I did not want to embarrass Carol."

Carol: "I thought my back was breaking. I really did. I kept yelling, 'My back is killing me!' The doctor just kept saying, 'Hold your breath. Press down.' Finally, it was all over."

Jane: "I cannot put words to it. I saw the baby's head start to come out and, apparently, it was turned a little bit awkward. Then, the child made a final turn and the head came out. Looking into the big mirror, I saw this big head of black hair. Now, Tom is black-haired, but Carol is blonde. I thought, 'Oh, it's not blonde.' Then, the rest of the body just flipped right out. The head came hard, but the body just flipped out. I saw that it was a boy, a big boy, and I thought, 'Well, this is it. The answer to our prayers.' The doctor took him and put him under the light and I was the next person to touch him. Carol said, 'I'm so happy for both of you.'"

Carol: "I could tell that Jane was very, very happy. Tom, too. I could see it in their eyes. Then I went to sleep."

Tom: "I guess I was stupid not to go into the delivery room. Jane tells me that once you see a baby being born, your baby, you'll never forget it."

Jane: "When did it hit me that we had done the impossible? Well, not until about three days later when we took Carol home. We picked her up at the hospital and the nurse put Carol in the front seat and handed her the baby. But Carol said, 'No, not me. That's Jane's baby. Give him to her.' So I took the baby. We drove Carol home and took her in the door and visited for a while. Then we went back to the car, Tom and myself and Tom, Jr.

"That's when it hit us. We had our baby. I was forty and Tom was thirty-eight and we had our baby. As we drove home, Tom and I never said a word. We just looked at each other and cried."

Well, as you can see, the difficult work was over. Sue and Carol had made believers out of Debbie and George and Tom and Jane. All I had to do now was to make sure that these extraordinary births would be followed by ordinary adoptions. Because that was all that Debbie and George wanted for Elizabeth Anne and Tom and Jane wanted for Tom, Jr. To adopt them and give them an ordinary upbringing.

I had been talking to my friends at Wayne County Probate Court, particularly Judge Lincoln. Mrs. Pfieffer and I felt encouraged. I knew it would be difficult, but I was confident that what these six people had accomplished through imagination, perseverance, and resourcefulness could certainly be given the protection of the law.

But these are legal issues. It was a time to be happy. Shortly after Tom and Jane took Carol home from the hospital, they showed up in my office with a visitor. Tom, Jr., who with black hair and flashing brown eyes, is the spitting image of his father. Jane, as usual, was crying.

That night I would tell my wife, "Honey, I got not one but two cigars!"

·5·

"Surrogate mothers may replace adoption and revolutionize how people go about having babies."

It WAS during 1978 that I had to confront the surrogate-motherhood phenomenon head on.

The children born to George and Debbie and Tom and Jane by surrogate mothers, who were motivated only by a desire to help barren women, made for inspiring stories. But I had to ask myself, were these births merely a curiosity or did they represent a new cause? Were they minor miracles that should be celebrated and forgotten or were they the beginning of a movement?

In short, should I stop while I was ahead or should I continue charting previously undiscovered legal, moral, and religious territories?

The answer would be provided by a television show. In late March 1978, Debbie, Sue, and George made a repeat performance on the Phil Donahue Show. But this time they brought a guest—two-month-old Elizabeth Anne.

The format was the same. Donahue worked the jam-packed crowd of women and fielded call-in questions. Debbie, Sue, and George sat down in front, the center of hundreds of eyes in the live studio audience and of millions across the country. But while their earlier appearance had prompted moral reservations and legal questions from the audience, this time there was only one focal point: Elizabeth Anne, blonde-haired, blue-eyed, and as real as a baby's yell, which she cut loose with a couple of times.

Debbie, Sue, and George might have previously stimulated discussion of abstract issues of fundamental social importance, but now there could be no doubt about their motivation. And happiness. Elizabeth Anne was clearly the apple of their eyes and she clearly won the hearts of the audience.

The show was one of Donahue's highest-rated ever and the audience came down firmly on the side of what Debbie, Sue, and George had done to bring Elizabeth Anne into the world.

I have always believed in publicity and the news media because I think it is the only way to truly find out what people are really thinking.

I knew the experts, from the Pope on down, would be against our unconventional idea. I was not disappointed. The doctors, lawyers, and social agencies did not want to be bothered. In a very real sense, it was the newspapers and the radio and TV shows that made all of this happen by reaching the people who were becoming very excited about surrogate motherhood.

After the Donahue show, the mail came into my office in a blizzard from every corner of the country. There were a few critical letters—very few. The vast majority were supportive of what Debbie, Sue, and George had done, and about half of the letter writers asked for help in doing the same thing.

When I managed to wrestle the letters away from my office manager, Martha, who was astonished at the outpouring, I took the better part of a day to sift slowly through them and reflect.

What it all meant, I realized, was this: People were very excited about the possibilities of surrogate motherhood and had no idea about what to do next.

The letters were addressed both to myself and to Debbie, Sue, George, and Elizabeth Anne. Some almost made me cry. Many were written on floral stationery in lovely handwriting. They expressed praise for the trio's courage, admiration for going public with their story, best wishes for the baby, and a plea for advice on how to find or become a surrogate mother and how to later deal psychologically with adopted children. This letter is typical:

"Dear George and Debbie: I have never written to anyone before. But after seeing you on the 'Phil Donahue Show,' your story really hit home with me. I want you to know how much I admire what you have done and how lucky I think Elizabeth Anne is to have Sue as a surrogate mother and you and George as parents. This is truly a loved child. I have been married six years and cannot have children. I feel very inadequate as a mother and woman. Can you ask your attorney to contact me if he thinks there is any way I might be able to pursue something like artificial insemination of a surrogate mother? . . . ."

And this:

"Dear George and Debbie: I think what you did is very wonderful and I admire you, for it must have taken a lot of courage. Certainly, your willingness to tell your story to the world puts you one step in front of your critics. Now, I have a question for you. I am sixteen and adopted. I realized I was adopted when I was about ten. My parents never told me and they have no idea that I know. I love them very much, but I would like someday to meet my real parents. What are my legal rights as an adopted child? How long should I wait before I tell my parents? . . . ."

Obviously, my friends had touched many deep feelings and provoked a wide range of emotions out there.

Everything that I knew so far about surrogate mothers I had learned on the job. (As I said, I had never even handled an adoption before.) But two factors had to be a part of the program if surrogate parenting was to become common and workable on a large scale.

First, we had to make sure that children born this way could be adopted. That is the worry of the infertile couple.

Second, we had to make it legal to pay a reasonable fee to the surrogate mother. That would be the only way there would ever be enough surrogate mothers to meet the demand from the infertile.

I decided I was going to see this cause through. To solve the first problem, I began the legal work to accomplish what would become a landmark adoption by Debbie and George of Elizabeth Anne. The same procedures would be used for the adoption of Tom, Jr. To solve the second problem, I began the legal work to sue the state of Michigan and overturn the ban on paying a surrogate mother.

The resolution of these legal issues, I knew, would determine whether or not there will be other children like Elizabeth Anne and Tom, Jr. in the future.

Biting this legal bullet meant that I would have a new purpose and emphasis to my legal practice. What had formerly been general practice would now become uniquely specialized. I was about to become the legal champion of surrogate mothers. And my old friends, the news reporters, would be back on my case.

In those early days, it was pretty heady stuff. Here I was, Noel Keane, the son of a factory worker from East Dearborn, Michigan, suddenly seeing myself in *Time* magazine and *People* magazine—and on national television.

But as I argued for the cause, there was always a nagging concern in the back of my mind. Assaulting as we were the most fundamental customs and strongest feelings of people, I knew that we had to proceed with the utmost caution. This new concept of surrogate parenting and the legal questions it raised would require great judgment on my part. And the people who got involved would also have to exercise the ultimate in judgment—and trust. Eventually, I thought, the best answer would be legislation and regulation through binding contracts by the state. But that was years away. In the meantime, there were people who were putting their lives on the line. And asking me for help.

In those early days, I was pretty flush with the success of Debbie, Sue, and George and Tom, Jane, and Carol. But as usual, my wife, Kathy, and the conscience of my office, Martha, would bring me back to earth. Part of our success, they pointed out, was pure luck. Things might have taken a different tack. After all, look at what is happening to Bill and Bridget.

My baptism of fire with this concept was the complicated case of Bill and Bridget and their surrogate mother from Tennessee, Diane. Throughout the summer of 1978, as other things proceeded smoothly, this case was a constant concern.

I had been very impressed by the parallels in our two earlier cases. Though the couples are years apart in age, both Debbie and George and Tom and Jane are hard-working people who subscribe to the simple virtues of home, hearth, and happiness. The men worked night shifts, the wife kept the house, and the only thing missing was children. Their surrogate mothers, Sue and Carol respectively, who were motivated by truly wanting to give the most precious of gifts to others, added children to the family equation. Trust was the glue that bound them together through the storm of disapproval. I was called in, really, to make legal and respectable what they had largely done themselves. Their stories are happy ones.

Bill and Bridget and Diane seemed to start out that way, too. But it was a mirage.

When Diane first called me on the phone, she sounded like a good prospect. She had seen the first Donahue show and she wanted to help an infertile couple. She was a thirty-one-year-old divorcee with a two-year-old son. I asked all the right questions and she gave all the right answers.

Now, I knew that Bill and Bridget were having a frustrating time. Time and again they thought they had the right surrogate mother only to have the woman walk out or demand money. I knew they were getting increasingly desperate. Their situation was truly dead-ended for every possibility except surrogate motherhood.

I had some qualms about letting them talk to Diane, distressed as they were, but she sounded OK. I had long ago decided that I could not choose the surrogate mothers. Not only for legal reasons, but simply because this is an intimate bond and what seems important in a potential surrogate mother to me may not to someone else. And vice versa. I would do the preliminary screening, but the choice—and responsibility—was between the couples and the surrogate mothers. Debbie and George and Tom and Jane had found their own surrogate mothers. In fact, I had at first recommended against the woman who gave birth to Jane and Tom's baby. So, I figured, let Bill and Bridget talk to Diane and let's see what happens.

"She seemed sincere," said Bill later on. "She really did. Boy, were we fooled."

It is late 1978, and Bill and Bridget are sitting in my office. They have their son, Bill, Jr., and he is tugging at my ficus plant. His father, Bill, the ex-Marine, has arms of steel but they are as gentle as silk as they wrap around Bill, Jr. Their story worked out, but the twists and turns had Bill on the verge of a nervous breakdown. "Noel," he said, "I knew you were concerned about how things were going, but you didn't know the half of it. I couldn't tell you everything because you would not have wanted to know. This woman put us through the wringer emotionally.

"As I said, Bridget and I both talked to Diane on the phone and she sounded fine. So we drove down to Tennessee to visit with her. She looked great—tall, blonde hair, soft brown eyes. Her boy, Anson, looked great. He was only about two years old, but she had a huge album of photos of him. I mean it must have been a week-by-week photo progress report. Normally, you don't have an album that big until your children graduate from college. She seemed like a good mother, like she really loved children, and like she really wanted to help us."

Bridget says, "She was divorced, and she said how important it was to her to have had a child. She said she wanted to help others have the same happiness. We believed her. We should have asked her more about her personal life, but we never did. That would come back to haunt us."

Bill says, "We got to her house at about ten in the morning and talked and talked until about three-thirty. Everything said go. She was older, thirty-one, and seemed mature, she already had a beautiful baby, and she wanted to help us. We decided to do the insemination right then. This was October 1977.

Bridget: "I did the insemination myself. Bill and I had talked to Debbie and George and they had told us it was really very simple. As a nice touch, Diane asked that I do it. She said she wanted me from the start to feel close to the baby. At Debbie's suggestion, Bill and I had abstained from sex for about ten days before. So Bill had no trouble ejaculating his sperm into the glass jar. Just like Debbie and George, we used a drugstore syringe to do the insemination."

Bill: "It was about forty days later when Diane called. She asked for me and said, 'Bill, you are going to be a father!' I was unbelievably happy. It seemed too good to be true. Diane said she was going to a female doctor, that she had explained everything to the doctor, that the doctor thought it was a fantastic idea, and that she would be sending us a medical statement confirming the pregnancy. Bridget and I were beside ourselves with joy. We had already told both our parents what we were trying to do, and now we got in the car to go tell them the good news. We had done it."

Bill: "Now, Noel, we followed the instructions on the legal forms Diane signed with Bridget and myself, but we haven't told you everything about the money. We knew that nothing could be paid to Diane except expenses and, at first, she seemed to agree to that. We told her that you had specifically ruled out any kind of a fee. Now, we were all pretty vague about it, but she said that since her son, Anson, was so young, not quite two, it didn't make a lot of sense for her to try to work. For one thing, she couldn't get a good job, and, for another, whatever she made would be eaten up by a babysitter. So she suggested that maybe we could help her get through the pregnancy, help pay for the rent and food and so on, and then, maybe after the baby was born, help her get back on her feet and get a better job. She was thinking of going to computer school. She also said that she was very close to her son and hated to leave him alone right now. Well, it all seemed pretty sensible, and we thought that she was helping us and we could help her. We never discussed dollar figures, but it was kind of understood that we would try to help her along those lines. We were more than happy."

Bridget: "We're not wealthy people, as you know. Bill is a butcher at the military commissary and I do clerical work there. If things get tight, I would be among the first to go. But we had our home and some money in the bank, and this baby was what we really wanted. It seemed only fair that we should help Diane pursue her dreams, too."

I had in front of me a copy of the Statement of Understanding that had been signed February 18, 1978, by Bill and Bridget and Diane. It read:

"That Bill and Bridget _____ of _____ , Michigan, are unable to bear their own child.

That Diane _____ of _____ , Tennessee, has consented to carry a child for them.

That as a result of that offer, Diane _____ was artificially inseminated with the semen of Bill _____ .

That as a result of that insemination, Diane _____ is now pregnant and expects to give birth in July 1978.

It is the understanding of all parties concerned that actual and legal custody will be given to Bill and Bridget _____ and that Diane _____ will cooperate in whatever manner necessary so that their understanding can be brought to a conclusion."

In a separate agreement among the three, I made it clear that only expenses—no fee—could be paid.

It all sounded nice and neat, but as I was to learn, it hardly worked out that way.

Bill said, "It started about Christmas 1977. We had all signed the standard agreement form and everything beyond that was simply on good faith. Diane had just gotten pregnant and it was Christmas and Bridget and I were very happy. So when Diane called one day to say she had not seen her mother, who lived in Boston, in quite a while and that she would like to see her and that neither she nor her mother had money to travel but could we help, we thought why not. We sent her money to cover the trip. When she came back after the first of the year, she called us and said how thrilled she had been to see her mother again and thanked us for making it possible."

Bridget: "I think that's what triggered her greed. That first request was met by us so quickly that she must have begun to think that we were the Tooth Fairies."

Bill: "We didn't hear from her again until March, though. Then she called one night in tears to say that she had been robbed. We had just sent her $400 to cover the rent, groceries, clothes for Anson, and so on and now she was telling us that she had cashed the check and somebody had robbed her. I said, 'Don't worry, we'll send you another $400 right away.' That was probably a mistake. She must have thought we were easy touches. And we were. We were scared to hurt her. Or upset her. After all, she was carrying our baby. Maybe she thought we were loaded. We are not. We both have to work to make ends meet."

Bridget: "From that time, she was calling us collect about every other night. It was always one thing or another, but the point was that she always needed money. More and more money."

Bill: "Christ, the stories she would come up with. One night, she said she had fallen down the steps and hurt her back and needed money to pay the doctor. A few nights later, she said she had smashed up her car and needed money to fix it. Like fools, we kept sending the money."

Bridget: "One night she called and I couldn't make out what she was saying because she was so high or drunk. I had to call Bill to the phone."

Bill: "She kept talking about her girl friend. She said she was living with a friend to help share expenses. And that the friend was giving her a hard time because of what she was doing for us. That it was bad and wrong and that she was no good. She said that the friend got mad one night and went berserk and busted out all her windows and slapped her and so on. I guess that should have been a tipoff to me as to what was going on, but it never registered. I'm pretty naïve, I guess. I just sent her more money."

Bill's remarks brought back a memory. One day, Martha had told me, "Noel, the surrogate mother for Bill and Bridget just called and she sounded drunk. I couldn't tell what she wants, but she said that she'd call back." She never did, of course. Why should she mess with me when she had Bill and Bridget right where she wanted them?

Bill: "Finally, I reached the breaking point. Our phone bill was running $300–$400 a month just to talk to her—all her calls were reversed charges—and every call she was boozed up or stoned on drugs or out of her mind with one thing or another. Now, she was carrying my baby and I didn't want the drugs and booze to hurt the kid. So I would beg her to straighten out, sober up. Diane would always say, 'Oh, Bill, I want to, but unless I get the money I can't straighten out and I'll have to kill myself or I will get myself worse and it will really mess up your baby.' "

Bridget: "She was threatening us, and we were too scared to call her bluff."

Bill: "In May or so, it was about her seventh or eighth month of pregnancy, and she called again, dead drunk, and I was just biting my tongue trying to keep her happy and then something snapped. You know, she had gone too far. I said, 'Diane, God damn it, I've had enough. I mean every time you call you're plastered. Jesus Christ, what do you mean take care of the kid. You're running around drunk and you can't even take care of yourself, let alone your son and our baby. All you want is damn money. We want to help you, too, but we aren't rich. Christ, you're supposed to help yourself, too.' Then, I hung up on her. I just slammed down the phone. I had snapped. I had to go out in the yard—it was Sunday—and play with the dog for awhile."

Bridget: "It almost broke up our marriage. Bill was starting to feel sorry for himself, to go into a shell. Every night, he would go off by himself into the den and start sipping on a bottle."

Bill: "It's true. I had never been much of a drinker before, but now it was the only way I could get through the night. We had had a big Christmas party at the house for our folks—we were celebrating Diane's pregnancy—and a lot of the booze was left over. Well, after March or so I started working on that booze and went right through it. Most nights, I was near tears. I didn't know what to do except try to hold on. Had Diane hurt our kid, I don't know what I would have done."

Bridget: "At one point, I almost left Bill. I can forgive him almost everything, but I cannot stand to see the sight of the man I love reduced to a crying, drunken baby. That's exactly what was happening, and, don't forget, my fifteen-year-old daughter and sixteen-year-old son from my first marriage were living with us. I had them to think of, too. My big husband—all six-foot-four, 250 pounds of him—wouldn't come out of the den. All he wanted to do was drink himself to sleep. I made plans to go live with my parents in Upper Michigan, but I finally realized that I just couldn't leave Bill. I was afraid of what he might do to himself."

Bill: "Well, Diane called back that Sunday after a few hours and said, 'Bill, I really am going to try to straighten out. Don't worry, your baby will be fine.' Naturally, I wanted to believe her. Of course, there was one condition. She needed more money. She said her back treatments were $22 each and she needed two a day. We sent the money."

Bill pushed toward me a shoebox of cancelled checks, Western Union drafts, and money-order stubs. He says, "It's all right there. I hate to look at it, but it's all here. By the time Bill, Jr. was born, we must have spent $12-$13,000 on her. She hit us for $3,000 right before he was born. Said she needed it to go to computer school. We didn't want to screw up the adoption papers or anything, so we paid it. Like I say, we were just trying to hold on."

Bridget: "We should have known something funny was going on, when you're out of state, it's hard to get to the bottom of things. And, of course, we really didn't want to know the worst. But one night I called and Diane's roommate, Vicky, answered the phone. She was very abusive to me and when Diane came to the phone she was crying. Apparently, Vicky and Diane had just had another fight. They were always fighting. It kind of went through my mind that there had to be more to Diane and Vicky than just roommates. I mean, roommates just don't stay at each other's throats like that. We found out soon enough, about two weeks before Bill, Jr. was born. It is a wild story, but I can't say that I was shocked."

Bill: "Here it was, two weeks before our baby is due, and we get a call one day at four in the morning. Diane is in jail on a drunk-driving charge and wants us to send bail money. Well, we had already bailed her out of one drunk-driving charge. We decided we might as well fly to Tennessee and stay with her until we had the baby. That's when we found out the truth about Diane."

Bridget: "We got there and got Diane out of jail—she was swollen with our baby—and she couldn't stop crying. She took me aside and said, 'Bridget, there is something I have to tell you. I am gay. And Vicky, my lover, is driving me crazy. That's why I am driving around drunk all the time. Trying to get away. And she's always on me to pressure you people for more money. I can't take it anymore.' I tried to calm her down. 'Diane,' I said, 'I had a feeling you might be gay. We don't hold it against you. I mean everybody has to do their own thing. This one's gay, this one's straight. Different strokes.' Oh, I tried to be calm with her, but when I got Bill alone, I have to admit I let him have it. 'Bill,' I screamed, 'do you realize that the woman you got pregnant is not only an alcoholic and drug addict but a lesbian!' "

Bill: "By this point, it was beyond me. I mean all I wanted was our baby. I tried to tune everything else out. We had planned to stay at the Holiday Inn, but Diane said no, she wanted us with her in case she had to be driven to the hospital in the middle of the night. And in case Vicky came back. She had dumped Vicky for a new girl, Regina, who had come up from Texas. Vicky was boiling mad."

Bridget: "We moved in with Diane and Regina. I had gotten over her being gay by now. What really bothered us was her ripping us off for money and not taking care of herself. But basically, she was a very strong person physically and this is what brought her through. And us. Diane and I had made plans to go to Lamaze classes together, so I could be in the hospital with her for a natural birth. It was a two-week class, but Bill, Jr. arrived within a week. I never made it to the delivery room—we got detained by a hospital shouting match with Vicky—but Bill and I were right there in the waiting room."

Bill: "Noel, the day our son was born you can't believe the scene. I mean, I'm not much of a reader but this is something out of Tennessee Williams. There we are having Sunday breakfast, me and Bridget and Diane and Regina! Suddenly, who comes to the door but Vicky! Diane won't let her in. Vicky starts to kick down the door. Regina opens the door and stands between Vicky and Diane. Now, Diane is almost nine months pregnant and looks pretty weak. Vicky and Regina are both big as bull mooses. Believe me, I've been in the Marines and heard a lot of barracks language, but I have never heard anything like the kind of foul language these two bull dykes were laying on each other. They had gone too far, because I could tell that Diane was getting sick. And she was carrying our baby. Well, I ran to the door and got pretty violent. Grabbing one in each arm, I said, 'Look, you two foul-mouthed bitches, if either one of you lays a hand on Diane and my baby, I'm going to kick your ass from here to Detroit and back.' I almost hit Vicky, but she backed off pretty quick. All bullies do, if you stand up to them."

Bridget: "About an hour later, Diane's water bag broke. She insisted that Regina drive her to the hospital. We followed in our rental car. And who should be right behind us but Vicky. She had been hanging around the house. Well, Vicky almost beat us to the hospital and went right to the OB nurse and started to tell her that Diane was no good and was on drugs and so on and so forth. She kept us from making it to the delivery room in time. But at four o'clock that afternoon, our boy was born."

Bill: "In a way, Vicky served a purpose. She meant to be malicious, but she alerted the medical staff to what was going on. Bill, Jr. was a little baby, only five pounds, fifteen ounces, and right after birth he had to be detoxified. He was quivering and shaking and he had diarrhea. The nurse told us it was withdrawal. But he was basically all right. He was healthy. And he was ours. I'll tell you this. The minute we saw him, it made everything all right. I forgave Diane for everything. I even tried to work up some good feelings for Vicky. We had been through a lot, but it was having a happy ending."

Bridget: "Of course, we just wanted to take the baby and get out of there as soon as possible. The doctor said, 'Well, when I was in the military, we let babies travel on a plane one day after birth. But we're going to keep your son here until he gets a little bit heavier and a little bit bigger and then we will release him.' The day after Bill, Jr. was born, Diane signed the release papers you gave us and then she went home. Like I say, she was basically a physically strong person. Thank God."

Bill: "We had told all the nurses that we were adopting the

baby and were the real parents. They knew all about the artificial insemination and that Diane had signed papers releasing the baby to Bridget and myself. The night the baby was born, Bridget and I checked into a Holiday Inn, which was right across the street from the hospital. After the second day or so, we would just walk across the street and were allowed to go right into the nursery, where we would change diapers on Bill, Jr., rock him, kiss him, play with him. We did that for five days until he was released in our custody. That night we took him back with us to the Holiday Inn."

Bridget: "It's funny, but Diane never even wanted to see the baby she had carried for nine months. The night we took our son back to the Holiday Inn, Diane called. We thought she might want to see the baby. No, she wanted more money."

Bill: "We were so overjoyed that we gave her all the money we had. I was having such a case of the guilts that, after all, she had had a baby for us and all, that I went down to the hotel lobby and cashed in all our travelers' checks, about $300 or so, and gave the money to her in the lobby. She didn't want to come up to the room, because she didn't want to see the baby. Well, I gave her the money, and she said it wasn't enough. She needed more. So I took all the pocket money I had, about $100, and gave her that. I kept only enough to get home with. I figured it was well worth the price. I've still got the hotel stationery, on which I asked her to sign a receipt that we had given her all this money for medical expenses. Let me tell you, when we got on that plane with Bill, Jr., it was well worth it. Even knowing what bad news Diane was, I would have done it all over again just to be able to carry my son home."

Bridget: "We thought we were home free, but what happened shortly after we got back really blew my mind. We get a bill from the hospital demanding payment for the birth of Bill, Jr. We give all that money to Diane, and she doesn't even have the decency to pay the hospital bill."

Bill: "We paid the bill. But Diane still doesn't let up. A month ago, she calls again, says she needs money to get through school. That if we don't send it to her, she's going to stop the adoption."

At this point, Bill looked at me with a pleading expression and said, "Noel, what do we do. We're at our wits' end. First, she wants more and more money, and, then, a few days ago she calls to say that now that's it's Christmas season, she realizes how terrible she is and how sorry she is to have put us through so much and will we forgive her and so on. But we're still afraid that tomorrow she'll change her tune and demand more money. Enough is enough. Hell, a birth certificate or an adoption approval is nothing but a piece of paper. We've got Bill, Jr. and that's what counts. I never want to see or hear from Diane again, if I can help it."

I had been listening to Bill and Bridget for an hour or so and the thought struck me; "Here we go again. The Keane circus." But beneath the melodrama of their story is a crucial need. I had to make sure that Bill and Bridget could legally adopt their son, and, beyond that, I had to make sure that what almost happened to them would never happen to anyone else. In short, we had to clean up the potential mess that threatened every person who sought out a surrogate mother.

"Bill," I said, "Let's review the document you signed with Diane right after the baby was born. I think that will do the trick." Carefully, we read the legal form I had prepared, called Consent to Remove Child from the State of Tennessee. It spelled out:

> I, Diane _____ , a citizen and resident of _____ , do hereby give to Bill _____ and his wife, Bridget _____ , my consent and permission to take with them from the state of Tennessee the baby boy born to me in _____ , Tennessee, on July 2, 1978, he having been given the name of Bill _____ , Jr. and having been conceived by me through artificial insemination on behalf of Bill _____ .
>
> It is further understood and agreed that Bill _____ and

his wife, Bridget _____, do fully intend to adopt Bill _____, Jr. as their own child, and I do hereby agree to sign any necessary surrender and consent to adoption hereafter forwarded to me by them.

The document was signed July 7, 1978, by Diane. I noticed that Bill, Jr.'s middle name was in honor of Bill's father. I knew we would have some problems in accomplishing the adoption because of a recent change in Tennessee law. About six months before Bridget and Bill's son was born, Tennessee passed a law stating that any child born to an unwed mother could not list the father's name on the birth certificate. The law was passed because many unwed mothers were simply naming just about anybody as the father and this caused a big headache for law enforcement officials as they tried to unravel who did what to whom. Thus, the best we could get from Bill and Bridget in the way of legal documents was the agreement and the consent to remove the child from Tennessee. However, the birth certificate, though it listed only Diane as the mother, with a blank space for the father, did give the baby's name as Bill _____, Jr., which, of course, was my client Bill's surname. I figured that this fact, plus the other documents and Diane's sorry record as a mother, would be plenty to accomplish an adoption for Bill and Bridget whether or not it came to a fight. Eventually, that is. I knew it would take time.

"Bill," I said, "I'm sorry about all this heartache. But you have what you want, and I'm going to see that everything works out. The first thing is to forget you have ever known Diane. It sounds like all she wants is money. The next time she calls, refer her to me. Turn off the money faucet. If we need her cooperation, I'll take care of it. But I doubt if we do. In the meantime, you've suffered enough. Forget her. Think about Billy."

The ex-Marine broke into a broad grin. "Noel," he said, "no hard feelings. All's well that ends well. Let us know if you need anything to speed things along." It was Saturday afternoon, and I had some Christmas shopping to do. I ushered Bill and Bridget out of my office with a big show of enthusiasm. But, privately, I was shaken.

I had helped these people get into this mess. And although, once again, a guardian angel had warded off disaster, I knew we could not long tempt the fates. We needed decisions on whether or not the law was going to protect infertile couples who chose surrogate motherhood to have a child. In other words, I had to press my lawsuit against the state of Michigan to allow the payment of a fee to surrogate mothers and others, and I had to press my petition to allow Debbie and George to adopt the baby born of their surrogate mother.

I reviewed the voluminous papers buttressing the lawsuit filed May 5, 1978, in Wayne County Circuit Court by myself and a legal associate, attorney Robert Harrison. The Preliminary Advisory opinion I had received from Judge Lincoln made clear that there were two distinct issues under Michigan law. Yes, a volunteer surrogate mother could legally bear a child for a couple to adopt, but no, the law did not allow the payment of fees to the mother for the service.

This meant, of course, that single people and those not choosing to adopt could with apparent legal immunity pay whatever fees they wanted to a surrogate mother. For those vast majority of couples, however, with an infertile wife and a strong need to adopt, this law meant that the supply of surrogate mothers available to them would be severely shrunken.

Bob and I reviewed the case law and decided that while "baby-selling"—the payment of fees to mothers who put their children up for adoption—is justifiably illegal in almost all states, the phenomenon of surrogate motherhood—using the husband's sperm and artificial insemination—is a special situation. Thus, in a thirty-page motion for summary judgment, we asked the Wayne County Circuit Court to enjoin the attorney general of Michigan and the Wayne County prosecutor from interfering in the payment of fees to surrogate mothers.

To my mind the question was, "Does the state have sufficient interest in this entire scheme, which overrides the right of privacy and the right to bear and beget children, to apply a sanction against fees?" Bob and I do not think it does.

In researching our lawsuit, we pondered those unanswered serious questions raised by surrogate mothers. If the surrogate mother decided to keep the baby, could she sue the father for child support? What if the couple divorced or if one or both died before the surrogate gave birth? If the birth mother suffered depression after giving up the baby, could she sue for damages?

I had the answers to none of the above, nor to the many other questions that could be posed. But it seemed to me that if the use of surrogate mothers was made legal, then it could be ruled and regulated by the state and binding contracts could be drawn to cover any and all eventualities.

That was our intention in May 1978, when we filed the lawsuit. It was now December, and the lawsuit was still dragging. I knew that the day of decision was years away and, beyond that, there would be appeals.

When we filed our lawsuit, the national news media, of course, jumped on it. There I was pictured in *Time* magazine, my forelock tumbling over my forehead and looking snappy in wirerimmed glasses, camel blazer, and paisley tie. All my friends got a kick out of it. *Time* noted that the case would require a difficult decision, since "it involves the sale of a child, or rather the sale of half a child, since one of the buyers is also the biological father."

Laws like Michigan's, of course, were specifically enacted to prevent "baby-selling," a heinous crime that was the furthest thing from my mind and the mind of everybody with whom I had been working. My clients were simply trying to circumvent their barrenness. To them, the surrogate mother concept offered new hope. But I also knew that to many the spectre of baby-selling was never far away. This is the challenge we had to overcome. Our unusual challenge to the traditional thinking about motherhood was capturing the nation's attention. Shortly after the *Time* article appeared, *People* magazine sought me out. And within a few weeks, there I was appearing in the pages of the magazine that is the most avidly read in my wife's beauty salon. The story featured the experience of Debbie, Sue, and George and the birth of Elizabeth Anne, and, among other photos, showed me, Kathy, and Doug and Chris shining up our family treasure, my 1950 lemon-yellow roadster, the car that I had promised myself if I ever managed to make it through law school.

Back in June 1978, I was becoming a pretty well-known guy. Heads would perk up when I stopped down to visit with Kathy at her beauty shop. I got respect when I checked in at my Dearborn racquet club. People noticed me on the street. My new restaurant-saloon was booming. Called "The Keane Place," it was an enterprise started as a hedge against the possible failure of a law practice suddenly dependent upon a "weird" idea. I was a pretty content guy.

But my December meeting with Bill and Bridget changed all that. I knew I could never rest until the legal issues raised by their near-fiasco were resolved. Compulsively, I began spending hours in the law library, researching adoption proceedings for Debbie and George.

Never far from my mind was the plaintive plea of Bridget to Bill: "Are you aware that the woman you got pregnant is not only an alcoholic and a drug addict but a lesbian!" It would have weighed me down, but my new friend, Mrs. Pfieffer, had a happier thought.

Blowing smoke rings from the little cigars she favored, she gazed off into the distance and said:

"Noel, nobody said it would be easy. But stick with it. Surrogate mothers may replace adoption and revolutionize how people go about having babies."

·6·
"He's always been ours.
Now, he's legally ours."

WHILE 1978 was a wild year of sudden fame and soap-opera melodrama, 1979 would find me turning to quieter pursuits, such as laying the legal foundation to support the surrogate-mother movement.

Heavy publicity marked the 1978 births of the first children brought into the world by surrogate mothers. Plus, in a related development, the birth that summer of England's "Baby Louise," the first true "test-tube," or *in vitro* baby, electrified the world. People were excited by these new frontiers in conception.

In 1979, the publicity died down. It was time for the real work: tackling the legal and moral dilemmas posed by the medical breakthroughs.

I had two major legal goals. The first was to argue my lawsuit against the state of Michigan to allow surrogate mothers to be paid. The second was to win adoptions for my first three clients.

The lawsuit, of course, was absolutely critical to public acceptance of the surrogate mother concept. If necessary, we intended to fight it all the way to the U.S. Supreme Court, so an ultimate decision remained years away.

The briefs in this controversial case were anything but brief, running hundreds of pages and citing hundreds of decisions. However, I will sum up our position in a sentence:

We are arguing that the Michigan adoption law barring payment to a surrogate mother violates state and federal constitutional guarantees of privacy.

At issue are Section 710.54 and 710.69 of the Michigan Probate Code. Section 710.54 stipulates that all fees paid as part of the adoption process must be approved by the court. Section 710.69 sets penalties for violation of this law—a misdemeanor for the first offense and a felony for subsequent offenses.

Now, we—attorney Bob Harrison and myself—have no problem with the intent of the law. The Michigan adoption law, like so many others around the country, was enacted for a very good purpose—to prevent the back-alley sale of babies for thousands of dollars. We believe the state should regulate adoptions.

However, at the time this statute, and others like it around the country, were enacted, no one ever dreamed of the surrogate-mother scenario. This is a far cry from baby-selling. The baby is the father's child. His wife is just adopting it.

The preliminary legal opinion submitted to me by Juvenile Court Judge James Lincoln discloses a striking paradox in the Michigan adoption law.

On the one hand, it appears to be perfectly permissible and proper to pay a surrogate mother to have the baby and then take the child and raise it, but, on the other, if you try to adopt the child, it becomes illegal. Payment to a surrogate mother is illegal only if you want to adopt.

Thus, people who choose not to adopt can presumably make whatever arrangements they want with a surrogate mother. Single men, for example, who would through artificial insemination be the father of a child born to a surrogate mother, would have no need to adopt and thus, could pay a fee. So could married and unmarried couples, if they chose to raise a child without the legal protection of adopting it. And finally, even single women, if they chose not to adopt, could pay a surrogate mother to be artificially inseminated (probably from a sperm bank, though some I know want the insemination to be done with the sperm of "prize" donors) and to deliver a child for them.

The only offenders under this law are that vast bulk of people who really need help—the married couples with an infertile wife who want to pay a surrogate mother a reasonable fee (probably $10,000, but it can vary widely) to give them a child they can adopt.

Our lawsuit, assigned Docket No. 78-815531, was first filed in May 1978, in Wayne County (Michigan) Circuit Court. We asked that the defendants, Frank J. Kelley, the Michigan attorney general, and William L. Cahalan, the Wayne County prosecutor be permanently enjoined from enforcing Section 710.54, since it is constitutionally overbroad and infringes upon the fundamental constitutional rights guaranteed to the plaintiffs by the United States and Michigan Constitutions.

The plaintiffs, identified as "Jane Doe, John Doe, and Mary Roe, and Jane X, John X, Jane Y, John Y, Jane Z, John Z," are pseudonyms for real people. We are arguing for the legal right to pursue this six-step arrangement:

1. JANE DOE and JOHN DOE will pay MARY ROE a sum of money in consideration for her promise to bear and deliver JOHN DOE'S child by means of artificial insemination;
2. That a licensed physician will conduct the artificial insemination process;
3. That prior to the delivery of said child, JOHN DOE will file a Notice of Intent to Claim Paternity;
4. That at the time the child is born, JOHN DOE will formally acknowledge the paternity of said child;
5. That MARY ROE will acknowledge that JOHN DOE is the father of said child;
6. That MARY ROE will consent to the adoption of said child by JOHN DOE and JANE DOE.

The suit stipulates that this arrangement is being pursued because "JANE DOE and JOHN DOE are both desirous of having children, that JANE DOE is biologically incapable of having children, and that JANE DOE and JOHN DOE want to have a child biologically related to JOHN DOE."

We need to know, of course, if this arrangement is lawful. In our legal language asking for relief from the Michigan adoption law, we argue, "Public confidence in the judiciary can hardly be served if the plaintiffs are to be excluded from the exercise of a fundamental right on the basis of an arbitrary and vexatious interpretation of a statute which fails to mark the boundaries of prohibitive behavior." Or, in other words, if you can adopt if you don't pay and pay if you don't adopt, then why not allow the obvious choice: pay and adopt?

As expected, our motion for an immediate, or declaratory, judgment was denied. The case then went to a formal bench trial before Wayne County Circuit Judge Roman S. Gribbs. Throughout 1979, Bob Harrison, myself, and other legal associates polished and presented our arguments on this crucial case. Simultaneously, I was doing the legal work on the adoptions for Debbie and George and Tom and Jane. Steps three through six of the surrogate-mother arrangement that we are trying to have declared legal are, of course, the same steps to be followed in the subsequent adoption.

Since Debbie and George had not paid a fee to Sue and Tom and Jane had not paid a fee to Carol and Bill and Bridget had not (in a strict sense) paid a fee to Diane, I did not anticipate great difficulty with the adoptions. However, I knew that if there were to be any more children provided by surrogate mothers for adoption, we would have to legalize the fee. If "Jane and John Doe" cannot find a woman who will be a surrogate mother for free, and if "Mary Roe" is a woman who will be their surrogate mother but only for a fee, then, we argue, we have a right to make that payment so we can receive a child. The current adoption law is preventing that.

The legal literature includes thousands of case-law examples, obscure and otherwise, that can be used to make our case for the right of privacy. And I diligently tracked them down to footnote our briefs. However, what really concerned me was something much more obvious. Judge Gibbs is a Roman Catholic. His brother is a priest. Now I know that this is not supposed to have any bearing on a matter of law and I am not saying that it did, but the judge's background hardly reassured me.

In my arguments, I tried to make the case that old adoption laws should give consideration to the new surrogate-mother arrangement.

We argued, "Plaintiffs do not contend that the State lacks a sufficient interest to enact laws regulating the insemination process and adoption process to insure the health of the child, but rather the State's interest in protecting newborn children and insuring an orderly adoption system does not justify a blanket prohibition against giving consideration to a surrogate mother. . . . To the extent Section 710.54 portends to prohibit the payment of money to a surrogate mother, it violates the exercise of plaintiffs' constitutional rights to personal autonomy, and would be unsupported under Michigan law."

In other words, the state lacks a sufficiently compelling interest to prevent a married couple from paying a surrogate mother for her promise to bear a child and consent to its adoption.

This is so, we argue, because the arrangement does not jeopardize the State's statutory responsibility to always act in the "best interest of the child." The surrogate-mother arrangement we describe stipulates that "Mary Roe" (the surrogate mother) will consent to terminate her parental rights; that "John Doe" (the natural father) will file a verified notice of intent to claim paternity; and that "Jane Doe" (the wife) will consent to adopt the child." Thus, our motion argues, "The State will accordingly be omnipresent to protect the best interests of the child." The motion adds, "In the event, MARY ROE [the surrogate mother] refuses to consent to terminate her rights, the Child Custody Act yields to the Court the power to determine the best interest of the child.

"Given the fact that current legislative enactments protect the best interests of the child in the given instance, any broad prohibition of the aforementioned arrangement by the Court, rationalized with the reference to the best interests of the child, would be constitutionally untenable."

We further argue that there is no Michigan public policy, as determined by its statutes or case laws, that prohibits the payment of a fee to a surrogate mother. In resting our case for the payment of a fee, we conclude:

"The Courts have shown that in matters that reflect the need to respond progressively and circumspectly to social and technological change, enlightened judicial solutions can be forthcoming without any abandonment of the traditional protections provided by the Courts."

In other words, let's see if the law cannot be equal to a resourceful solution to infertility.

The State, of course, had other ideas. And arguments. The defense briefs argued that Michigan's adoption laws, including the penalty provisions, are constitutional, and the surrogate-mother arrangement we proposed is against the public policy of Michigan.

The brief of Wayne County Prosecutor William L. Cahalan argued that, "Plaintiff's right of privacy to conceive, bear, and raise a child does *not* include a right to use the public statutory adoption process to legitimatize the child born as a consequence of their private acts." And, further, "The State has a substantial compelling interest that outweighs any fundamental rights possessed by plaintiffs regarding the statutory adoption process."

Cahalan's brief concludes, "This defendant believes that plaintiffs' ultimate goal of providing a method for an infertile couple to have a child biologically related to one of them and legally belonging to them both through adoption is admirable. Nevertheless, the method they propose is fraught with danger to the welfare of society. The legislature has recognized the grave consequences inherent in the arrangement proposed by plaintiffs; for legitimate and compelling reasons, they have made such actions against the law. That law is not unconstitutional. If there is to be any change in the law so as to permit an arrangement similar to that proposed by plaintiffs, it is properly a subject for the Legislature, which can fully balance the dangers against the benefits and provide safeguards. It is not a matter for the Courts."

We are in agreement with this defense brief on one key point. The ultimate answer to the questions raised by surrogate mothers is to be found in enabling legislation and state regulation. Cahalan and Kelley are both saying the same thing. We enforce the laws, we don't make them. But while the wheels of justice grind slowly, the wheels of legislation grind even slower.

I knew that before the legislature even got around to considering this idea, there were going to be hundreds of people growing too old to act on it. Thus, we had to move first in the courts.

As the legal arguments stretched on, I also pursued some happier business—the adoptions.

The first, of course, would be the adoption of Elizabeth Anne by Debbie and George. We had been working on it for more than a year.

Not everything went perfect in those first days at Oakwood Hospital when Elizabeth Anne was born. We had arranged through Susan's doctor, Dr. Keith Curtis, and the hospital administration for Debbie to take complete charge of the child immediately after it was born. However, the word never made it down to some of the obstetrical ward nurses, and Debbie was not allowed to feed the baby. Sue said, "Well, if you are not going to let Debbie come in and take care of her baby, then I am not going to feed her either." The OB nurses had to do the first feedings before we finally managed to straighten things out and get permission for Debbie to take over. This was accomplished by consulting with the hospital's attorneys and having Debbie, Sue, and George sign releases that exempted the hospital from any liability arising from the unusual arrangement. Then, Debbie was allowed to walk right into the nursery, and, of course, things went smoothly.

The first birth certificate for Elizabeth Anne had only Susan's name on it, reading "Baby Girl _____." So my first step was to have George file a Notice of Intent to Claim Paternity. This was done in January 1978, and the form noted that both George and Sue were living at the same address in Dearborn Heights, Michigan. The corrected birth certificate then read that "George _____ " is the father and "Susan _____ " the mother.

The next step was to formally petition for adoption, which we did in February 1978. This petition for the adoption of "Baby Girl _____ " had one unusual feature seldom seen on the standard form. It noted that the adoptee "is related to petitioner George _____ , being his natural child." The form listed Susan as the mother and George as the father.

This petition was unique, of course, because under Michigan law George, as the blood relative of the child, could petition the court directly for adoption without going through a private agency. That is how couples using surrogate mothers can adopt quickly while others—as George and Debbie would have been forced to—are now waiting up to seven years or more for a newborn white infant.

The next step in the adoption process was to meet Probate Court's requirement for court approval of all payments and exchanges between an adopting couple and the mother of the adoptee. In March 1978, Debbie and George filed with Probate Court their "Statement describing money or other consideration paid or exchanged, request for approval and order." It had cost them exactly $423.50 to achieve their impossible dream. The breakdown was as follows:

- Dr. Keith L. Curtis—pre/post natal care, $310.
- Oakwood Hospital (not covered by Blue Cross-Blue Shield), $60.
- Prescriptions, $30
- Certification fee—Notice of Intent to Claim Paternity, $2.50.
- Petition fee, $19.
- Birth certificate fee, $2.

A third required form was filed in June 1978. That was the

Legitimation and Acknowledgment of Paternity signed by George and Susan as the birth parents of Elizabeth Anne.

Since in 1978 we had scrupulously followed all of Judge Lincoln's instructions, I in 1979 expected little difficulty in accomplishing the adoption of Elizabeth Anne, otherwise known as, "The Matter of Minor #54373."

However, there was one little thing. By 1979, Judge Lincoln had retired, as he had told me he would, and the judge who would be hearing our adoption petition was Juvenile Court Judge Y. Gladys Barsamian, a lady of somber manner and strict adherence to procedures. She was well aware of the controversy included in this adoption case, and was determined that everything would be done right to the letter.

Which was fine with us. We felt we had an airtight case. Extraordinary as the social situation might seem, the facts were simple. Susan had out of friendship given her best friend, Debbie, a gift—a baby conceived through artificial insemination from George's sperm, and carried, delivered, and surrendered by Sue. There was no money involved, and there were no sexual relations between Sue and George, though some cynics suspected both motives. The amazing fact is that the trio never even remotely considered either of these choices.

We were concerned, however, that Judge Barsamian might be put off by one thing. "Auntie Sue" was still living with Debbie and George and helping to care for Elizabeth Anne. Some social workers—and psychiatrists—might find this unhealthy, and we worried that the judge might make the adoption contingent upon Susan's leaving.

The hearings before Judge Barsamian were private, but they were very formal. The judge found surrogate motherhood to be neither amusing nor enjoyable. She had her legal reputation to think about.

Blood tests were ordered for Elizabeth Anne, George, and Susan. Judge Barsamian was a little skeptical about this wild scenario she was being asked to believe.

For George and Debbie, this was the hardest thing, having to watch the blood being drawn from their one-year-old daughter. It was a painful process and Elizabeth Anne screamed in fright. It cost about $500 to produce the three blood samples.

Now Judge Barsamian wanted to make sure of two things. First, that Elizabeth Anne was, indeed, the child of Susan and George, and second, that the pregnancy could have resulted from artificial insemination. She felt she needed a court-appointed expert and turned for advice to Dr. S.J. Behrman, a nationally known expert in the field of human fertility.

There were some ironies involved. Dr. Behrman told the court that, yes, it was perfectly possible for Susan to have been artificially inseminated by Debbie with George's sperm, just the way they described it. Having said this, however, Dr. Behrman observed to Debbie, "Do you know you were practicing medicine without a license?" I jumped right in, "Now, wait just a minute, Doctor. You know, as well as I do, that we have approached several doctors, including yourself, to perform these inseminations and the doctors simply don't want to get involved. The next case I have I am going to ask you to do the artificial insemination, so we won't have laymen practicing medicine without a license." He simply shook his head.

The legalities of the use of artificial insemination upon a surrogate mother had been tested in Michigan. While George could petition the court on the grounds that the AI child was his, the law would allow the petition to be subject to court interpretation. But Judge Barsamian, though apparently put off by the thought, accepted Dr. Behrman's testimony that Debbie, Sue, and George could very easily have accomplished an AI pregnancy exactly as they described it.

We are now at the crucial point of the hearing; the interpretation of the blood tests. Dr. Behrman said the results indicated a probability of 99.7 percent that George was the father of Susan's child.

Judge Barsamian would be forced to grant the adoption, but we still worried that she might make it contingent upon Susan's moving out. I knew that Debbie and George would not sit still for that. Debbie and George are a very religious couple, and Debbie had been very active in her church, being elected to her parish's governing board. When her involvement in surrogate motherhood became known, however, she was asked to relinquish her post and resign from the parish. This blow was causing Debbie and George to relocate to a new parish. Having been kicked around by the Church, I knew that the couple was not going to be told to kick out their friend.

We never had to face the dilemma. Our friends, the news reporters, again came to our rescue. This adoption was a legal landmark, the first adoption of a child born to a surrogate mother, and on the day the adoption was to be granted there were about fifty photographers and TV cameras in the lobby of Juvenile Court Hall waiting to record the event. I think that the Judge wanted to order Susan out—a court-appointed social worker had recommended against the unusual living arrangement—but she was afraid to take on the press.

On March 28, 1979, the Order of Adoption was signed for Minor #54373 and Elizabeth Anne was legally George and Debbie's. In short order, we obtained a new birth certificate naming Debbie and George as the parents of Elizabeth Anne, with no mention of Susan. Her rights are terminated once and for all. Those rights can never be regained unless Susan could show she was defrauded or under mental duress. But, for all practical purposes, Susan's legal relationship with Elizabeth Anne is terminated and she can never again claim Elizabeth Anne as her child.

Judge Barsamian was not excited about all of this. In fact, she called her own news conference to denounce the intrusion of the press upon a private judicial matter. Meanwhile, the wire services carried the story around the world. The headline read COUPLE ADOPT HUSBAND'S CHILD CARRIED BY SURROGATE MOTHER The photo showed a smiling fourteen-month-old Elizabeth Anne playing patty-cake with her mother's cheek while George looked on lovingly. Susan was not on hand for the final proceedings, but she was not forgotten. George told reporters, "It's incredible. She did it just for Debbie."

The adoption had taken eight months from the time hearings began, fifteen months from the time we first filed a formal petition. Debbie and George had won legal irrevocable custody of a child born to a surrogate mother, the first time such custody had ever been granted and the first time it had ever been sought. I kept my remarks to the reporters brief and to the point.

"This adoption is unique," I said, "because it's finally been brought right out into the open that a surrogate mother has carried a child for another couple, unlike some earlier cases where people might have entered into this type of arrangement without telling anyone.

"The artificial insemination was performed by the couple and the surrogate mother because no doctor would take the case. Blood tests were conducted to authenticate the child's parentage.

"Elizabeth Anne is truly a gift child. Debbie and Sue are close friends, and Sue wanted to give Debbie what she couldn't otherwise have."

This landmark adoption was exhilarating for me. The East Dearborn kid who wasn't smart enough for college and who had not too many years ago been working as a midnight booking clerk for a police station had made legal history. But even more important, the adoption was the perfect way to conclude the remarkable story of Debbie, Sue, and George. I have never taken a fee from Debbie, Sue, and George, and, in fact, have absorbed the costs myself because I have enjoyed working with their case so much, which, of course, was among my very first. But I got all the payment I needed when Elizabeth Anne kissed me on the courthouse steps, right in front of God and everybody. I love that little girl. I was never again to hear from Judge Barsamian.

Meanwhile, I turned my mind to the other two adoptions. Tom and Jane, I figured, would be extremely easy; Bill and Bridget extremely difficult. I was right on both counts.

Having done my homework for the adoption of Elizabeth

Anne, we simply retraced our steps right down the line for the adoption of Tom, Jr. First, Tom filed a Notice of Intent to Claim Paternity; then Tom and Jane filed a petition for adoption and a statement describing the court-approved expenses they had paid for surrogate mother Carol; and, finally, Tom and Carol signed a Legitimation and Acknowledgment of Paternity. Unlike the adoption of Elizabeth Anne, which required meticulous legal procedures and prompted heavy publicity, we simply walked right through the adoption of Tom, Jr. By now, it was old hat.

Bill and Bridget's case, I knew, would be a battle, but after what they'd gone through I figured they deserved all that could be done.

To give their surrogate mother credit, we should acknowledge that she gave Bill and Bridget a beautiful baby boy, Bill, Jr. The child is with Bill and Bridget and they all are very happy. But Diane's personal life has complicated the adoption process incredibly. Additionally, she lives out of state, which has created yet another problem.

Diane signed with Bill and Bridget both a statement of understanding and a release to allow the child she delivered to be taken out of state. However, Tennessee law forbids the use of Bill's name as the father on the birth certificate. This law was recently enacted to prevent unwed mothers from irresponsibly blaming any man they chose. This is a drawback, but the birth certificate does give the boy Bill's surname, a procedure Tennessee apparently invoked to allow a statement of paternity if the alleged father will consent to have the baby bear his last name. So we have a birth certificate in which the boy's middle name is the same as Bill's father's first name and the boy's last name is the same as Bill's.

That should be enough to straighten things out, but, for right now, the child is in legal limbo. He has Bill's last name but nowhere is he legally connected to Bill. He has no legal relationship with his mother Bridget. And he probably will never see his birth mother (or natural mother: the woman who biologically gave birth to him) Diane.

What is needed is to have Bill file a Notice of Intent to Claim

Paternity and then have both Bill and Diane sign a Legitimation and Acknowledgment of Paternity.

I promptly had Bill file in Michigan a paternity action against Diane to get his name on the birth certificate. Once that is accomplished, we can have Bridget acknowledged as the adoptive mother. But first, Diane had to acknowledge Bill's paternity.

It seemed simple enough until I tried to get in touch with Diane. She had since become embroiled in a custody fight over her son, Anson, with the Tennessee Department of Human Services, which called her an unfit mother. Panicking, she packed up and fled to Florida, whether with Vicky or Regina I do not know. She left no forwarding information.

However, I am working with government and law-enforcement officials in Tennessee to resolve the impasse. I am told the matter will be resolved successfully, either through Diane's cooperation or by default.

One night, as I explained all this to Bill and Bridget, little Bill, Jr. awoke from his nap and started exploring the living room where we were seated. He is a curious child and was fascinated by my tape recorder, particularly the cord that plugged into the wall. Several times, in fact, he took the cord out of the socket for a closer inspection, thus stopping our recorded conversation.

"Well, Bill," I said, "we've got to get this mess cleaned up before your boy needs a birth certificate to get in school. We'll make it."

Bill added a new chapter to the ongoing saga of surrogate mother Diane. This big ex-Marine just sat there and said, "Noel, I'm OK now. I've pulled out of it. But after Bridget and I left your office that last time after Billy was born, things were even worse.

"You know I've always said I hated melodrama and now I find myself living one. Diane never let up. Right after we came home with Billy, she started calling again and asking for money. I guess I should have taken your advice and referred her to you, but I was afraid the adoption wouldn't go through. So we tried to help her out. After all, we had Billy.

"One night, she got into another fight with Vicky. I guess she lived in a gay neighborhood, one of the few sections that would rent to gays. But this was so bad that the neighbors called the cops. Then pretty soon people were telling Diane to get out of town. They wanted to take Anson away from her. At that point, she called us and asked for money. She said if she didn't get it, she'd lose Anson and she'd come to Michigan to take away Billy. She asked me to send a letter to the court saying that she was a good mother. Can you imagine that? I sent the letter, but they took her son anyway. But she was told that if she straightened up and got a job and showed signs she was back on the right track, she could have Anson back. Of course, she needed money to get back on her feet. We sent it to her. In the meantime, she wouldn't sign any of the forms you gave me because she didn't want to complicate her custody fight over Anson. She was about to lose her own kid if she helped me adopt mine.

"Everything was hitting rock bottom. My dad died and we had always been close. My mother saw Bill and said, 'Oh, son, I've been waiting thirty-five years for this!' That made me really feel guilty. I mean she waits thirty-five years and I have to screw it up like this. I'm a butcher, a civilian worker, at the military commissary, and things are getting tight. I was demoted and Bridget was laid off. By April 1979—Billy was nine months old—our savings were shot. We were almost forced to miss a house payment. I had to borrow from my mother. I was becoming a weekend alcoholic. I would be fine at work, but all I wanted to do at night was drink. My stepson is sixteen now and into cars. One night, he took our car and smashed it up. Everything was magnified. I was cracking again. Every time I heard the phone ring, I would wince. Diane again. Once I asked her, 'Diane, why is it always bad news with you. Never anything good. Damn it. What does it take to make you happy?' She said, 'Oh, maybe $100,000. If you're going to adopt your son, why not adopt me and Anson, too?' I thought she would never let up, that she would always hold over our head the threat to take away Billy. One night, I started to cry on Bridget's shoulder. Real tears. Here I am an ex-Marine and this crazy gay woman has got me going over the wall. Bridget finally pulled me out of it."

Bridget says, "Noel, I had to warn him again that if he couldn't pull himself together, I was going to take Billy and leave. I could never leave Billy, but I didn't have to see his father disintegrate. That did it. Gradually, Bill pulled himself together."

Bill says, "I was feeling sorry for myself once while Billy was sleeping. I'd look at him in the crib and think, 'Boy, I'm sure some kind of father. I can't even get the little guy a birth certificate.' But then I decided, 'Hell, it really is only a piece of paper. What really counts is giving him a home. And he's going to have that. And if Diane comes after him, she's in for a hell of a fight.' I don't know whether it's luck or what, but she hasn't called since April 1979, when we finally just called her bluff and told her to do her worst. As Christmas approaches, I imagine we'll hear from her again. She seems to get sentimental around Christmas. But this I've accepted. It's out of our hands. We're just going to raise our boy."

I had heard enough. "Bill," I said, "give yourself a break. Diane cannot hurt you. You are hurting yourself. One way or another, this adoption is going to go through. Billy is yours. Period. I'll take care of it. Leave the legal work to me. And, Bill, if Diane calls even one more time you refer her to me. Got that?"

By now it was ten P.M., late for me. I am a morning person and it is a rare night when I'm not in bed by then. I had an hour's drive ahead of me to get from Bill's house to mine. Plenty of time to think about the ongoing mess that had just been described to me.

Bill, I knew, was a believer in working your own way out of your problems, but he had simply gotten in over his head. I wished he'd confided in me earlier about Diane's extortions and the way they were ripping him apart. But I guess Marines are trained to fight their own battles. Bridget did not call because in her mind she would have been betraying Bill.

Anytime you get two high-strung personalities like Bill and Diane involved in something like having a baby through artificial insemination, you're going to have some trouble. Add Diane's history of booze, drugs, and emotional distress, and you have an episode for "Days of Our Lives" or any Grade-B melodrama.

Should it have happened? Could, or should, I have prevented it? Maybe.

But this I know. We're going to work things out for Bill and Bridget and Bill, Jr. Who knows what the experience meant to Diane. She, apparently, has been "lost to follow-up," as the researchers like to say.

Two things were certain. The only way to prevent this type of thing from happening again is to pay the surrogate mother a reasonable fee upfront and bind both surrogate mother and adoptive couple by an enforceable contract. In other words, win our lawsuit and fight for legislation. The other certainty is that Bill and Bridget, given the result, would knowingly do it all over again with Diane, strange as that may sound.

Bill's final words rang through my mind:

"Noel, if my choice were doing it all over again or not have Billy, I would do it. He has made it all worthwhile. He has been a terrific little guy and he has been one heck of a joy to us. It has worked because of him turning out so beautiful. I mean he has a great little personality. It's hard to say. I guess anyone speaks great of their own, but he is and always has been worth it. Even the money part. We are not the type who are striving to have a big boat someday or anything like that. Bridget's three children from her first marriage, including my stepson, all love Billy. Those photos above the fireplace are the two children of Bridget's oldest son. They come and play with Billy. That's Billy in the middle picture, Billy in the bottom picture, Billy in the top picture. Everytime Sears has one of those photo specials, we go and get another picture made of Billy. Believe me, he's worth it."

You want to go to bat for a guy like Bill, I decided. I could live with whatever mistakes had been made in this case. But I was a little down when I finally got home.

It was Christmas time again, and Kathy was waiting up for me. "Noel," she said, "here's a letter you should read."

As they had so many times before, Tom and Jane were about to renew my faith in the surrogate mother idea. Their adoption for Tom, Jr. had recently been approved and Jane was writing to thank me and Kathy. She was thanking my wife because she knew without Kathy's support, I would have abandoned the field long ago.

It was a long, lovely letter. Jane is a very religious lady and she regularly goes to a Bible study class. She wrote,

"Noel, you know one of the hardest things about this whole experience is that you don't share your secret with any but your closest friends. But there were nine of us ladies in Bible study class a few weeks ago when another woman came in and said, "Say, did you see the Phil Donahue Show recently. There was this couple that went out and got a surrogate mother and. . . ." She went on and on and there I was with my friend Barbara, who is a neighbor and who knows our story, and we were right on top of what she was talking about, and yet we didn't say a word. I don't want the publicity or the glory or whatever, but it's a funny thing to be on the inside of something and not be able to talk about it.

But, Noel, I want you and Kathy to know this. We want to share our happiness with you. It is so wonderful to have a son that now we truly know how much we were missing before. The adoption is frosting on the cake.

He's always been ours. Now, he's legally ours. God bless you!"

·7·

"Noel Keane, are you my savior?"

I WAS IN it for keeps. As 1979 drew to a close, I realized that representing surrogate motherhood had become a dominant part of my law practice. What three years before had been simply a strange idea was now a full-time involvement.

My birthday is December 18th and, traditionally, our law office throws a big party on that date, both to mark my getting older and to celebrate the start of the holiday partying. I turned forty-one in 1979, and our eleventh-floor suite and surrounding areas were jammed with people helping me celebrate.

These are my people from East Dearborn, where I grew up. It was a strange mixture. Law clients and law colleagues, policemen and vice detectives, friends and relatives, wives and husbands, girl-friends and boyfriends.

Most of these people had known me for twenty years or so. As the music blared and the liquor flowed, it struck me how easily these people had accepted my new mission in life. A few years ago, most had never heard of a surrogate mother and, even today, many were turned off by the concept, but since they accepted me, they accepted what I was doing. Which is why they are my friends.

By now, of course, "surrogate mother" was becoming part of

the language. The news coverage assured that. The question was how far and how fast the concept would catch on.

All in all, though, I was pretty content with myself as the new year beckoned. I was still enjoying the challenges posed by surrogate parenting and I was still looking forward to helping other people who otherwise could not have children. My only real concern, in fact, is that my involvement not in any way come back to harm my sons. I had a long talk with the priest of my parish and felt very reassured. He took the position that it is too early to make any hard-and-fast judgments about surrogate parenting and that we all should just wait and see what happens. One could not ask for any more.

During 1979, I had mostly pursued the adoptions and the lawsuit. I figured that we should first clear the air legally before involving other people in this risky new area. So in that entire year, I accepted only one other couple to represent, and they were to become one of my happiest stories. Richard and Aralee are a professional couple, both Ph.D.s from Virginia. He, ironically, is a professor of genetics at a university and she is a microbiologist employed by a hospital. I put them in touch with Sally, a Detroit-area stewardess who wanted to become a surrogate mother "so I will not miss out on this important experience." All three are wonderful people and would spend much of 1979 unsuccessfully trying to get Sally pregnant. But before I get into their story, I want to tell you about the five couples I could not help. Because each represented a unique example of the risks and uncertainties of this new field.

First, I had some consultations with a couple from the Midwest. We'll call them the Smiths. The wife could not conceive a child, but she could carry one. She wanted to know if there were any way that her husband's sperm could be used to artificially fertilize another woman's egg and then have that egg implanted in her uterus to carry to term. Just like Tom and Jane, this couple knew exactly what they wanted to do. The question to me was simple: Was it possible?

Many of the developments in this field are coincidental and, by happenstance, I had had a call only weeks before from Randolph Seed, M.D., and Richard Seed, Ph.D., who run the Reproduction and Fertility Clinic in Chicago. They have been working for years to try to perfect techniques to do exactly that. Find a donor woman, a surrogate mother in effect, who will agree to be artificially inseminated with the sperm of the husband of a barren woman. The doctors then flush the womb of the surrogate mother to try to recover a fertilized egg. In theory, the fertilized egg could then be implanted into the womb of a woman like Mrs. Smith, who cannot produce her own egg. If successful, this procedure would be the ultimate in biological involvement for an otherwise infertile couple. Not only would the husband be the birth father (biological father) but the mother would actually carry and give birth to the child. Legally, of course, there would be a conundrum. Who is the real mother of such a child? The woman who donated the egg and who left her genetic signature, or the woman who carried the baby inside her for nine months and gave birth?

We will not know the answer to this question for some time. The technology, unfortunately, is not yet equal to the challenge. Despite years of work and considerable success in the cattle-breeding industry, the Seed brothers have not yet perfected a successful method for humans. Transferring a fertilized egg from one woman to another is an incredibly difficult procedure. So far, doctors working in the field have recovered just three eggs—only one fertilized—and they are not ready to attempt a transfer.

The Smiths, however, are a young couple and they chose to run the risk of working with the Seed brothers rather than search for a conventional surrogate-mother arrangement. I am following their case, and the other patients at the Seed Clinic, with great interest. If ever proven practicable, the embryo-transfer procedure can be an enormous boon to women who cannot produce an egg and, thus, cannot conceive but who can carry a child. It also would minimize the time and hardship required of the surrogate mother. However, the emerging embryo-transfer procedures are at least as difficult as the older technology for "test-tube babies."

To be eligible for a test-tube baby, a married woman must be able to produce an egg, although a defect in her reproductive parts prevent it from being released into the Fallopian tube for natural fertilization. For test-tube, or *in vitro,* fertilization, doctors must perform a laparoscopy. A laparoscope, or viewing device, is inserted into the body via the navel and doctors look through it to locate the egg inside the ovary's follicle sac. Through another incision, the ovary is held in place with a forceps while the delicate search proceeds. Doctors use a hollow needle to extract the egg from the follicle sac and they then draw it through an attached aspirator tube. The entire procedure takes only eighty seconds. The recovered egg is allowed to mature for several hours in an incubator and then is combined with a few drops of the husband's sperm in a solution in a Petri dish. If fertilization occurs, then at the eight-cell stage the embryo is ready to implant in the uterus with a nylon catheter. The fetus's development then progresses in a normal manner. This is the procedure that British doctors Patrick C. Steptoe and Robert G. Edwards used to help provide the world its first *in vitro* baby, Louise Brown, who was born July 25, 1978, in England. Her mother had been trying to have a baby for twelve years and the birth of Baby Louise caught the world by storm. The procedure, however, remains shrouded in mystery. Physicians cannot explain why it works in some cases, but not in most.

The embryo-transfer procedure, which offers hope to women who cannot produce an egg, may be even more difficult than the test-tube procedures. The Seeds are trying to perform human artificial embryonation in four steps:

First, over a period of months, they attempt to hormonally synchronize the menstrual cycles of donor and recipient. Their wombs must be in accord so that when the donor ovulates and her uterus readies itself to receive the fertilized egg, the uterus of the recipient is also preparing to have and hold an egg.

Then, when the doctors think the women are in sync, they will inseminate the donor with the sperm of the recipient's husband.

The third step is to, four days after the insemination, flush out the uterus with a plastic catheter—a five minute-procedure—hoping that an embryo is washed out. The flushing is done four days after the insemination because it takes about three days for an egg to pass through the Fallopian tubes from the ovary to the uterus. If fertilized during that time, it will float freely for another two or three days before attaching to the uterine wall.

Finally, if a fertilized egg is recovered from the donor, then it can be transferred to the recipient's womb.

So delicate is the required timing for synchronization, fertilization, and egg retrieval that as yet the doctors have not even attempted a transfer. However, the Seeds are working with several couples, including the Smiths, and corresponding donors. They say the procedure will cost each couple "as much as a new car," and there are no guarantees. Donors are used again and again and are paid $50 a flush, with a $200 bonus if a fertilized egg is recovered.

My client, the Smiths, are determined to stick with the embryo-transfer attempts "at least for a year." I wish them well, but my advice to most childless couples is that a surrogate mother offers a much more immediate and realistic hope than either embryo transfers or test-tube babies. Both the work being done by the Seeds and the *in vitro* work here and abroad is highly experimental and highly restrictive. In this country, it is under the purview of the Ethics Advisory Board of the U.S. Department of Health and Human Services, and bureaucratic delays and obstacles are a certainty. It will probably be at least a decade before either of these procedures is a viable hope for most barren couples. If ever. Most couples do not have that much time. Or prefer not to take the gamble.

While I referred the Smiths to a complex option, the embryo transfer, I thought I had an easier solution for Jim and Kathy Walker, who came to me looking for a surrogate mother. He is a university professor and she is a nurse. Unfortunately, there were no surrogate mothers to be found. About this time, however, a client came to me looking for help in placing for adoption a child his unwed daughter was about to have. The Walkers are from Minnesota, a state which allows direct, or private, adoptions. I thought it would be possible to have the Walkers adopt the baby about to be born to my client's daughter, and sought advice from Michigan state officials on how to handle an out-of-state adoption.

Everything seemed in order until the Walkers told a Minnesota adoption agency what we were about to do. The Minnesota people were outraged that an out-of-state attorney was involved in an adoption in their state and put tremendous pressure on the Walkers. In fact, they almost drove them to tears with threats of one kind or another. The Walkers had previously applied to adopt a Korean child—the only babies available without a long wait— and now were told that this application was in jeopardy if they didn't immediately cease and desist. Well, the Walkers wanted to live in Minnesota and they decided they had no choice but to knuckle under to what the adoption agency demanded. Plans were dropped to adopt my client's child and, in time, the Walkers did adopt a Korean child. Their hassles with the adoption agency is but one example of many brought to my attention. One of the biggest reasons for the popularity of the surrogate mother is the simple fact that people are fed up with the high-handed dealings of most U.S. adoption agencies. The agencies act as if they are doing people a favor just to talk to them, when, in fact, talk is about all they have to offer. People looking for babies need assistance and a listening ear, not a bureaucratic shuffle and moralizing.

In two other cases, I became briefly involved with people whose motives I distrusted.

One couple seemed a mismatch in motivation. The man was obsessed with having a child, but his wife, who was rather sickly, seemed to care less, although she said all the proper things. The woman had diabetes and kidney problems and it was a full-time job for her to take care of herself. Nevertheless, her husband insisted that they wanted to find a surrogate mother. About two weeks after their first visit, the case was closed. The wife just up and left to live with a former boyfriend in Florida. She left a note saying that she could not stand the pressure being put on her to have a child.

The other case was even more bizarre. A couple from Manhattan with a frenetic lifestyle thought they needed a child to cement what was a sagging marriage. I had received a call from a potential surrogate mother in Brooklyn, so I put these three New Yorkers in touch with each other. Next, I heard from a hysterical wife. Seems like the husband and surrogate mother went to a motel to attempt the insemination and decided, what the hell, why not try it the good old-fashioned way? They liked it so well they ran off with each other. I have a feeling, though, that had this couple not self-destructed over a surrogate mother, they would have found another excuse. Their story is, however, another powerful argument for state regulation of the business.

I was spared from extensive involvement in the fifth case, thank God, by a doctor's advice. This couple, Adam and Olive May (their real first names), was from Indiana. Now Olive May, God bless her, was sixty years old and obsessed with somehow providing a child for her husband, Adam, who at age forty was a generation younger.

I have become fairly adept at screening potential adoptive couples and surrogate mothers over the telephone. The idea does attract some people on the fringes. And if the voice on the other end of the telephone sounds as if it required a third party to dial the call, I make quick work of the conversation. But Olive May sounded pretty together. And she lied about her age. So I scheduled an appointment.

When they walked into my office, Martha saw them first. "Noel," she told me, closing the door, "if you represent this couple, count me out." It didn't take me long to agree with Martha. Not only was Olive May sixty, but she looked older. She looked, in fact, as if she had one foot in the grave. Adam, on the other hand, had trouble spelling his name. He literally was a half-wit. Well, they had sent me a check before coming to the office, and I promptly handed it back to them, pointing out that we could proceed only if their priest or family physician would approve of their participation. A few weeks later, their family doctor sent along a curt note. "In my opinion," the doctor wrote, "Mrs.

_____ is not a good candidate for this particular conception. She is a diabetic and too mature, age sixty. Thank you. Dr. _____." And thank *you*, doctor. Olive May later wrote me a nice note, saying how disappointed they were but that they were pleased they had tried.

While these five cases came and went, I kept close tabs on Richard and Aralee and their surrogate-mother-in-waiting, Sally. She simply could not get pregnant. As a stewardess, Sally had free flying privileges and each month she would fly to Virginia for another artificial insemination. But despite keeping temperature charts and doing repeated inseminations, nothing seemed to work. How ironic, I thought, because if ever a trio went into the surrogate mother arrangement with informed consent, it was these three. Yet, in a year of trying, they still did not have a pregnancy. Were Adam and Olive May to have found a surrogate mother, I am sure that the insemination would have taken on the first try. Fate does play curious games.

At the time they met Sally, Richard and Aralee had been looking for a way to have children for eight years. Aralee had a hysterectomy in 1971, so her options were two. Adopt or find a surrogate mother. But in 1971, no one had ever heard of surrogate mothers. At a 1974 conference on human genetics, however, Richard heard a lecturer discuss the use of surrogate mothers in certain genetic experiments. He had always kept this possibility in the back of his mind and in 1978—when he was told the adoption waiting list was ten years—he called the lecturer. She disavowed any knowledge of surrogate parenting and told them, "You're at least ten years ahead of your time. This area is simply too sticky for people to get involved."

In the meantime, they had seen me on the Phil Donahue shows and, in 1978, gave me a call. We arranged to go on an NBC-TV show, "America Alive," with Art Linkletter. At the time, it seemed the only way to find a surrogate mother. Richard was thirty-two and Aralee thirty-one, and they were getting anxious. Right after the show was scheduled, the NBC programming people got the idea that it would be a great idea to put a potential surrogate mother on the show if one would volunteer. Well, as it happened, this young woman, whom we'll call Jill, did volunteer. She sounded a little theatrical to me, but NBC insisted on her as a condition to do the show. It was to be a very dramatic moment, sort of a "This Is Your Life" type of thing. Jill came on stage to confront Richard and Aralee, who had never seen her before, and everybody seemed to hit it off. She was blonde and beautiful and bright. She appeared to be everything a couple could ask for in a potential surrogate mother.

It was to turn out, however, that Jill's real interest was not in babies, but in being a TV star. She milked the publicity and then backed out of a scheduled artificial insemination with the excuse of—what else?—a heart murmur.

Richard and Aralee are both private people and it had taken a lot for them to go on TV at all. Then to have spent months working with a woman whose real interest was celebrity, not humanity, had really crushed them. They were ready to forget the whole thing. Richard told me, "Noel, I sometimes think that if I were to walk through Times Square carrying a placard on my back, we could find a surrogate mother. Or if I took out an ad in *The New York Times* (which along with several other newspapers, however, has steadfastly refused to carry ads for surrogate mothers). But we're not about to do either."

It was early in 1979 that Sally came to me seeking to be a surrogate mother, and I immediately knew she was the match for Richard and Aralee.

Unlike Jill, Sally wanted nothing to do with TV or any other kind of publicity. She simply wanted the experience of being pregnant and giving birth and, inexplicably, her past had always for one reason or another conspired against her doing that. Being a surrogate mother seemed to her the perfect solution.

"I'm thirty now," Sally told me. "I'm an instinctual person, and my instincts tell me that being a surrogate mother is the right thing for me to do.

"I was married for seven years and worked to put my husband through law school. He didn't want children because he said he felt uncomfortable around them. Then the funniest thing happened. We divorced, and he turned right around and married another woman with two small children. I guess I was pretty bitter. I married on the rebound and made a mistake. I figured it was better to admit the mistake and get out, rather than compound it with a child. Now, my current boyfriend, whom I dearly love, just doesn't want to get married. He's financially able to support a family, but he says he's not emotionally ready to have children. I've been anxious to have children for years, but I've never been with the right man at the right time. I want to stay with my boyfriend, but I'm afraid if I did and it deprived me of ever having children, I would in later years come to resent him. So being a surrogate mother seems right to both of us. My boyfriend is supporting me all the way."

Richard and Aralee met Sally in my office and it was instant rapport.

Sally would later recall, "Aralee reminds me of a girl I went to kindergarten with and whom I've known all my life. Aralee could almost be a twin to this friend of mine. And Aralee is also a microbiologist. At the time I got this idea to be a surrogate mother, I was studying microbiology. I figured, 'Well, this is meant to be. . . . this has got to be a good omen.' "

Richard is very sophisticated about the new science of genetic counseling, but he recalls, "Aralee and I approved of Sally instantly. She was very charming and she was very sincere. We could tell from a simple conversation that she was obviously intelligent. Her appearance was perfectly normal. She said there are no medical or mental problems in her family, and we took her word.

"Now, I'm a professor of genetics, but let's face it, unless there are some very obvious genetic diseases in a family, everything is up for grabs anyway. If we had convened a panel of ten eminent geneticists and put Sally through a seven-day battery of tests, I doubt if we would have found anything other than what our common sense told us. We are lucky to have such a fine woman to carry a child for us. Genetics is an incredibly complex process, anyway. If Farrah Fawcett were to volunteer to be a surrogate mother for a million dollars or so, I doubt if anybody in their right mind would take her on, even if the money were no object. The odds are that Farrah Fawcett's daughter would be no better or worse than one born to the average woman."

So immediate was the bond between Richard and Aralee and Sally that they decided to attempt an insemination the afternoon they met, which, coincidentally, fell within Sally's fertile period. That insemination, however, did not take, and neither did the next nine or ten. During all of 1979, Sally was futilely trying to get pregnant.

From my standpoint, their case was almost textbook-perfect, with the crucial exception that we could not produce a pregnancy. Legally, everything was in order.

First, I had the trio sign a six-point "Agreement of Understanding," as follows:

1. That SALLY will be artificially inseminated with the sperm of RICHARD;
2. That RICHARD will file with the Wayne County Probate Court an Intent to Claim Paternity;
3. That all necessary costs will be paid by RICHARD and ARALEE, his wife, with the approval of the court having jurisdiction;
4. That SALLY will give *immediate* custody of the child to RICHARD and will further sign all necessary forms to relinquish any and all legal rights she may have to the child;
5. That there will be no fee paid to SALLY and that nothing of value will be given in lieu of a fee;
6. It is expressly understood by SALLY that she will be severing any and all ties to said child.

I made arrangements with a Dearborn, Michigan, osteopath to assist with the inseminations, if desired. Richard, Aralee, and Sally all signed "hold harmless" agreements exempting the osteopathic physician from any potential liability. The agreement stipulated that as Sally artificially inseminated herself, "the doctor was present *solely* for the purpose of acting as a witness." We still could not persuade a doctor to do the *actual* insemination, although now they would tell the women how.

My legal fees to Richard and Aralee were $2,000 and the agreement I signed with them was by now fairly standard. It read:

> Mr. and Mrs. _____ have contacted Noel P. Keane and requested to locate a surrogate mother to be artificially inseminated with the semen of Richard _____ , and who will deliver a child and then return the child to Mr. and Mrs. _____ by means of adoption.
>
> Mr. and Mrs. _____ have agreed to pay to Noel P. Keane the sum of $2,000 as attorney fees.
>
> It is expressly understood that Mr. Keane *has not* guaranteed any of the following:
>
> A. That in fact a surrogate mother will be found;
> B. That Mr. and Mrs. _____ will, in fact, receive a child;
> C. That the surrogate mother, if found, is artificially inseminated and does deliver a child, that she, in fact, will give the child to Mr. and Mrs. _____ .
>
> It is further understood that any and all expenses paid to the surrogate mother must be approved by the court that has jurisdiction over the matter.
>
> It is further understood between Mr. and Mrs. _____ and Noel P. Keane that they shall hold Noel P. Keane harmless from any and all liability associated with this undertaking.

As you can see, this legal agreement clearly spells out the hazards of the surrogate-mother search and guarantees absolutely nothing. For $2,000, the couple gets a hope and a prayer. But I had learned my lesson with Bill and Bridget and their sorry experience with

Diane. This is the state of the art. We all were simply taking a leap into the unknown with only faith to guide us. When everything is said and done, I realized, there is no substitute for the calibre of the woman you find to be the surrogate mother. Richard and Aralee, I thought, were extremely fortunate to have Sally as a volunteer. Now, if they could only get her pregnant.

The trio had discussed all the related questions that cannot be spelled out in a contract and were in agreement.

What if the child is born deformed?

Said Richard, "Well, that is a risk you face on every birth. We are willing to accept whatever comes. For better or worse, this will be our child. If it is deformed and becomes a financial burden, then it is our family burden. We are taking a chance."

He added, "Another very obvious fear is that if the surrogate mother decides to keep the child, she probably can and there is nothing we could do about it. And since I have signed a statement of paternity, I could be strapped with $500 a month or whatever in child support. It all gets down to the fact that you have to be convinced that your surrogate mother knows what she is getting into. She has to be absolutely reliable.

"In time, as this concept expands, it will have to be regulated. I see it as the flip side of artificially inseminating women from sperm banks. Sperm banks are regulated. And, for that matter, male donors to sperm banks are paid. Since the effort required of a surrogate mother is considerably greater than that required of a male donor to a sperm bank, I think the surrogate mother should legally be paid a reasonable fee. And I think the state should step in and regulate the transaction, just as it regulates sperm banks."

My sentiments exactly, Richard.

Sally said, "I know I will never have any problem giving up this child, because from the start I have thought of it as a project, something I am doing for another couple. To complete my life and feel like a total woman, I feel like I need this experience. I feel that Richard and Aralee are doing me a favor by allowing me to have the one experience I have so far been denied. If I were never to have a pregnancy, I think I would feel cheated. I must admit that a part of me hopes that my boyfriend will see how happy I am and that maybe two years from now we can have our own child. But this baby will be Richard and Aralee's. I am simply harboring a gift for them."

Sally's concern was, "What if Richard and Aralee would be killed in a car crash or something? I would feel like the child is an orphan and that I have a responsibility." I explained that Richard and Aralee, like all parents, would designate someone, a brother or sister or other close relative, to take over in such a case. And that she would not have a say in it. Sally said she accepted this, "though I would want to know that the child had a loving home." She added, "If the baby were born with enormous medical complications, let's say congenital heart problems, I would feel a responsibility to help them out." I told her, "You understand, of course, that once the baby is born, it's out of your hands." Sally said she accepted this, "though I would always want to know the baby is being taken care of and that, if necessary, I would be allowed to help."

Sally is a very independent woman and only two opinions were important to her as she embarked on this adventure—her mother's and her boyfriend's.

"My mother is a very grandmotherly type," Sally said, "and, at first, it really distressed her to know that there would be a child in her family who really wasn't in her family. She has four grandchildren, and, of course, this would be her fifth grandchild—except it wouldn't be—and it was tough to explain. I finally told my mother that, 'Look, it's better that you have a grandchild by me who lives somewhere else than that you never have a grandchild by me at all.' She supports me and said that she wants to be in the labor room with me when I give birth, since this will be my first baby. And I have also told my two sisters and my grandmother. The women understand. It is a woman's story. I have not told my father. He would not understand. I have to admit that I feel closer to Aralee than to Richard. I am doing this for her because of the experience that she cannot have and that I will have for both of us."

The adoption proceedings would be easy for Richard and Aralee. I had seen to that. Since Richard would claim paternity and Sally would release custody to the father, Richard would simply take his child home with him to Virginia. Then, his wife, Aralee, would immediately adopt in Virginia, so that if anything happened to Richard, the mother, Aralee, would have legal custody.

I was pretty pleased with my work with Richard and Aralee and Sally. If ever a group deserved success, it was this trio.

So at my birthday party in 1979, I could look back on some solid achievements in the field of surrogate mothering.

First, my attorney associate, Bob Harrison, and I had strongly argued our precedent-setting lawsuit asking that a fee for surrogate mothers be made legal. A preliminary decision was due in early 1980. Second, we had accomplished landmark adoptions for the children born to Debbie, Sue, and George and Jane, Carol, and Tom, and had created a system to assure that future adoptions would be quick and painless.

Third, the continuing news publicity was making "surrogate mother" a household word. More importantly, it was becoming respectable among the legal fraternity. In the fall of 1979, I gave a lecture on the surrogate-mother phenomenon to the annual meeting of the American College of Legal Medicine. Afterwards, I was astonished to find out that the legal questions posed by the surrogate mother had become a test question on the Family Law Section of an exam at a prestigious law school. The answers I had had to grope for on my own were now being written down in little blue books by ambitious law students.

People from law schools across the country were contacting me. Professors wanted information for their classes; students wanted information for their papers. The *National Law Journal* profiled me in a page-one story headlined "The Babymaker." One law student with whom I corresponded early on in my involvement would later write me a nice letter and observe, "Little did I know that I would be dealing with a national celebrity." The *National Catholic Reporter* even asked me to write an article—for $40—on the controversy. "You are the nation's chief legal authority in this new source of hope for the infertile," read the cover letter.

Clearly, I had become just that. The national legal overseer of a happening that was making instant celebrities of everyone who touched it. I am as a big a ham as the next guy and I have to admit that I have enjoyed the limelight, but I also know that I would not be in the field if it were not for the continuing challenge and the continuing opportunities to truly help people.

The movement was now going national. Early in 1979, I met a young obstetrician-gynecologist from Louisville, Kentucky. Richard Levin, M.D., who questioned me about everything I had learned in three years of working with surrogate mothers. Dr. Levin told me, "I see these people every single day. You get tired of infertile couples sitting on the other side of your desk crying. For them other options are just not feasible. I'm interested in the surrogate mother."

Having been rebuffed by so many other physicians, I found Dr. Levin's views refreshing and cooperated wholeheartedly in explaining to him everything I had learned. I certainly did not intend to seek a monopoly on anything so important.

The state where Dr. Levin practices, Kentucky, does not specifically outlaw the payment of a fee to a surrogate mother. With this in mind, he began working with Kentucky lawyers and created during 1979 the Surrogate Parenting Associates, Inc., a medical practice intended to recruit—and pay—surrogate mothers to have children for infertile couples. By the end of 1979, Dr. Levin was just beginning to get his unusual practice off the ground, and I was working closely with him and his attorney, Katie Brophy, to help smooth the way. The addition of a full-time physician to the field could mean only one thing: the surrogate mother was here to stay.

Dr. Levin's cases were still ahead of him. I had three years of cases to look back on, and the twists and turns continued.

Incredibly, both of my first two threesomes—Debbie, Sue, and George, and Jane, Carol, and Tom—decided during 1979 to at-

tempt the impossible. To duplicate their earlier collaborations.
Surrogate mothers Sue and Carol were about to try to get pregnant again through artificial insemination.

Carol never made it. After the first insemination failed to take,
Tom and Jane put their heads together and made a decision.
"Noel," Jane would later tell me, "I think that maybe the Good
Lord is trying to tell us something. Leave well enough alone.
Carol has given us one child and our lives will never again be the
same. One miracle is enough. Tom and I decided to call it off.
Carol was willing to do it for us again, but we decided that she
and God had already given us enough for a lifetime."

Debbie, Sue, and George, however, with typical persistence,
simply went out and repeated their entire scenario. By November
1979, there was a baby boy, Paul James, to join Elizabeth Anne.
Again, the birth was by Caesarian to surrogate mother Sue, who
remains a virgin. Auntie Sue continues to live with Debbie and
George and their two children, and I visited with them shortly
after the second birth in their "new" forty-year-old aluminum-
sided home. Paul James, it appeared, would grow up to be a
football player. He is muscular and active. Debbie and Sue are
talking about starting a day-care center. George is thinking of
quitting his job as a pressman and going to work for the post office
("no night work and more regular hours"). By now, Debbie and
George are known as "that couple," and some of their neighbors
are upset by the notoriety. But Debbie, Sue, and George seem
perfectly comfortable. Both with what they have done and what
they continue to do by living together. An unusual *ménage à trois*.
Clearly, Debbie is the mother and runs the household. Sue is
essentially a boarder and friend. The only real change I noticed is
that George has put on a little weight, which is not unbecoming.
His father still is not speaking to him.

I was certain of one thing. The adoption of Paul James would be
a piece of cake. The work we had done for Elizabeth Anne assured
that.

In the meantime, I was laying the groundwork to eventually
accomplish the difficult adoption for Bill and Bridget. We are

filing papers in Michigan and Tennessee to simultaneously establish Bill's paternity and to terminate the legal rights of surrogate mother Diane, who has dropped out of sight. Once these two things are accomplished, then Bill and Bridget can adopt Billy Jr.

I was musing to myself that at the time our lawsuit was to be decided early next year, Elizabeth Anne, the first child born to a surrogate mother, would already be two years old.

The partygoers were spilling throughout my office suite. Clients were telling dirty jokes behind closed doors in my private office. Suddenly, my partner Chuck Fellrath, called me aside. "Noel," he said, "there are two women on the phone trying to reach you. Should I tell them to call back tomorrow?"

I was flying pretty high—it was eight P.M. by now—but I took the calls.

The first was from Sally. She was finally pregnant. And overjoyed.

The second call was to commence my strangest case yet in the remarkable saga of the surrogate mother.

Her name was Lorelei, and she spoke in a rich, lilting voice that carried the thousand miles from her Connecticut home as if she were standing next to me. Her opening line caught me off guard. "Noel Keane," she began, "are you my savior?"

She was married, unable to have children, and wanted me to find her a surrogate mother. Her husband was tall, dark, and handsome, and they both were gainfully employed. She would send me a check as a legal retainer first thing in the morning.

And, oh yes, one more thing. She is a transsexual. For the first twenty-one years of her life, she had been a boy.

I told her to send me a letter explaining all this. Then, I headed for the bar. I bumped into my closest friend, Stan Bromley, a national executive for the Hyatt Hotel chain.

"Well, Noel," he began. "I guess by now this surrogate mother stuff is getting to be old hat?"

I slowly stirred my scotch and soda and said softly, "No, Stan, believe me. It's anything but old hat!"

ꞏ8ꞏ

"The evils attendant to the mix of lucre and the adoption process are self-evident."

THINGS happened fast in the new year. It was during 1980 that the full potential of the surrogate mother began to be accepted.

People were coming to me for help in greatly increasing numbers. In addition, Dr. Levin was getting his Surrogate Parenting Associates business off the ground. The publicity over both our cases was driving home to the public the realization that the surrogate mother is not about to disappear.

The first news of the new year, however, was disappointing. We lost the first round of our lawsuit to have the payment of a fee to a surrogate mother declared legal.

I cannot say I was that surprised. As I mentioned before, the presiding judge, Wayne County (Michigan) Circuit Judge Roman S. Gribbs is a strong Catholic, and his brother is a priest.

In a fourteen-page opinion, Judge Gribbs ruled that paying a surrogate mother violates Michigan's adoption laws and is illegal. The court ruling was the first legal decision in the nation on this controversial subject, and the fact that it was disappointing does not deter Bob Harrison or myself. Not only are we appealing

Judge Gribbs' decision, but we both feel the issue eventually will
be decided by the U.S. Supreme Court.

Our lawsuit, brought on behalf of childless couples and surrogate mothers, argued that the Michigan adoption law is unconstitutional and violates the plaintiffs' right to privacy and that the
surrogate-mother arrangement we propose is not against the public policy in Michigan.

The lawsuit, which is now three years old, raises three broad
questions:

✓ Are the Michigan laws barring the payment of a fee to a surrogate mother, when an adoption process is involved, unconstitutional?
✓ Is the penalty provision making payment of such a fee as part of
  the adoption process a misdemeanor and imposing criminal
  sanctions constitutional?
✓ Is the arrangement we propose whereby the surrogate mother
  could be paid a fee as part of the adoption process against the
  public policy in Michigan?

In each case, of course, the state says "yes" and we say "no."

The current Michigan adoption law says that judicial approval
is required of expenses paid in connection with an adoption, and
that the probate court disapproves of any payments to the natural
mother for giving up her child to adoption.

The legal papers and references buttressing our arguments run
hundreds of pages, but, essentially, we are saying that the Michigan adoption statutes violate the rights of privacy of the natural
mother and the adoption couple; that the statutes are constitutionally overbroad and create a constitutionally underinclusive classi-
fication affecting certain infertile women; and that the statutes are
unconstitutionally vague.

Most important for the future, we argue that the Michigan
public policy does not preclude the surrogate-mother agreement,
in which the surrogate mother, for a fee, will bear a child to a man

through artificial insemination and then relinquish that child to the man and, in most cases, his wife by adoption.

Judge Gribbs, however, did not agree.

For arguing purposes, attorneys had set the fee to be paid to a prospective surrogate mother at $5,000.

Judge Gribbs upheld the constitutionality of the adoption law and its prohibition of payment of any money in connection with the adoption of a child except for those approved by the Probate Court. He pointed out that a couple in adopting a child born to a surrogate mother would be relying on the same adoption law the lawsuit is trying to upset. Addressing himself to the proposed fee of $5,000, the judge said:

"The right to adopt a child based on the payment of $5,000 is not a fundamental personal right and not within the constitutional protection of the right of privacy as defined by the U.S. Supreme Court."

In later telling reporters that we would appeal the decision, my legal associate, Bob Harrison, said:

"We do not subscribe to back-alley sales of babies for thousands of dollars. We believe the state should control adoptions. But this isn't the selling of babies. It is the father's child. His wife is just adopting the child."

The heart of our argument is this attack upon the strange paradox in the adoption law. Harrison told reporters:

"It's curious that it would be permissible and proper to pay a surrogate mother to have the baby, and for the couple to take the child and raise it, but when the couple tries to adopt the child, it becomes illegal."

We are saying, in effect, that the adoption law is obsolete and is in no way responsive to the unexpected phenomenon of the surrogate mother. The Michigan law is from another era—the era of sordid bartering for babies. It is sadly dated in regard to today's new frontiers in conception and their accompanying medical breakthroughs and moral dilemmas.

The judge did not see it that way.

Since his ruling is the first legal decision ever handed down about the surrogate mother, other than the advisory opinion I solicited from now-retired Juvenile Court Judge James Lincoln, I shall quote at length from relevant portions of Judge Gribbs' opinion. He found:

" 'Baby bartering' is against the public policy of this State, and the State's interest in preventing such conduct is sufficiently compelling and meets the test set forth in *Roe* (our lawsuit).

"Mercenary considerations used to create a parent-child relationship and its impact upon the family unit strikes at the very foundation of human society and is patently and necessarily injurious to the community.

"It is a fundamental principle that children should not and cannot be bought and sold. The sale of children is illegal in all states. The brief of the Attorney General (a co-defendant) cites this elementary rule:

" 'Parents have no property rights, in the ordinary sense of that term, in or to their minor children, and, accordingly, a parent's right of control or custody of a minor child is not a property right which may be bargained, sold, or otherwise disposed of.'

"The evils attendant to the mix of lucre and the adoption process are self-evident, and the temptations of dealing in 'money-market babies' exist whether the parties be strangers or friends. The statute seeks to prevent a money market for the adoption of babies. The defendant prosecuting attorney concedes that the plaintiff natural mother (Roe) and the plantiff couple (Doe) are free to 'conceive a child, bear it, and raise it as they agree among themselves because these acts are guaranteed by the right to privacy.' The defendant prosecuting attorney argues perceptively when he asks: 'How much money will it take for a particular mother's will to be overborne, and when does her decision turn from voluntary to involuntary?'

"In their brief and in oral arguments, plaintiffs vigorously argue that they are in this Court motivated by good will and with the best of intentions seek the Court's approval of their proposed course of action. The prosecuting attorney pointedly responds as follows:

" 'Plaintiffs seek to convince this Court that the 'surrogate mother' would act out of altruistic rather than pecuniary motives. If that were so, no monetary payment would be necessary because under MCLA 710.54 she can still be reimbursed for fees and expenses. What plaintiffs seek is to provide her with a sum of money ($5,000) over and above the reasonable expenses she has incurred. Even if some of this money goes for legitimate expenses unrecognized by MCLA 710.54, the fact remains that the primary purpose of this money is to encourage women to volunteer to be 'surrogate mothers.' Plaintiffs have initiated this lawsuit because few women would be willing to volunteer the use of their bodies for nine months if the only thing they gained was the joy of making someone else happy by letting that couple adopt and raise her child. Thus, contrary to plaintiffs' exhortations, in all but the rarest of situations, the money plaintiffs seek to pay the 'surrogate mother' is intended as an inducement for her to conceive a child she would not normally want to conceive, carry for nine months a child she would normally not want to carry, give birth to a child she would not normally want to give birth to, and, then, because of this monetary reward, relinquish her parental rights to a child whom she bore."

Judge Gribbs concluded:

"The personal desires and intentions of plaintiffs are not in queston, and their good faith is conceded. Nonetheless, public policy is established to guide all the people of this State, of whatever intent.

"A desire to change the established stated public policy that meets constitutional muster is properly addressed to the Legislature and not to the courts."

I found the reasoning of the attorney general rather cynical in implying that "in all cases but the rarest situations," a woman would be a surrogate mother only for money. Obviously, he had never met Susan and Carol, my first two surrogate mothers and two women who truly did it as a gift to others.

But Judge Gribbs did concede our good faith in pursuing a legal remedy to the situation. Beyond that, he put his finger on the real solution in suggesting, "A desire to change the established stated public policy that meets constitutional muster is properly addressed to the Legislature. . . ."

We know the ultimate answer must come from state legislation and state regulation. We are working on this, but it is a long way down the road.

In the meantime, Bob Harrison and I immediately began work on our legal appeal. Round One, at the trial-court level, was lost. We now moved to the Court of Appeals, which is a three-judge panel. That decision, however, would be at least a year away.

While the legal outlook remained fuzzy, the demand for surrogate mothers was coming through loud and clear. I began to pick up my pace in representing both those who wanted children and those who wanted to be surrogate mothers.

The fun—and the frustration—were only beginning. I am a lover of old-time music, and most appropriate to the months ahead is the old Al Jolson lyric, "You ain't seen nothing yet!"

·9·

"If she's bright, beautiful, and talented and wants $50,000, why not?"

THINGS opened up in 1980. Suddenly, some of my clients were legally offering $10,000 fees to find surrogate mothers. Introduced into the drama of surrogate parenting were, among others, a transsexual housewife, a single male Hollywood scriptwriter who wanted a son through sperm-splitting and sex-selection techniques, an East Coast "tomboy," a celebrity couple big in films and country music, a Texas midwife with a cause, a California forest ranger, an immigrant couple with everything but a baby, and a physician-supervised clinic specializing in surrogate mothers.

Five of my new cases in 1980 represented the unusual cross-section of people that now are seeking out this new option. Each represented a new challenge for me. There were:

John and Lorelei, a married couple from Connecticut. Lorelei is a transsexual. This couple had to institute a cross-country hunt to Southern California to find a surrogate mother. And Rita, the woman they thought was the answer to their prayers, was to make their lives a nightmare. It was Bill and Bridget and Diane all over again. After John and Lorelei suffered great anguish and expense Rita became pregnant. But, in a dramatic turnaround, she then vowed never to give up the baby. The baby is due in the spring of 1981, and I think that this case will make legal history. Unless Rita changes her mind, a court will be asked to decide whether the baby born to a surrogate mother belongs to the natural mother or to the natural father and his wife.

Joseph, a single man from Hollywood, California, who is both a student and scriptwriter. At the age of thirty, he decided he was ready to start a family, but there was one catch. He was not yet ready to get romantically involved with a woman. He wanted a surrogate mother to give him a child. Beyond that, he wanted a son. To increase the probability of having a son, he wanted to have his sperm split in a laboratory procedure to enhance the male-carrying chromosomes and to have the surrogate mother inseminated with the male-enriched sperm. Since he would not have to adopt (he would already be the father) he is legally able to pay a fee and is prepared to pay what is becoming the standard rate at Dr. Levin's new clinic in Kentucky—$10,000. (Joseph, however, as a single man would not be eligible to find a surrogate mother at Dr. Levin's clinic, which works only with married couples.) Since Joseph's case adds three unorthodox new dimensions—the payment of a fee, the splitting of sperm for sex-selection, and single parenthood—to what is already a controversial subject, I knew there was but one way to argue Joseph's cause: on television. Sure enough, when Joseph spent an hour on "The Phil Donahue Show," the female audience began by wanting to eat him alive. But by the show's end, they had come around to his point of view. A few even volunteered to be the surrogate mother! But Joseph is a fastidious man, and we were to find the search for the surrogate mother to be slow going.

Thomas and Cindy Sue, a film couple from Manhattan. He is a producer of enormously successful TV commercials and industrial films and she is a Southern belle who is well known on the country music scene. They were to spend frustrating months trying to impregnate their surrogate mother, Donna, an East Coast "tomboy" who grew up on a farm and desperately wanted to get pregnant for someone else. The only problem was that she either couldn't get pregnant, or, on two occasions when she did, she could not carry a child to term. It was to be a case of extreme determination and extreme frustration.

Andy and Nancy, a laid back couple from the mountains of eastern California. The surrogate mother they found, Jeannette, is unusual for two reasons. She is married and entered into the agreement with her husband's blessing. And she is a midwife who publicly announced her decision in an effort to spread the good news about midwifery. This case represents the ultimate in coincidence. Andy and Nancy called me one afternoon looking for a surrogate mother, and, ironically, Jeannette had contacted me that same morning to volunteer as a surrogate mother. Within days, Jeannette was inseminated by Nancy with Andy's sperm and, it subsequently was confirmed, became preganant.

Stefan and Nadia, an immigrant couple from Yugoslavia on whom time was running out in their relentless search for a baby. The surrogate mother was their last resort, and they had the money to pay a fee. This was the first couple I sent to Dr. Levin in Kentucky to be matched with a surrogate mother, who would remain anonymous to the adoptive couple. Their baby, I am happy to say, is also due this spring and you would have to look far and wide to find a happier couple.

These five new cases are a mixed bag of motives and personalities that run the gamut of human experience. The surrogate-mother marketplace is becoming a rather exotic bazaar.

I will describe these cases in detail but they are only the tip of the iceberg. Calls and letters come in daily from people representing every aspect of the human condition. There are a lot of people who want babies by surrogate mothers and there are a lot of surrogate mothers who—both with and without a fee—want to have these babies. This is not only my experience, but it is also the experience of surrogate mothers in Dr. Levin's clinic.

Each new case represented to me a new legal nuance, a new challenge to be surmounted. But, in addition to the legal intricacies, I have been fascinated by the motives of the people involved, both those who want to have children and those want to carry them. Through the surrogate-mother issue, I have met more interesting people than I have in all my other legal work combined.

When you talk to people about having babies, you are unlocking their strongest feelings. In discussing their hopes, the people in these pages bared their souls so that others like them might have it a little easier.

One factor that should not be overlooked in the surrogate-mother story is the extraordinary effort required on the part of everyone involved, often against enormous odds.

It took surrogate mother Sally a full year of repeated monthly inseminations before she finally became pregnant. And she was prepared to go another year, including visits to a fertility clinic if necessary. She was not paid a penny, other than routine expenses, by adoptive couple Richard and Aralee who had been looking for a way for them to have a baby for years before even hearing of a surrogate mother. (Their first candidate for a surrogate mother, Jill, strung them along before bowing out with an alleged heart murmur.) They persisted with Sally and their hopes—and efforts—never wavered.

I was absolutely delighted when Sally told me she was pregnant. Later, Richard would explain to me how trying their quest had been.

"Sally had free flying privileges and would often fly down to Virginia for the inseminations," he said. "But just as often, Aralee and I or just myself would fly to Detroit. It was becoming very expensive, and we are not wealthy people. Although we both have professional positions, let's face it, the universities do not pay that much. And we both are still paying off heavy educational debts.

"Sally's cycle was so irregular that it was very difficult to calculate her fertile period. We tried temperature charts to pinpoint the precise time of ovulation, but it was all very haphazard. The first two inseminations were witnessed by the Detroit doctor, but that procedure got to be very inconvenient. The most opportune times were often on the weekends, and the doctor would be out of town or off duty. The doctor wasn't doing anything we couldn't do for ourselves, so we just started to do it ourselves. We even went to a fertility clinic in Virginia to get some added advice.

"Sally would perform the inseminations herself. If it were being done in Detroit in a motel, which was another expense, I would discreetly go into the bathroom and fill a syringe and bring it to her and then leave the room. If it were being done in our home in Virginia, I would give the syringe to my wife and she would take it into the other bedroom to Sally.

"Then would begin the long wait. We knew that Sally's period is usually around the first of the month. So we would just sit around and wait for the phone to ring. Every time it rang around the first of the month, we would think, 'Oh, no, that's Sally calling to say she's started her period. We have to do it all over again.' That was the pattern month after month.

"But Aralee and I both believe in extraordinary effort for the things that we want. We are prepared to pour all our energy and money into something worth having. We never gave up, and, fortunately, never did Sally. She did get a little discouraged. At one point, she was feeling guilty, thinking that maybe she wasn't capable of conceiving and that she was wasting our time. She went to a gynecologist, who said there was no apparent problem, but that, perhaps, there was some subtle technique that needed to be worked out. Sally decided that if things didn't hit by the end of 1979, she would go to a fertility clinic in Michigan. I was prepared to go back to the fertility clinic in Virginia to see if there was some extra technique or medication we could try.

"But December was our month. The phone never rang when we feared it might, and we started to cross our fingers. About a week later, Sally called. Our hearts sank. We thought, 'She's calling to say her period was a week late.' But, no, she said, 'Nothing yet, keep your fingers crossed.' She had bought a home pregnancy kit and was going to do the test the following week. It was positive, and her doctor later verified it. Her next call was what we had been waiting to hear for years. 'We've done it! I'm pregnant.' What a Christmas present! Aralee and I have been all smiles ever since.

"And, Noel, you know Sally called us on the night of December 18th. She said she had called your home, too, but your son said you were at an office party. Sally didn't want to bother you, but Aralee and I insisted. We knew you would want to know as soon as possible. After all, you helped make this whole thing possible."

I spent very little time worrying about how Richard and Aralee and Sally would come out. I knew they were right on. My five new cases, however, were not moving so smoothly.

Lorelei sent me a long letter, lovingly handwritten on floral stationery. She said, in effect, that nature had played her a "dirty trick," that for twenty-one years she had the soul of a woman imprisoned in the body of a man, but that the minute she came of age corrective surgery was performed to change her gender. I am neither a physician nor a psychiatrist and was in no position to appraise the validity of her claims. She was recently married and wanted children. With her background, there was but one real option—the surrogate mother. I told her my fee was $2,000—nonrefundable—and that I would require personal interviews with her and her husband, and affidavits from her parents and physicians.

"Do you still want to proceed?" I asked. Lorelei shot back, "You've got it. This is the answer to our prayers."

An appointment was scheduled, but before Lorelei and John came to Detroit, I received a letter from her father. Knowing that Lorelei Michele spent the first twenty-one years of her life as Loren Michael, I was curious as to what her father made of this. His letter was both touching and reassuring.

Hello, Mr. Keane,
My daughter, Lorelei Michele _____ , nee Loren Michael _____ , informs me that you have requested a letter from

my wife and me, saying, in effect, that we know all about what she did and is doing, and approve. In view of the fact that Lorelei is twenty-six years old and a married woman, I assume that this is professional courtesy on your part and not a requirement.

Of course, we approve. Surrogate parenthood runs in the family. I am an adopted son, and Lorelei's older brother is also adopted. That is to say, in both cases there were a natural mother and second-husband father. But I could not have been more loved nor better reared than I was by my Dad, Mom's second husband. And my oldest son is a source of great pride and joy to me. I think my wife and I must have done something right. All our kids still love us. And we them.

What this all boils down to is, again, a philosophical conviction that parental love doesn't happen biologically. It is a creation of minds and hearts interacting over months and years, giving and receiving to and from each other. My parents believed and demonstrated that. My wife and I have always believed it, and I think we have passed it on to our children. If I am right, then it's an accomplishment I take pride in.

Lorelei, therefore, will certainly have no difficulty loving for and rearing 'another woman's child,' because being the kind of person she is and having the background she has, she will never think of the child as anyone's but hers and John's. The fact that half the chromosomes will be John's is mere icing on the cake.

And speaking for my wife and me, the child will certainly have doting grandparents to visit and get spoiled by."

The letter was signed by both father and mother. I noticed that in Lorelei's formal application to me, she described her father as a decorated fighter pilot during World War II. He was a big Swede, six-foot-three and 245 pounds. Ironic, I thought, that his son should turn out to be a girl.

Whatever remaining doubts I might have had about Lorelei

disappeared when I interviewed her and her husband. They are good folks and happily married. Period. However, I had to ask them some tough questions.

John is a big dark man and Lorelei is a big blond woman. To the untrained eye, she would certainly "pass" as a normal woman, though a trifle big-boned. Her disposition, however, is decidedly feminine. She speaks quickly and without affectation. Hers is a particularly moving and unusual story.

"I spent the first twenty-one years of my life as a boy," she began. "And I was a very strange-looking boy, OK. In high school, I finally got to the point where I stood there in front of the nurse and said, 'Is this the body of a boy?' And she said, 'Have you seen a doctor?' And I said, 'Well, no, I have never been sick.' She said, 'You have never had a medical examination?' I replied, 'Not since I was six. In my family, you just don't go for medical checkups unless you are sick. A little cold or flu going around, we don't go to the doctor.' My family couldn't afford it. I had never been sick. Well, the nurse wrote a note to my gym teacher excusing me from gym class because it had gotten to the point where I was looking pretty strange, you know. Nothing was developing as it should and some things were developing that shouldn't have been.

"So, when I was twenty, I started preparing for the fact that at twenty-one I would legally be able to do anything to my body that I wanted. I went to a doctor and asked for hormone tests. I told the doctor, 'I think like a woman, walk like a woman, and act like a woman. If there is something wrong with me, I want to know it. I cannot live my life as a man, much less as a boy.' He took hormone tests and, sure enough, I was semi-hermaphroditic. Later, the doctors approved me for corrective surgery to cross genders and become a woman. At the time I went in for the surgery, I was performing in a dance company as a female. I was pretty much naked most of the time on stage, skimpy leotards and tights, and I was with all the girls in the dressing room, and no one ever had an idea that it was going to take surgery to make me a real woman. I was the featured dancer in this show—I had been a theatre major in college—and when I went to the hospital for the surgery, the whole dance company would come to my room for rehearsals. They all thought I was there to have fibroid tumors removed.

"What was I like as a boy? Well, I was thoroughly celibate. One of the doctors asked me, 'Have you ever been to bed with a woman?' I replied, 'Are you kidding? I may be a lot of things, but I am not a lesbian!' Physically, I simply did not develop as a man. I sang soprano in the choirs. I was terrific in gymnastics. I was good in swimming. I had Daddy's hands and Daddy's feet. My life going through school was pure hell. You know how cruel kids can be. I always felt like a girl in the boy's locker room. I spent my entire life in fear of being brutalized by the bullies. I would wait in the school library until the bus came and then make a mad dash for the bus. I was terrified. When I was fifteen, I almost had a nervous breakdown. How I got through it, I will never know. But I was in school plays and other dramatic arts. I made a name for myself within the school.

"You know, my father and my two brothers are all big Swedish horses. Very athletic, very macho. My older brother is a doctor now, and he never paid that much attention to me. But I think my younger brother always knew my problem, because I always babied him. After I had the surgery, he told me, 'I've always thought of you as more of a sister than a brother.' That's because I always acted like a mother to him. Our mom worked and when she came home from work, she was exhausted. I was trained as a little girl. I did all the cooking, all the cleaning. My older brother, the doctor today, would have nothing of it and my little brother was too young, so I did all the housework. I bathed the dog. I did everything. I was a housewife from the time I was seven. I fed the baby, and when my younger brother started to toddle, I took him around with me. I taught him the things I learned from church and school. You know how little girls like to play Mama. Well, that's what I did.

"When the doctors told me what my problem was, I wanted the surgery right away. Normally, it is a two-year wait, but for me they waived it to six months, the absolute minimum. I had suffered enough, they told me. While I was waiting, I moved out of state and took a job as a beautician. In my off hours, I sang in a band and danced in a road show. I worked myself to death. I dreamed of making it big in Los Angeles. The surgery took seven-and-a-half hours and was incredibly painful, but I was euphoric. Free at last. When they cut the stitches—they were metal because they had to form the labia from what they had to work with—the nurses were amazed that I didn't scream in pain. But I had already done the real screaming during those first twenty-one years of hell. The doctors said I was a joy to work on because the dancing had put me in good physical condition. I lost twenty pounds in the hospital. Before I had always looked like a tall, thin, hairless, feminine boy. Now, I looked like death on a cheese cracker. I was very skinny—it's only since I became a happy housewife that I've been fat. But anyway, when I left the hospital, I was very, very happy.

"I met my husband while tending bar. I was filling in for a girlfriend. It was a beer-and-wine type place. No problem. John came in with a buddy, and both were pretty looped. He asked me out and I said no. The next night, he came in and asked me out again. I said no. This must have gone on five or six times. Just to get him off my back, I said OK. The rest is history. We hit it off right away.

"He is a good man. Very intelligent. I am absolutely crazy about my husband. He's a terrific person."

I looked across the desk at John, this big, good-looking bull of a man, and started to ask the obvious, when Lorelei anticipated my question.

"Well, after about two months of dating, he finally coaxed me into the sack. After a few weeks of sleeping together, I was staying overnight at his place and going to work from there. He said, 'Are you on the pill, or something?' I said, "Oh, no." He asked, 'Well, what if you get pregnant? Will you keep the baby?' He was thinking of us as a married couple. It was obvious he had no idea of my background. I decided I had to tell him before he decided he was in love with me. I didn't want to hurt him. So, one night I made a big dinner, and told him, 'Look, it's time I told you something. . . .'

"Step by step, I started to tell him the whole thing. Halfway through, he cut me off. 'I've heard enough,' he said. 'I need some time to think about it. But let's face it, I've been to bed with you and I don't know the difference. I find it difficult to believe and I don't know why you bothered to tell me, but. . . .' Now, I cut him off. 'Because,' I said, 'there are people in this town who know and I don't want you to learn from them.'

"The next day, he called and said, 'It makes no difference to me. I love you [this was the first time he had told me he loved me]. You are a woman to me. You have never been anything different. I don't need to know or hear anything else about it."

I looked at John. He simply nodded in agreement. Lorelei added, "That dinner was in May. Two months later, we were married.

"We knew we could never have children, but at first it was no big deal. John said, 'Maybe someday we can adopt.' After a couple years, I started to bug him, 'Are we ready to adopt a baby?' He hedged and then said, 'Well, I would like to have my own child.'

"Now, I really don't know why, but somehow the term 'surrogate mother' had stuck in my mind. But I couldn't remember where. So I called the library. They looked up a back copy of *People* magazine and your name was in it. And here we are."

Knowing what Lorelei had gone through and how sincere she is, I made a snap judgment. I would try to help them, bizarre background or not. Lorelei is as solid a housewife as I have met in a long time. And their marriage seemed secure.

They did not have a lot of money. They had owned a saloon, but the lease ran out. Lorelei was a dispatcher for the police department and John was a driver for the Salvation Army. ("He ran the rag route," Lorelei joked. "You know, driving around and picking up old clothes that people donate. But, don't worry, next month he moves on to bigger things. The appliance route.") Lorelei concluded, "We are not wealthy people, but we can afford the things we really want. And this is what we really want."

Their $2,000 check to me wiped out two years of savings. "It's worth it," Lorelei said. "Worth double that. Now, we have hope."

I shuffled through the papers on my desk and came up with the letter from Rita. She lived in Southern California and had recently written to me volunteering as a surrogate mother. She does not want money, I thought. Carefully, I read her letter.

"I have been wanting to do this for some time," Rita had written in that first letter, "and thought perhaps you could help me as I don't know how to find a couple who are looking for a surrogate mother. Do you know of any couples who are interested? I would appreciate your help very much. Thank you. Very sincerely. Rita _____."

There was a phone number at the bottom of the letter. It was now four P.M. in Detroit, one P.M. on the West Coast. I dialed the number. Rita seemed very cool and very decisive about what she wanted to do. I would later think that she sounded very much like surrogate mother Diane. All good con artists have the ability to fool you. But at the time, I was anxious to help the couple sitting in front of me. Rita said she was twenty-seven, divorced with three children. She said that having children was very easy and very pleasurable for her, and that she wanted to help a couple who could not have this pleasure.

I called in Martha and dictated a letter:

Dear Ms. _____ :

To confirm our telephone conversation, you are hereby authorizing me to give your name to a couple who are in need of a surrogate. I would also like to repeat myself in that you will not receive a fee for being a surrogate mother, but that all expenses will be paid by the couple.

Sincerely,

Noel P. Keane.

I handed a copy of Rita's letter to Lorelei and John. The phone number was included. "Think about it for a while,' I said. "Then, let me know what to do."

They floated out of my office. Martha took a long, hard look at Lorelei, but by now she was not one to judge. "Noel", she said, "all your cases are unusual. Let's hope your luck holds."

In this case, it did not, but we are getting ahead of the story.

Money was not a problem with my next two clients, Joseph, the single student and scriptwriter from Hollywood, and Thomas and Cindy Sue, the celebrity couple from Manhattan. But still, they were to have the same problem as Lorelei and John. Finding the right surrogate mother.

When Joseph called me with his proposal, I knew we would be breaking new ground. On the surface, his request seemed outrageously selfish. All he wanted was to stay single, find a woman who would give him a child, find a sex-selection specialist who would split his sperm so there would be maximum potential for that child to be a boy, and, oh yes, the woman had to be superperfect. He was prepared to pay a fee and since he would not have to adopt, I could legally assist him in paying a fee.

By now, I was accustomed to doing fairly in-depth interviewing of all potential adoptive couples. I wanted to assure myself that they were mature enough to take on the responsibilities. Now, the obvious question is: Why didn't we also go into the motives of the potential surrogate mothers? That would have eliminated someone like Diane. Well, as an attorney, I was representing the people who wanted to find a surrogate mother. I would do preliminary screening by phone and questionnaire of the potential surrogate mother, and I would give advice but the buck stopped with the people who wanted a baby. They had to choose their own surrogate mother. For reasons of law and common sense, I did not think I should make the decision for them.

Joseph came to Detroit for a consultation, and I liked him immediately. I knew that critics would say we were playing God, but I believed his reasoning that he was simply trying to find a practical solution to his own situation.

Joseph is slender and attractive. A New York Yankees baseball cap covers the beginnings of his hair transplant. He is an occasional actor who is pursuing a doctorate in political science and writing a screenplay.

He began telling me about himself, "I would like to settle down and have a family. Now, it so happens that I have not fallen in love. I haven't met the right woman, and I don't think I should be restricted by the traditional guidelines set by society. I want a boy because I know the trials and tribulations of growing up as a boy. If it is a girl—wonderful, fantastic. I want to artificially inseminate because I would have a very difficult time doing it otherwise. After all, we are talking about getting into a situation with a woman I do not know."

Why did he want a child, especially a boy?

"I think the psychological vacuum of growing up without my father has a lot to do with my decision. My father was a famous actor and comedian—the 'Charlie Chaplin of Puerto Rico,' they used to call him. He was a beloved figure. His casket was carried through the town square, streets are named after him.

"I never really got to know him. He died when I was six years old, struck down by a brain aneurysm when he was only forty-seven. I only know what other people tell me about him.

"I guess that is the biggest regret of my life, never getting a chance to know my father. But I loved him. He was a theatre man, a life of wine, women, and song. The stories they tell about him! He had his tombstone engraved, 'Excuse me for not getting up!' He was somewhat of a rake, and my mother was his third wife. She would get on him about this womanizing, and he once told her, 'Dear, to me you are like a great cathedral. All the other women are but country churches.' I mean you have to like a man like that.

"I want to give my son all the loving I never received from a father."

Was he sure?

"This is a very cold and calculated decision, to have a child. I want to have one now—at thirty—while I'm still young enough to share things. Unfortunately, I'm not ready to settle down with a woman yet and may not be for five or ten years. Why should I wait? This decision is very calculated. But all calculations and coldness stop when I have my son. I have a lot of love to give and this will be a loved child."

Could he afford a child?

"Money will not be a problem. I am not wealthy, but I am comfortable. Comfortable. I had a very privileged upbringing— European vacations, school in Switzerland and all that. I have invested my money wisely. Everything in my life is being structured to care for a child. I will work and study out of my home. Everthing will be built around my son."

Why didn't he find a woman first?

"Maybe I'm selfish right now and simply do not want to share my son with anybody else. I realize it would be easy to put down my motives. To say I'm being narcissistic. But that isn't the way I work. Music, the theatre, and sports are my passions. I have a $50,000 stereo setup, not because it costs that much but because I wanted the best in music. I drive an old car and wear old clothes. The hair transplant is for professional reasons. Why should I look thirty-five when I am thirty? I go all out for the things I care for. That's why my stereo system is the best money can buy. I love to listen to good music. And I get up many mornings at four A.M. to play the piano. What kind of woman is going to want to put up with that?

"I have seen a lot of unhappiness in marriage. I saw that with my parents, brothers, and relatives. When there are children, divorce hurts them. Relationships can be sticky and messy. I'm a neat person. I guess I want to be in control of my situation."

What if something went wrong?

"My mother is very worried for me, that things may not turn out. But I have made up my mind. If the child is born retarded, that is still my child. I accept the risk."

I had no more questions. Joseph, it seemed to me, knew what he wanted to do.

To find a woman for this new twist to the surrogate mother story, we went on "The Phil Donahue Show." It was to prove one of Donahue's highest-rated shows since Debbie, Sue, and George returned with their "gift child," Elizabeth Anne.

We sat there right in front of hundreds of astonished women, Joseph in his Yankee baseball cap, myself in a three-piece suit (Kathy, who was sitting a few feet away, had selected it for me), and Ronald Ericcson, Ph.D., president of Gametrics, Inc., a reproductive biology clinic in Sausalito, Calif., that among other things separates sperm for sex-selection.

The audience quickly went to the attack.

"What makes him think he is going to be a good parent?" one woman asked.

In his inimitable style, Donahue responded, "Why wouldn't he be a good parent?" Added Joseph, "How did you know you were going to be a good parent?"

Another woman listened to Dr. Ericcson's description of sperm-splitting to try to get a boy and envisioned "a 'brave new world' where everybody wants the perfect kid."

Donahue joked, "Hey, if you can get the perfect kid, why not?"

As Dr. Ericcson described the lab techniques to separate and capture the male-carrying Y chromosomes, the audience broke into an uproar. One woman asked Joseph, "What kind of qualities are you looking for in a woman?"

Joseph: "She has to be attractive. She has to be psychologically sound. She has to be. . . . ."

Audience uproar.

Another question: "Why don't you just do what comes naturally—get married and have children?"

Audience uproar.

And, "Why artificially inseminate? Why not just pick out a woman and, you know, it would be more fun, wouldn't it?"

Audience uproar.

Buzzing swept up and down the studio crowd and questions swept down to the three of us throughout the full hour of prime TV time.

"Why don't you adopt? There are now single adopting parents." And, "I think you want the love of a child when you should first be looking for the love of a woman." And, "You have to question the emotional stability of a woman who could let herself be used this way." And, "It is adultery for a woman to be artifically inseminated with your sperm."

Patiently, Joseph answered one and all. He had anticipated the questions. After all, we had already discussed most of them in my office. Slowly, he won over the crowd of women.

The clincher came from a caller to the show. It was a man and he said, "This man wants a family based on love. There are plenty of single women who do it—raise children on their own, provide a loving home, care for their kids, take the full responsibility. I can't believe you people are against a man doing it, too."

Audience uproar.

As we drove down Chicago's Kennedy Expressway from Donahue's studio at WGN-TV on the city's northwest side to the Merchandise Mart offices of NBC-TV for a network "Today Show" taping of the same topic, Kathy told me, "Noel, you're finally getting it down. Today, you looked good on camera. And, you sounded halfway good, too."

I had now been on Donahue five times, plus countless other TV appearances, and the thrill had long ago worn off. I now went on shows like Donahue for a simple reason. Other than placing classified ads, the only effective way of finding surrogate mothers was through television and news articles. The true fathers of the surrogate-mother story, perhaps, are the Phil Donahue Show and *People* magazine. Time and again, people have come to me for help with the opening, "I read about you in *People* magazine," or, "I saw you on Donahue." This TV show and this magazine have built their success on knowing what people want to know. And, clearly, the people continue to want to know about surrogate mothers.

We had said that Joseph was prepared to pay $10,000 for a surrogate mother. Now we would have to sit back and wait.

Finding a surrogate mother is one problem. Getting her pregnant, as we were to find with Richard and Aralee and Sally, is another. And, as we were to find with Thomas and Cindy Sue and their surrogate mother, Donna, keeping her pregnant is yet a third. The fourth and biggest problem, of course, is keeping her happily pregnant. But again, we are getting ahead of our stories.

Money was of small matter to Thomas and Cindy Sue, the Manhattan film couple. They had plenty. Once Thomas said jokingly, "Noel, when we find a surrogate mother, why don't we just send her to France. I have a small place in Paris, and she can stay there until she's ready to give birth." I was firm. "No, you people will want to adopt and there's no way you can give a surrogate mother anything of value and then adopt her baby. You can pay expenses, period."

Thomas was forty-two, Cindy Sue forty-one, and their time was running out. They had put their hopes on Donna, the tomboy from the East Coast.

By definition, most surrogate mothers are pretty independent women. But of all the actual and potential surrogate mothers I have met, none are as strong-willed as Donna.

Her father wanted a boy, and he never let her forget it. She grew up on a farm and in a determined effort to win her father's approval learned to out-macho the boys. As I talked to her, she was alternately sunny and sullen, insightful and flip. She had answered an ad I placed in the *Washington Post*.

Why did Donna want to be a surrogate mother?

"I really don't know what is driving me, except there is this woman who cannot have a baby. I can—at least as far as I know. When I was growing up [she is now twenty-one], a friend of my mother's could never have children. I remember how upset she was and during my early teens I used to think, 'If I ever get pregnant, I'll give the baby to her.' Now, I had never heard of 'surrogate mother,' but that's what I wanted to be. When I saw your ad, I thought, 'Fantastic.' I mean this is what I want to do. I believe in it.

"Now, I would never want to get paid. I believe in it too much to take money. And I would never do it for an anonymous couple. I have to know and like the couple for whom I am having a baby."

She had started out trying to be surrogate mother for a Delaware dentist and his wife and became pregnant on the first insemination. But nine weeks later, the child was stillborn. Donna was crushed, but she tried twice more for the dentist and his wife. In the meantime, a resourceful reporter who had noticed our ad called to see if there had been any takers. I asked Donna if she wanted to talk with this reporter. She did, and a few days later her story and high school graduation picture were on the front page of the *Washington Post*.

Instant notoriety. The dentist, a private professional, was aghast. He had words with Donna. This was shortly after her traumatic miscarriage, and she wanted support, not criticism. She broke off the arrangement. Months later, she called and said, "Noel, get me another couple. I'm ready to try again." Thomas and Cindy Sue were waiting in the wings. For six consecutive months now, Donna had flown to Manhattan to be artificially inseminated at the Idant sperm bank with the frozen sperm deposited by Thomas. For six consecutive months, nothing happened. She was back in town for another attempt and as we sat in a midtown Manhattan hotel, I wondered how long her resolve would hold. She had been at it for better than a year now. She is an attractive, sexy woman and, in all her time of trying to be a surrogate mother, she had sworn off sex. Or at least sexual intercourse. She was under tremendous pressure from her friends and family to forget this crazy idea.

What did her parents think?

"When my parents first found out, it was a complete disaster. When my mother found out I was pregnant, she thought it was a boyfriend or something like that. When I told them what I was doing, they wanted me out of the house. My father threw me around, beat me up. After the miscarriage, though, they just kind of accepted it. I mean, they wish someone else were doing it, but at least they have quit abusing me. They think surrogate motherhood is a great idea, but not for their daughter. Every time I get my period, my father applauds. He tells me, 'Congratulations!' They keep hoping I'll come to my senses.

"I guess all my problems go back to one thing. I was the first-born and I was a girl. My father wanted a boy. The birth announcements were made up by a friend of my father's. The front cover had a blue baby outfit, blue rattle, blue hat, blue booties, and it read, 'We knew he was coming.' You open the card and on the inside there are pink booties and things. It reads, 'And here she is.' No doubt about it, he wanted a boy."

Donna is crying, but she continues.

"My father coaches football and track. I guess I made up my mind to be my father's son. I knew he could never tolerate anyone weak. I am a very strong person. I grew up with the guys. I used to go to all the practices with him. I ran on the track team. I lifted weights. There wasn't a guy around I couldn't beat up. I could outlift them, outplay them, outrun them. Almost all my friends were boys.

"But I never really dated or anything like that. My father wouldn't let me. I was dating this guy named Jim for awhile. He was gorgeous, or at least I thought he was. He ran track and he was one of the fastest kids around. Jim's parents were divorced and his father lived in Florida, so my father kind of took him under his wing. He sort of adopted him. But my father restricted me from seeing Jim. It was a way of punishing me. But I was a pretty rebellious girl. I saw Jim anyway. I was going to show my father. We grew up on a farm and it was fantastic. I used to ride horses every day. At one time, I wanted to train show horses. I would get on the tractor and plow the fields. I played football. I would wrestle with the guys. I was one of the gutsiest girls you would ever want to meet. I was going to prove things to my father. But when he wouldn't let me go out with Jim, that really hurt. In fact, it probably hurt me more than anything, other than the miscarriage.

"The miscarriage was absolutely horrible. I am a nurse and I believe in abortion and I see aborted fetuses every day, but this really got to me. I was bleeding and getting ready to go to the hospital. Every time I would urinate, the bleeding would get worse. So I refused to go to the bathroom. Finally, I had to. I figured I better go before I left for the hospital. When I did, that's when I lost the baby. I could feel it wrench within me. I screamed for my mother. When she walked in, I was kneeling down at the toilet with the fetus in my hand. It was about ten weeks old and maybe an inch or two long. It was unmistakably human. What happened? I really don't know. I had been running, riding horses, dancing, being active. Maybe it was just God's will. I can't describe the feeling. I was really down. There are two parts to my head. The nurse part said 'It's good that you lost it. It must not have been normal.' But the woman part said, 'Oh, my God, I've lost my baby.' I asked my mother for a plastic container, and I took the fetus with me to the hospital. I was surprised at how powerful my feelings were. I mean, I had been saying to myself all along, 'It's their baby. It's Judy's baby. I am only carrying it for them.' But when I lost the baby, I was depressed for weeks. That was the beginning of the end for me and the dentist and his wife. I guess I expected them to send me a flower or a card or at least ask, 'Donna, how are you?' But it was like they didn't give a damn. I tried twice again to get pregnant for them, but my heart wasn't in it. After the second time when the insemination didn't take, I told them, 'I don't want to do this anymore.' We didn't have a contract or anything, just the written agreement you prepared. Well, the dentist got down on his knees and begged. 'I want to have a baby. We want you to have a baby for us. Please. Please. Please.' I cannot stand a weak man. My father's influence, I guess. He was begging. I just walked away.

"Then, through you I met Thomas and Cindy Sue. They care about me, and it shows. I really want to give them a baby."

I asked, "How about the men in your life?"

"I have no use for men. Well, I mean, I do only once in a while. I do not want a full-time relationship with a man. I do not want to get married, until I'm seventy or eighty, anyway. I have plenty of male friends, but I do not need a steady relationship. I have been trying to get pregnant as a surrogate mother for one year now. It would not be fair to get involved with a man. I mean I could not go to bed with him. I am prepared to go another year to have a baby for Thomas and Cindy Sue.

"Do my parents respect me? I don't know. I don't respect them. I hate my father and I hate my mother. My mother is very, very weak—she takes whatever my father dishes out—and my father never shows any affection at all. I cannot stand them.

"But this I know. I want to be a surrogate mother. I am a very strong-willed person, and I always get what I want. Always."

There you have it, a conversation with surrogate mother-hopeful Donna. What would the psychiatrists say? Would they want her as a surrogate mother? Was she a good risk?

I had my doubts if surrogate motherhood were in her best interests. Certainly, with her enormous drive, Donna could have been a success at anything, once she pulled herself together. For now, she seemed determined to have a baby for someone else. I decided, all right, let's try it one more time. But, privately, I was developing serious reservations about her participation.

So unusual are the motivations of these first three cases—Lorelei, the transsexual housewife; Joseph, the single man who wants a surrogate mother, sex-selection, and a son; and Donna, the surrogate mother as crucified avenger—that it almost makes my other cases seem serene by contrast. But three of these—Richard, Aralee, and Sally; Andy, Nancy, and Jeannette, their Texas midwife turned surrogate mother; and the Yugoslavian couple referred to Dr. Levin's Kentucky clinic—also added new dimensions to the story.

The Andy-Nancy-Jeannette linkup is unusual in the legal challenge—Andy and Nancy's California adoption must overcome the Texas legal presumption that Jeannette's husband, Marshall, is the father of the child—and in the missionary zeal with which the surrogate mother approaches her task. Jeannette wants nothing less than the "perfect birth." But I'll let her explain.

"My husband and I have a private joke that we would like to give birth over and over again until we got it right, but what in the world would we do with all the kids. At that time, of course, we had never heard of the 'surrogate mothers,' that there actually were women who gave birth and then gave the babies away. When our son, Christopher, was born, we both felt that several things had gone wrong. I ended up in the hospital, for one thing, and I wanted to give birth at home, attended by a midwife. The baby was separated from us for two to four hours for an observation period, and we do not approve of that. And he was given supplemental vitamin injections, which we didn't think were necessary. So, all in all, we didn't think it had been a 'perfect birth.'

"About two weeks after the birth, I saw you on the Phil Donahue show and heard about 'surrogate mothers' for the first time. My husband, Marshall, said, 'Well, here it is, the chance to have the perfect birth. Why don't you give him a call?'

"Now, I'm one of the last of the great procrastinators. Two years went by, and then I happened to pick up a copy of *Science Digest*. I had never heard of the magazine before, but it happened to have an article about Noel Keane and the surrogate mothers. The topic had always been in the back of my mind and I mentioned it to Marshall. He said, 'Call him.' Two weeks went by and, still, I did nothing. But Marshall kept reminding me. Finally,

I called your office, and your office manager, Martha, told me to write a long letter describing myself and my motivations. I sat down that very afternoon, wrote the letter, and life has never been the same since."

Jeannette's letter ran fourteen handwritten pages and is a model of purposefulness and thoroughness. It covered everything from her family and medical history to her strongly held beliefs on how a surrogate-mother pregnancy and birth should be conducted. Enclosed was a photo of her and her son Christopher. I read the letter one morning, and called Jeannette to get verbal permission to give her name to prospective adoptive couples. Then I went to lunch. The minute I walked back into my office, the phone rang.

It was Andy, calling from California. He and his wife, Nancy, had just seen a rerun of the CBS television documentary, "The Babymakers," which featured a segment about myself and surrogate mothers. Nancy had two teenaged daughters from a first marriage, but a subsequent hysterectomy ruled out children for her and Andy.

At first, this did not bother Andy, but as he got older, he began to want his own child. He was a father to Nancy's two daughters, but he also wanted his own.

I asked, "Have you tried to adopt?"

Andy replied, "Yes, and they told me it would take at least three years just to get on the list. Then, once on the list, there is a probationary period of at least a year. Then, you wait for a baby, and you will be lucky if you get one. I'm thirty and my wife is thirty-five. Besides, I have two stepdaughters from my wife's previous marriage. That's sort of like adopting right there. The only reason I haven't adopted them is because their natural father is dead and the children collect Social Security. I have a desire and a need for my own child."

I said, "Well, by coincidence, I just talked this morning to a woman in Texas who thinks she would like to have a baby for another couple. Let me read you her letter."

Andy listened patiently to Jeannette's recitation of why and how she wanted to be a surrogate mother. Then, his voice almost cracked, "I knew that somewhere in the world there had to be a woman who would understand," he said. "I had no idea it might happen so quick."

"Would you like her number?," I asked.

"You bet."

I read off the Texas telephone number. Within a week, Andy's baby would be on the way, carried by surrogate mother Jeannette. Their story is a model, I think, of how the surrogate-mother arrangement can work. Andy and Nancy are poor people, and there is no way they could have paid a fee. But Jeannette would not have heard of a fee. She was doing this for her own intensely personal reasons. All she asked was that the adoptive couple care about children and be able to care for them. Her only financial request is payment for the services of a midwife.

The human story is a warm one. The legal story is complicated, but I think we are on top of it.

But at the end of that call, I simply told Andy, "Let me know what happens."

The story of Stefan and Nadia is one of persistence and eventual success. He is forty-three, she thirty-nine. They came to Detroit from Yugoslavia eleven years ago, and both have good jobs in the auto industry.

He is the oldest of five children, she of eight. They had been trying to have their own children for eighteen years.

As they sat across my desk, Nadia recalled their ordeal.

"We never gave up," she said. "Never. The problem is blocked Fallopian tubes. I have had four major surgeries. One tube was completely removed. But I still had the other. The doctors told me it was very bad, but there was a slight chance I could get pregnant. I went to the fertility clinics and took the medication. Nothing happened. Once I had a tubal pregnancy. This was my last tube. The doctor repaired the tube, and said it was still OK. But I never got pregnant. Twice more, the doctor opened me up to check the tube and see if it were possible for me to have a baby. The second time, he told me, 'I don't want you to try to get pregnant anymore.'

"I quit seeing the doctor for three or four years. I kept hoping a miracle would happen. But nothing did. So, this year, I made an appointment with one of the best fertility experts in the country, (S.J. Behrman, M.D. who testified during the adoption proceedings for Elizabeth Anne and Debbie, Sue, and George). He put me in the hospital, opened my navel, and checked the tube. 'Give up,' he said, 'The tube is really diseased. And you are too old.' We have been married eighteen years, eighteen years of trying to have children, and he tells us to give up."

Stefan adds, "The doctor took us back to his office and had a long talk with us. He explained we shouldn't try anymore. It was terrible. Nadia was crying. And, I am not ashamed to admit, I cried, too. We sat there and cried like babies."

Nadia: "Before I made the appointment with Dr. Behrman, I had written a letter to England, asking about the 'test-tube' babies. I got a letter back saying they were not accepting any candidates over thirty-six. Then, I wrote to the clinic in Norfolk, Virginia, where they are studying test-tube procedures, and they told me the same thing—'We are not accepting anyone over thirty-three.' I had heard of Dr. Seed and the embryo-transfer procedures in Chicago, so I called him. This seemed the absolute last hope. The answer was the same. The technology is too new and I am too old."

Stefan: "It was like a miracle. We turned on the TV one day, and we saw you talking about surrogate mothers. My wife wrote down the phone number."

Nadia pulls from her purse a tattered, yellowed clipping. It is the 1978 *People* magazine article about my involvement with Debbie, Sue, and George. I am pictured tossing Elizabeth Anne into the air, and, in another photo, out in the frontyard with Kathy and my sons hosing down my vintage roadster. Nadia said, "I read about you two years ago, about how that lady had a baby for her friend and how you helped them. I have never left that clipping out of my sight.

"After Dr. Behrman told me there was really nothing left, I gave up. I was very upset. It was like my life was over. All my friends and family tried to comfort me. They felt sorry for me because they knew what I had gone through with the four surgeries. Most women would never have gone through what I did to try to have children. Really, I was desperate to have a child. Even my doctor said, 'I have never seen such courage.' He was amazed that I would go through all the pain.

"And for nothing. There was nothing left. We are too old to adopt. Then, I saw you on TV a few nights ago. I got out the magazine article and read it again. Very carefully. I thought that, 'Well, maybe, here is a new hope.' That is why we are here."

I explained to them the basic procedures, and emphasized there are no guarantees. A surrogate mother, if found, can always change her mind. They were ready to run the risk.

As one consequence of not having children, Stefan and Nadia are fairly well off. They own two homes, several cars, and a large boat. They could afford to pay a surrogate mother. And, by this time, Dr. Levin's Surrogate Parenting Associates, Inc. was ready for business in Kentucky.

"Are you prepared to spend some money to find a mother for your baby?" I asked.

They were.

Quickly, I figured it up. "It will cost you up to $22,000," I said. "That's $10,000 for the surrogate mother, $5,000 for the medical care, $5,000 for the legal fees, including the services of an attorney in Kentucky, and $2,000 in miscellaneous expenses. Plus, you'll have to sell your house and move to Kentucky. If you're going to adopt your baby, you'll have to first become residents of Kentucky."

Stefan said, "What is $22,000? A car costs $15-$16,000 and what have you got? One wrong turn and it's smashed up. It is nothing of real value. This is a human life. We will go anywhere and do anything."

I had had some preliminary talks with Dr. Levin and his attorney, Katie Brophy, and knew the general outlines of their program. The physician's intention was to limit surrogate mothers to married women with children, to pay them $10,000 and to keep them anonymous to the adoptive couple. The cost to the adoptive couple, covering air fares to Kentucky, psychiatric evaluations, insurance policies to protect surrogate mother and child, and medical and legal fees, would run between $13,000 and $20,000. And up.

Of course, first he had to find surrogate mothers. How?

I asked Stefan, "If you are prepared to go, we'll start by placing an ad. That's the first step in finding a surrogate mother. Should we do it?"

"Go."

I called Katie Brophy, and, together, we quickly worked out the wording of an ad to be placed in the *Louisville Courier-Journal*.

The search for my second paid surrogate mother was on. The other one, of course, is to find a surrogate mother for Joseph.

The surrogate-mother trail was now at a broad fork in the road.

In one direction, there were the traditional steps I had been following of trying to find a volunteer who would be a surrogate mother for medical expenses and the chance to help somebody else.

In the other, there were the steps opening up in Kentucky—and everywhere if we win our lawsuit—of being able to pay a woman to become a surrogate mother.

We were going to have to blaze both trails, I decided. There is merit in both approaches and different people want different options.

In the coming months, my clients would see me as both sinner and savior. Some of them found success and some found only sawdust. Some of those paying money found happiness and some did not.

The money angle, however, was putting a new perspective—and new publicity—on the issue. In one perhaps prophetic remark, Katie Brophy told a reporter, "Well, if a potential surrogate mother volunteers and she's bright, beautiful, and talented and wants $50,000, why not?"

Well, for one thing, I thought, because the kind of people I got into this to help them can never afford $5,000, let alone $50,000. Others could; however, I was very concerned that this hope of last resort for the barren not be limited to those with the highest barter.

In the meantime, I continued to work with my new clients. Some I helped, some not yet. Let's take the bad news first. As everyone keeps telling me, "Noel, no one ever said it would be easy!"

ᛉ10ᛧ
"You got yours, didn't you?"

FALL 1980. It was the best of times, the worst of times.

On the one hand, the surrogate-parenting business was growing. Continuing publicity prompted hundreds of calls and letters to my office from people who wanted to find a surrogate mother.

The requests were coming from all walks of life—physicians, business executives, policemen, black entertainers, career women, tenured university professors. Most were married, though some were single. They all wanted a child—their own child. They could adopt or choose not to adopt. Now I could offer them two broad choices. If money were a problem, we could try to find a woman who would do it solely for medical expenses and other court-approved fees. If they were prepared to pay a fee of $10,000 and were prepared to establish a legal residency in Kentucky—sometimes requiring actual relocation—we could try to find a woman who preferred to be paid. The people seeking the surrogate mother would have a choice of dealing directly with the woman who would carry their child. Or, after making the selection from detailed applications, a review of the potential surrogate mother's family and medical history, and telephone and personal interviews, they could keep the rest of the transaction anonymous.

This latter approach is the one established by Dr. Levin's clinic in Kentucky. He found it best to limit the surrogate mothers to married women who already have children, to require that adoptive couples pay the surrogate mother a fee, usually $10,000, and to insist on total anonymity between adoptive couple and surrogate mother, after the initial choice is made.

I thought it best to offer both choices. Some people, I know, cannot afford a fee. Some excellent surrogate mothers will not accept a fee. One potential surrogate mother, for example, is a gynecologist. She volunteered because, 'The experience of giving birth will make me a better doctor." She added, "I do not need any money." Some adoptive couples prefer to choose and become close to the surrogate mother. Some surrogate mothers insist on knowing and approving the adoptive couples. All of my initial cases had been between adoptive couples and surrogate mothers who dealt directly with each other and, usually, became close friends in the process. But now I was establishing a partnership in Kentucky with another attorney to create a system so that those who can afford it can legally pay a surrogate mother. This latter option, I knew, would assure an ample supply of surrogate mothers. Already, I was accumulating a backlog of surrogate mother applicants. And, beyond that, of course, we would advertise.

Despite these events, several of my long-standing cases were grinding to a standstill. Or, worse, a confrontation.

We found a surrogate mother for Joseph. She was a bright, beautiful divorced mother of two bright, beautiful children, who said she wanted to do it as "her own private protest against abortion." Everything seemed fine, but after the first two inseminations failed, she, inexplicably, started making demands that forced the arrangement to collapse. The search continues.

Meanwhile, surrogate mother Donna became pregnant again— this time for Thomas and Cindy Sue. But, sadly, she miscarried again. I decided enough was enough for her and tried—unsuccessfully—to convince her to call off her crusade. She continues as a potential surrogate mother, but I have severed the relationship.

And Lorelei, the transsexual housewife, and her husband John found a surrogate mother, Rita, impregnated her, and sat back in expectation. What they got, however, as did I, was a traumatic shock. The pregnant surrogate mother decided she would keep the baby, which is due in the spring of 1981. This confrontation will apparently have to be decided in court. A judge will have to rule on who deserves custody of the child—the man who fathered the child or the surrogate mother. Legally, it is a crucial case. Personally, it is a tragedy for Lorelei and John, though we all have our fingers crossed that either Rita will relent or that the court case will be decided in our favor.

Since these cases represent three of the essential frustrations in working with surrogate mothers: difficulty in getting her pregnant; keeping her pregnant; and keeping her happily pregnant— let's look at each in detail. Each frustration underlines the central legal truth of this book: Until we get definitive court decisions and/or legislation and binding regulations, there are no guarantees concerning surrogate motherhood.

Let's look at some examples of what I mean:

Kay is a medical technologist in Detroit. She had read stories about my involvement with other surrogate mothers and had seen Joseph's plea for a surrogate mother on the Donahue show.

She called me one morning and explained why the idea intrigued her:

"We would joke about surrogate mothers, my girlfriends and I. Once, I told a girlfriend, 'Here's something I can always do if I'm out of a job—have a baby!'

"Having babies is very easy for me. My two daughters, ages seven and nine, are both beautiful, healthy, and bright. Their IQs are in the 140s, and one is in a school for the gifted. You can knock me for a lot of things, but don't knock my mothering. I take it very seriously.

"Both my pregnancies were very easy. Both my daughters are very healthy. Not even any cavities. A few years ago, when one of my friends had a hysterectomy, I thought, 'Maybe, I should have a baby for her.' It's so easy for me and a baby would mean so much to her. It would be the greatest gift I could ever give her. But I realized it might not work out since we were so close to each other.

"Anyway, I've read about you and your work with surrogate mothers. Last summer, I saw one of your want ads. For weeks, I carried that want ad around in my purse. Then, I saw you and Joseph on Donahue. The idea intrigued me. That's why I'm calling."

For an hour or so, I probed Kay's motives. She seemed perfectly sincere. I asked her to send me a letter about herself, plus photos. The letter was a model of detail and thoroughness; the photos showed a beautiful woman with her two beautiful daughters.

I picked up the phone and dialed the West Coast. "Joseph," I began. "I think we have your surrogate mother. But come and see for yourself."

A week later, we sat in my law office, Joseph, Kay, and myself. Kay is an attractive woman, with a good figure and flashing green eyes. She had brought her daughters with her and they were darling. Joseph, a particular man, was impressed.

"Kay," I asked, "why do you want to do this?"

There was a long pause, and then she said softly:

"You know why I really decided to do this. I work in a hospital and every day I see aborted fetuses. Oh, they call them 'products of conception,' but what they really are are unborn babies. I guess this is my own private protest against abortion."

"What do your friends and family think?"

"You know, it's funny how people have reacted to my decision. The feedback is divided, but everybody has an opinion. What's surprising is how different people react. My mother is very supportive. She comes from a large family and in her day women sometimes had babies for infertile relatives. So she understands. My ex-husband, who is not into fathering, thinks it's the dumbest mistake I have ever made. He said, 'You'll lose your figure and be out of commission for a year or so.' I said, 'What does it matter to you? It's my life.'

"I've been dating two guys. One, a policeman, said 'Forget this, or you'll never see me again.' Well, I'll never see him again. The other, a teacher, has been very supportive. He thinks it's wonderful."

Joseph said, "I would like to handle some of the medical details. Maybe help pick the doctor, help pick the hospital. Maybe, I can even come to Michigan during the last stages of your pregnancy."

Kay's answer was to the point:

"Look, I will not interfere with you after the baby is born, so you cannot interfere with me during the pregnancy. It has to be my program. My doctor, my hospital, my procedures."

Joseph leaned back in his chair, smiled, and nodded agreement. He had met his match in perfectionism.

"Kay," I said, "you know that Joseph would like a son. Are you willing to go to the extra trouble of trying to split the sperm and increase our chances of having a boy?"

"Sure. If he wants a son, well, it's an ego thing, but why not? I hope it is a boy. I'm doing this strictly as a volunteer. It's like giving blood or donating a kidney."

I drew up a simple agreement stating that Kay would give custody of the child to Joseph. It was agreed that Joseph would pay Kay $10,000 plus expenses. This was perfectly permissible, since Joseph as the father had no need to adopt. If you do not adopt, you do not break any law in paying a surrogate mother.

Joseph said, "I will tell the child the truth about his mother as soon as he's old enough to understand. Kay, I may even keep a photo of you to show him. But I will expect you not to interfere in any way with my raising of the child."

"Kay," I said, "Is that understood? You will not interfere with Joseph's raising of the child? And, Joseph, you understand, of course, that this agreement is not worth the paper it's printed on. We're flying blind on trust. You will not adopt and if Kay chooses to contest custody, she has a case. A strong case."

Joseph said, "This is my son and if there is a custody fight I will go three times to every court in the land." Then, with a gallant smile toward Kay, "Of course, I know this eventuality will never arise."

Kay replied, "There is no need to worry. Normally, it would be hard for a woman to give up a child she has carried. But I am getting pregnant with the plan of doing exactly that. No problem."

It was time to go. It was Saturday afternoon, and both my sons had football games. An hour's drive apart. Joseph and I left for the games, Kay for the hospital and work. Joseph was elated. I was formulating plans on how to go about the sperm-splitting for sex selection. That night, Joseph came to my house for a big dinner prepared by Kathy. He brought champagne.

Days later, Kay called. She was having second thoughts. About the fee. "Noel," she said, "you know, at first I thought the $10,000 would be a big help. I want to go back to school and get my RN. I have a master's degree in public health, but I want to go into nursing. The money would help, but I started to see the words 'wombs for hire' flashing around in my mind. I cannot take a fee. I think it will be unethical. I am doing this for humanitarian reasons. I am impressed with Joseph's sincerity. This is a gift I will give to Joseph."

I called Joseph and the three of us hooked up on the telephone. Kay, a woman with a mind of her own, had an alternative idea.

"I have insurance to pay for the medical bills," she said. "I want to get pregnant this fall, so I can deliver next summer and be free next fall to resume my nursing education. Joseph, if you will agree to pay my expenses for six months after the baby is born—so I can recover without immediately having to return to work, we can do it that way. You will pay me only what I would have been paid at work, OK?"

Later, Martha, a practical woman, would observe, "Well, Noel, it seems to me that no matter how you slice it, it comes out to be $10,000. It seems like Kay has to have everything go her way, or she wants out. But if she feels better viewing it this way, why not?"

The next week, we were in Omaha, Nebraska, of all places, for what the newspaper editorials would later criticize as a "bit of *Brave New World*."

I had found B. C. Bhattacharya, Ph.D., a fertility expert from India, who agreed to split Joseph's sperm and inseminate Kay. My colleague from the Phil Donahue show, Ronald Ericcson, Ph.D., was unable for legal reasons to attempt the same procedure.

Dr. Bhattacharya, who is president of Applied Genetics Lab, Inc., took a sample of Joseph's sperm. Then, in an intricate electromagnetic technique, the doctor split the sample into X and Y chromosomes. He took the sperm, enriched to 92 percent male-carrying Y chromosomes, and in two separate procedures inseminated Kay.

With a broad smile, the scientist said, "This technology was developed for the cattle-breeding industry. In previous human attempts, we have been 80 percent successful in producing males."

My friends from Associated Press, United Press International, and the local television people were on hand for this latest chapter in the surrogate-mother controversy. "I feel like we hit the bull's eye," Kay told reporters. "If so, by next summer, Joseph will have his son." Joseph added, "If we didn't this time, we're going back to Omaha and do it again and again until we do."

Joseph returned to California, Kay to Detroit, myself to the law practice. The unusual insemination had triggered a new outburst of concern. The Omaha newspapers were polling people on whether they approved. To my mind, there were only two opinions that counted. And Joseph and Kay both approved.

We were all euphoric on that first attempt, but the adventure soon turned sour.

The insemination did not take. We came back in November 1980 and tried again. No luck.

Then, Kay began to make demands. First, she wanted Joseph to pay for her daughters to accompany her to Omaha. Then, she wanted expenses paid for her boyfriend—the policeman who had initially opposed her and whom supposedly she had dropped. It was a surprising turnaround. Joseph is soft-spoken, but has a will of steel.

"Kay," he said, "It seems as if your heart is no longer really in this. You have to be absolutely sure, absolutely reliable. Anything less is doomed to failure. Let's forget it."

I should have known better, I guess. From the start, Martha was skeptical of Kay's ability to carry out the arrangement. And as Martha goes, so goes my law office.

"Joseph," I said, "We're back to Square One. I will be in touch."

Meanwhile, I was off to New York, For more bad news.

From across the table in a small Italian restaurant in midtown Manhattan, the candlelight gave a soft glow to the rosy cheeks of Donna, the woman who would be a surrogate mother. But the words of this forlorn tomboy were anything but rosy. In Donna's twenty-one years, there had been very few roses.

She desperately wanted to have a a a baby for someone else. She had been at it now for a solid year. Her reward so far—two miscarriages.

This second miscarriage, losing the child intended for Thomas and Cindy Sue, had Donna in tears. She could not understand it, let alone accept it.

Gently, I reviewed Donna's past and tried to probe her motives. I am no psychiatrist, but I did not want this woman to persist in folly, if that were the case.

"Donna," I said, "Now, let's make sure I have it straight. Things were not working out for you before you saw our blind ad for a surrogate mother. Particularly things with men. Your father would not let you see Jim, but you did, anyway. Then, you rejected Jim because he didn't trust you. Your parents threw you out of the house and you moved in with another man, Larry, who physically abused you and then left you to marry another woman he was already engaged to. You say, 'I could have killed him, he was such a bastard.' To get away from it all, you ran off to Florida to live with a friend. But you missed the farmland, so you came home. You went to work for a group of doctors, but left when 'one of the old men pinched me on the ass. I cannot tolerate that kind of treatment.' You have not worked since; it's been a year since you've had a job. It was right after you left the job with the doctors, that you saw our ad. Since then, you have been pregnant and miscarried for two different couples. With the dentist and his wife, you got pregnant on the first try, but miscarried at ten weeks. The next two attempts to get pregnant again for him failed, and then you called the arrangement off, although he and his wife wanted to continue. You linked up with Thomas and Cindy Sue, but the first six inseminations failed. Then, you got pregnant, only to miscarry again at ten weeks. You have been at this now for a full year, and it seems as if you are knocking your head against a brick wall. Yet, you tell me you want to continue. Why?"

As I went through the dreary recital, Donna had been slowly nodding her head in agreement. Now she smiled.

"It does seem strange, doesn't it? I really can't explain what has a grip on me, why I feel I have to do this.

"Everybody is putting pressure on me to drop out. A few days ago, a neighbor lady told me, 'God does not want you to be pregnant.' I know that's what my parents think. My brother told me, 'Face it, Donna, you're a failure.' Our pastor came over one day to tell me, 'We are praying for you, that you will come to your senses.'

"All I know is that if I cannot get pregnant—and stay pregnant—I am going to be a very, very unhappy lady. The two times I have been pregnant, however briefly, I could feel the 'glow,' the special feeling you get from knowing a baby is growing inside you. I want that feeling again.

"Now, my parents say that if I get pregnant again, they will throw me out. So what? Then I'll have to get a job. I'll just find a new place to live. I want to have a baby for Thomas and Cindy Sue. I want to give them a baby. Then, I will have my own baby.

Then, if Thomas and Cindy Sue would like another baby, I will give them another one.

"I would prefer to have a girl to give to Thomas and Cindy Sue. But my child will be a boy. A boy to keep. I don't know how I'll have my boy, but it won't be through marriage or a steady relationship. Some of my friends, I know, will father a child for me, if I ask. But maybe I'll just go to a sperm bank and get artificially inseminated. I might even try to find one of these guys who split the sperm to make sure I will have a boy. I just don't want a daughter. Sons are easier to raise. I have lived on a farm all my life. I guess I am what you call a tomboy. I would get along better with a boy, I am sure. As to how I have my boy, I have not given it a lot of thought. I really don't care what other people might think. I do what I want to do. I know I love children. I grew up thinking that someday I would like to have thirteen of my own.

"I would raise my children with love. I think love has to be equal, that both partners need to play fair with each other. That's why I'm through with men, at least right now in terms of a steady relationship. My parents were very unfair to me, I think. My younger sister is the apple of their eye and can do no wrong. My younger brother, they're always giving gifts to. Last week, they gave him an $11,000 jeep. Yet I can't even borrow the family car."

I cut in. "Donna," I said, "it seems as if you're paying a high price for your independence."

She replied, "Well, so what? I figure I'm still on top because my parents still have to put up with me. And I can be a real bitch on wheels.

"Like I say, I do what I mean to do. I cut off the dentist and his wife because I did not think they really cared about me as a person. They just wanted to use me. I could never go to Dr. Levin's clinic in Kentucky and take a fee because I think that kind of operation is nothing but a baby factory. I think that being a surrogate mother should be something special. You have to care about the people you are doing it for and they have to care about you. I think that

Cindy Sue and I are a lot alike—we're both Leos and I put a lot of faith in astrology. And Thomas always takes the time to ask how I am. That's why I want to help them. They care about me."

I knew that Thomas and Cindy Sue were impatient with Donna, that in fact they no longer wanted her as their surrogate mother.

I asked, "What will you do if it doesn't work out with Thomas and Cindy Sue? If they get tired of the whole thing and back out?"

"Who knows? Maybe, I'll just take out my own ad and offer myself as a surrogate mother to whomever is interested."

"Maybe," I suggested, "you should just forget it. Some things are not meant to be. Maybe you should take all this time to get your head on straight and figure out what you really want to do. What do you thing about that?"

"Not much. This is what I want to do right now. I am an impulsive person and I do crazy things on impulse. I once dove off a cliff just to show up the boys. I had a rose tattooed on my ass because one day in the hospital I saw a woman with a butterfly tattoo on her thigh and I thought, 'Wow, that's neat.' So, I got into this on impulse. But I have given my word to Thomas and Cindy Sue. I think everybody should be as good as their word. My word is as good as gold. I have given my word that I will be a surrogate mother, and I will be a surrogate mother. That's all I have right now. I'm basically a loner. I stay at home and ride my horses and read my books and keep my diary. I'm writing a book about all this, you know. Mostly, it's been good, except for the publicity. The publicity has almost driven me nuts. Most of these reporters just want to use you to sell papers. They really don't care about you at all. I've grown up a lot in the last year."

Thomas and Cindy Sue had been sending Donna $350 a month to live at home and try to become their surrogate mother. They also picked up the tab for all these trips to New York and the inseminations at Idant. All that would be coming to an end. They wanted out with Donna and a chance to find a new surrogate mother. Donna apparently could not bring herself to relinquish the idea of being a surrogate mother. It seemed to me that by being a surrogate mother, Donna was looking for the love and acceptance she had never found in conventional ways. I would have to give her the bad news. We were now on the cappuccino and we both were tired.

"Donna," I said, "It's simply not going to work. Thomas and Cindy Sue do not want to continue with you. And I think that's best for you. Give yourself a break. Forget this. At least for now. Get your own life in order."

She cried, but she did not seem surprised. It may have been wishful thinking, but I imagined she looked relieved. This was one burden that, perhaps, she no longer would have to carry. In any event, my mind was set. She would not be a surrogate mother for any clients I represented.

We stepped out into the brisk Manhattan night and hailed a taxi. It was time to say goodbye.

The next morning I left New York and flew to meet Lorelei at her small New England town. Since her home was a hour and a half away, we had agreed to conduct our business right at the airport.

That business was not to be pleasant.

Lorelei's first call to me had led with the question, "Noel Keane, are you my savior?" Hardly, I now thought, months later.

In the weeks since that first telephone call, Lorelei and her husband John had excitedly made plans to try to find a surrogate mother and have their baby. My file on this case included several long letters from Lorelei, handwritten on floral stationery in flowing, feminine strokes. Each would close with a felicitation in Swedish and the comment, "It may be all Swedish to you, but no matter, we love you!"

Lorelei's recent letters, however, had been typed and terse. The dream was turning to dust. Or ashes. They had found a surrogate mother, Rita, a divorced mother of three from Southern California. She had been artificially inseminated with John's sperm, was pregnant, and due to deliver next spring. There was one catch, however. After first demanding money, which we had made clear could not be paid, Rita then decided she was either going to abort the baby or keep it. To Lorelei, either choice would be a blow to the heart. When Rita's nasty ultimatum arrived, it put Lorelei on the verge of a nervous breakdown. In tears, she called me at home and begged me to come out East to talk to her. So here I was.

I arrived at eight A. M., and headed straight for the coffee shop, which was the only thing open. It is a small airport, but the coffee shop was already crowded—pilots, stewardesses, maintenance people, passengers. Heads turned when Lorelei, tall, blonde, Scandinavian, and striking, walked through the door in denim jeans, halter top, and clogs to meet the bespectacled attorney in his three-piece grey suit. We sat at the back of the room. I noticed Lorelei's eyes were red from crying.

"It's really getting to you, isn't it?" I asked.

"Worse. My best friend was just killed. I work the night shift doing dispatch at the police station. I took a call about a car that swerved off the road, hit a tree, and killed the driver. As I took down the license number and car description, I thought, 'My God, that sounds just like Jimmy's car.' It was. Jimmy is the only friend I had left from the days when I was a boy. He's the only one in this town who really understood me and knows what I have been through. All the rest of the people from my past, I just washed right out. I mean, after my surgery I told them what had happened and they were just mean, catty, and vicious. They are all gay and their only interest in me had been as a 'drag queen.' I looked the part, so they thought I could be just another 'trick.' Well, I wouldn't have any of it then and I wasn't having any of it now. I was celibate until I met my husband. I saw them for what they are—worthless. I don't belong anywhere near people like that. Jimmy was the only gay friend left from my days as a boy who understood me. He was truly a friend. And now he's dead."

I thought, "Well, we're off to a great start. Lorelei hasn't slept all night, her best friend just got killed—she had come right from the morgue—and here we were to discuss what to do about a surrogate mother who says she'll keep Lorelei's child. A great way to start breakfast."

Lorelei was tired and distraught. Her words came out in torrents as she described her dealings with surrogate mother Rita. Ears picked up around the airport cafe, but Lorelei went on, intent only on talking out her pain.

"Noel," she began, "This thing is turning into a nightmare. You know when we first talked to Rita on the telephone, she sounded just wonderful. We never met her and, of course, this is turning out to be a big mistake. But on the phone, she sounded like a wonderful mother, a fantastic mother. She said she was divorced and had three children. She sent photos of the children, and they all look great. Rita herself is tall, slim, maybe five-foot-seven, blue eyes, light-brown hair. She is tall like me. Her photos looked fine, but at this point we were so excited, we probably would have accepted someone with purple skin from Mozambique. We wanted a baby.

"When we paid your legal fee of $2,000, that came right out of our savings. We were left with maybe $3,000 in savings. That was quickly eaten up to accomplish the insemination. We couldn't afford to fly both John and myself to California, so we took your advice and decided to fly Rita to New York for insemination at Idant. However, my husband and I work different shifts. He works from nine until five, I work five until midnight.

"Anyway, we just couldn't arrange our schedules so we both could fly down to New York at the time of Rita's fertile period. Or should I say what Rita thought was her fertile period. She said she always got pregnant right after her period. Now, that didn't sound right to me, but I figured the lady has three kids, she must know. So we set a time for Rita to fly to New York for the insemination. John and I had to go down first to leave his sperm and have it frozen.

"Now, that turned into a real adventure. Our flight is late and we arrive at Idant only minutes before they close at three P. M.

Thank God, I have a knowledge of Manhattan because otherwise we would never have gotten there on time. This was during the transportation strike in the spring of 1980, and we ended up running fifteen blocks to the Idant Corporation. It was hot in the city and we were miserable. John was in a business suit and by the time we arrived, he was hot, sweating, uncomfortable, and nervous. But they were about to close. We had to move fast. They put John in a little room with a tacky print on the wall and some erotic literature. And they expected him to masturbate one-two-three. Well, as nervous and upset as he was, he couldn't. So they sent me in to help. I did hand springs, but nothing worked. The girl was very curt and cold. 'You have to hurry,' she said, 'because the specimen must be in by three P. M.' It was now 2:57. John said, 'Well, I am not a machine, you know.'

"Now, the other office girl named Nancy turned out to be a lifesaver. She said, 'Take all the time you want. I will wait.' But John just couldn't do it. I felt helpless, like it was my baby but I couldn't do anything to move things along. Finally, John said, 'I can't. I simply can't do it.' I told him, 'Well, we are not leaving here until you do.' Then, Nancy said, 'Why don't you go out and have a drink. Maybe that will relax you.' So we did. Went to the Blarney Stone and threw down some quick drinks and went back to Idant. It was still no go. It had been too much of a day for John. He is scared to fly for one thing. He had never been to New York City before. And the rushing and pressure and all was too much. Nancy said, 'Well, why don't you take this specimen bottle, get a hotel room, and bring it in tomorrow.'

"That's what we did, and it worked out great. The next morning I brought it in. I had to come alone because John wouldn't go near Idant again. Now, Idant is on Madison Avenue, right in the heart of Manhattan. I had tucked the bottle of sperm sample between my legs and panties to keep it at room temperature. There I was waddling down Madison Avenue with this bottle of sperm tucked in my panties and determined to deliver it safe and sound to Idant. Anyway, I got the sperm there and Idant froze it.

"A few days later, Rita flew in with her son from California. She insisted on bringing her son. Well, we were so grateful to her, that we said, 'Fine, bring him along.' We put them both up in a hotel, and I even gave Rita a little extra money for meals and to get out and see New York. It's such a beautiful city, if you know where to go. Well, of course, she never got pregnant. It wasn't the time when she was ovulating.

"We were all very disappointed, especially Rita. She seemed to be really into getting pregnant for us. She started reading everything she could on fertility. We couldn't afford to fly her back to New York, so Idant suggested we send sperm to California and have a physician do it out there. We shipped a nitrogen tank of John's frozen sperm to California—that cost us $600 right there—and Rita found a physician in Pasadena to do the artificial insemination. Of course, we all had to sign 'hold harmless' agreements before the doctor would do this.

"This insemination took. Rita called to tell us she was pregnant and that the baby was due next spring. We were jumping with joy.

"Now, as the weeks went by, I would call her from time to time to chat. Apparently, she had a history of nausea with her other three pregnancies, but this one was the worst. She was very, very ill, and had to call her mother into help with her three kids. Then, for a long time, I could never reach her on the phone. There was simply no answer. I guess she was too sick to come to the phone."

At this point in time, I realized a coincidence may have helped push tired, nauseous Rita over the brink. One of Dr. Levin's first surrogate mothers decided to go public with her story. The Illinois woman known as "Elizabeth Kane" talked to *People* magazine and Phil Donahue about her decision to have a baby for an infertile couple. Part of the story was that Elizabeth Kane is being paid $10,000 for her efforts. Apparently, Rita got wind of this from her friends and family or through subsequent news stories. She thought she was being cheated. Lorelei picks up the narrative.

"One day, I got a letter from Rita. Now, her earlier letters had all been very chatty, very warm. This one was cold and to the point. She said she wanted $7,500, half now and half by November 1st, 'if the deal is to materialize any further.'

"I tried to stall her along. I figured that past twelve weeks or so, she wouldn't dare attempt an abortion. But then when I thought about her having an abortion, I would get physically sick. I mean that's my baby she is killing. One day, I finally reached her on the phone. I was doing the laundry, and I just let the phone ring and ring. When I picked it up again, she was on the other end. I said, 'Rita, I have been trying to reach you for weeks. Are you OK?' She said, 'Well, Lorelei, I guess I have been trying to avoid you.' I said, 'What's wrong.' She replied, 'Oh, Lorelei, I just don't want to do it. Besides, you are not going to give me any money, so it is not worth it to me.'

"Now, Rita had never said anything about money before. It had always been she was doing it for 'humanitarian reasons, because she had three beautiful children and wanted to help one who couldn't have children,' and so on, blah, blah, blah. Now, she wanted $7,500 period. I said, 'Rita, you are telling me now after all this time that you don't want to go through with it. It is so humiliating.' I explained to her about the Kentucky program and how, unlike down there, we were not legally allowed to pay her a fee. But I promised, 'I'll check into it, Rita, and if it can be done, we'll do it.' "

Lorelei had told me about Rita's demands at this point, and I had warned her, "Medical expenses only. If you pay her anything approaching a fee, count me out. I am dropping the case."

Lorelei said, "It got so bad that I considered breaking the law. I was afraid of Rita. I thought of paying her $7,500, but we don't have the money. My husband and I clear maybe $12,000 a year total, and we've spent $8,000 so far on getting Rita pregnant. I've become a fantastic juggler, letting the rent slide to the middle of the month, missing a car payment. Both our parents have helped out a little. I can vegetables and fruit from our backyard to save money on food. All so we can send money to Rita for her medical expenses.

"One day, she had told me over the phone how her prenatal vitamins cost eight dollars and other stuff came to such and such. Well, I sat right down and wrote her a check for twenty-five dollars. Now, I am generous to a fault and I figured that twenty-five dollars was three or four dollars over the bills, and she could use it for something. That twenty-five dollars meant our phone bill would have to wait a day or two. But I sent it off to Rita. A week later, she sends me a letter with the check torn in two. She wrote, 'I am returning this check because it is not for the right amount. I told you on the phone the prenatal vitamins were eight dollars and. . . . that comes to $26.35. You are so tight you don't even want to pay the medical bills. You must need the money more than I do, so keep it.'

"Noel, can you believe it? For $1.35, she is calling me a liar and sending the check back. Things have gotten so bad that I cannot talk to her anymore.

"I think this turnaround is so sudden because she is ill and people are putting a bug in her ear, telling her she is crazy not to get paid like that other woman was paid. It's not her friends—I don't think she has any friends—but her family. Her mother and sister. They are telling her she is crazy, she shouldn't do it for free, she should get money.

"Well, I went out to see if I could give her money. First, I tried the banks. Noel, I am here to tell you that banks will not accept as collateral the pregnancy of a surrogate mother. I thought of borrowing from friends. Thank God, I finally came to my senses. First, I don't want to go to jail. Second, we can't afford it. When the baby comes, there will be so many unexpected bills. Plus, I plan to take some time off right after the baby is born and stay at home. That's more money out of our pocket. Lately, it seems as if I simply cannot communicate with Rita. She hangs up on me when I call. She never answers my letters. But I sat down, and wrote her one last, long letter. I explained how excited we are about the baby, how we have put our life savings on the line, how we would pay her whatever we could if it were legally possible, and how grateful we are to her.

"I never got an answer."

Lorelei concludes the tale of woe. "You know, Noel, I'm amazed that I'm still standing. I think that if it weren't for everything I've been through all my life, I would crack. But I'm pretty strong psychologically.

"The hardest part is going it alone. I try to keep from John as many of the gory details as possible. He's there when I need him, but he thinks this is my responsibility. So I shield him from the heavy-duty stuff. But he knows. One day, he picked up the phone when I was talking to Rita and said, 'What's wrong with you? You're driving my wife crazy.'

"My job is high-stress. I have to make split-second decisions on that dispatch radio or some unfortunate things will happen. There'll be a robbery and the police will be sent to the wrong part of town. I can't afford to have something on my mind when I'm working. I'm taking stress counseling to help cope with the job. A little Puerto Rican woman I work with knows what's going on and she tells me, 'Every day, I say a prayer for you.' Things like that help. Plus, I exercise a lot, stay active, dance, work in the garden. That's what keeps me going.

"My husband and I seldom get to see each other. He works days, and by the time he gets home, I'm off to work. He'll usually nap in the early evening and then I'll wake him when I get home at midnight. I'll fix dinner and that's the the only quality time we have together. Dinner and conversation right before we go to bed.

"But everythng is being readied for the baby. I've applied for the day dispatch shift, so I can be home at night with John and the baby. Our folks can watch him or her during the day while we work. They're both super-excited.

"I am optimistic because nothing can dampen my spririts once I have something in my head. I dream about my baby every day.

John and I are always starting sentences, 'When the baby comes. . . .' I have the nursery started. I have things started for him or her. Bottle warmers, getting the names of pediatricians in my area, reading everything I can about babies and child care, taking hand-me-down baby clothes from friends.

"I have been dreaming about this for so long. I figure that John and I will be the best darn parents. That's because we both had good parents, we had good training, you know. We have so much love to give a child. And then I see some of these women with children. These slobs, these three-hundred-pound gross, filthy women waddling down the street with a trail of kids behind them like ducks, and all the kids are dirty and filthy and shabby and underfed and skinny and the mother is as big as a house. I mean it is just so unfair. Why, just the other night, a mother left a baby on someone's doorstep. I had to dispatch a police car to pick the baby up. I don't think it's fair that God gave women like these the plumbing to have a child and he did not give it to me.

"It is not fair because I am an intelligent woman. John is an intelligent man. We are both college graduates. We both desperately want to be parents. Boy or girl, it doesn't matter. We want to raise a child and give it love. By the time he or she is twelve, I want my child to speak three languages—English, German, and Swedish.

"What will I do if Rita has an abortion or leaves town and we can't trace her or if she decides to keep the child? Well, that's my baby, either Adam James or Erica Leath. It's amazing, but I have developed the killer mother instinct. I will do anything to have that baby. If it means tracking Rita down to the ends of the earth, I will do it. If it means a court fight, I will rob a bank or prostitute my body on the street to get money to fight.

"I am exaggerating a little maybe, but, Noel, as you can see, I mean business. I refuse to believe that she would have an abortion, kill my baby. I cannot believe anyone would be that cruel.

"We're totally strapped for money now, but John and I would pay double what we have for what my husband calls, 'Operation

Little One.' I can't tell you how happy it makes me to hear my big macho husband say how, 'I can't wait to change the diapers on the little angel. . . .'

"It's things like that that keep me going. Every day, I do some little detail to prepare for this baby, I cannot let myself believe that it is not to be."

Lorelei had been holding forth nonstop for about an hour. I merely sat there and nodded. And fetched coffee from time to time. People had long since quit staring at us, pegging us, no doubt, as a crazy pair with some crazy problem. Which, I guess, is close to the truth. So there we sat in an airport coffee shop and tried to figure our way clear of this potential catastrophe.

My file on Lorelei is quite thick, and I slowly rifled through the pages.

There is good news for our cause.

The initial letter from Rita clearly spells out her desire to volunteer as a surrogate mother. And my reply made it clear that a fee could not and would not be paid to her.

The letter from the Pasadena physician who performed the artificial insemination on Rita with John's sperm indicates he is working for the success of the arrangement. First, he discouraged Lorelei from using Medi-Cal (the state's medical welfare program) facilities because "I feel totally responsible for Rita's care. We do not take Medi-Cal, as it doesn't even cover our office overhead. I don't feel Medi-Cal payment justifies the amount of work necessary to take care of a patient like Rita, therefore we will continue her care with our original agreement we made with the _____ family, as regard to payment." In an attempt to cut corners, Lorelei had thought of using welfare funds for the medical care of Rita (who was not working and thus eligible), but the physician had convinced Lorelei that private medical care would be best for everyone concerned. Clearly, Lorelei had Rita's medical interests at heart. Second, the physician wrote that Rita, "at one point during her pregnancy came in for consultation considering therapeutic abortion. She has been bothered by both severe nausea and vomiting, which we have been treating with both oral and IM (intramuscular) medication. We firmly discouraged the abortion, as the patient's agreement and responsibility was thoroughly reviewed." So the physician, too, reminded Rita of what she had originally agreed to do. Rita, Lorelei, and John had all signed hold harmless agreements empowering the doctor to do the insemination.

But there was also bad news.

Most distressing, perhaps, was the preliminary report I had from a detective who was trying to trace Rita. In the past few weeks, she had simply up and disappeared. It also turned out that Rita is but one of several names she uses. This information was obtained from her Medi-Cal records. Her first husband, who was from India, had fathered one child and then committed suicide. Rita's next two children were born out of wedlock to two different men.

The detective's interviews with Rita's neighbors were hardly reassuring.

"Rita kept to herself," one neighbor recalled. "She was never seen, except late at night when she would bring her kids in. Sometimes, this would be as late as eleven P. M. and she has young children." Another said, "Rita did not take good care of her children. Once, I saw her slap her oldest daughter because the girl had stepped on Rita's toe. Another time, I heard loud slapping coming from Rita's apartment, followed by loud screaming. When I looked through an open door, I could see a baby sitting on the floor and screaming hysterically. When she saw me, Rita simply slammed the door shut."

The detective's report noted that Rita "has disappeared, with no apparent forwarding address. It may be, however, that her mother or another relative, remains in the apartment. We are checking out this angle."

Sitting stoically, Lorelei merely nodded in acknowledgement of this grim twist. "Well, Noel," she said, "Like I say, she seemed

OK. Plus, we were so excited we would have taken someone with purple skin from Mozambique. Just so Rita has our baby and the baby is healthy and we can take custody, that is all we want. I'm praying."

The last papers in the file were copies of the agreement to be signed by Lorelei, John, and Rita. As soon as Lorelei had told me Rita was pregnant, I had sent off the routine forms. John and Lorelei's was signed; Rita's was blank.

I knew that, legally, it could mean the whole ball game. If Rita stuck to her threat to keep the child, then we would have a court fight. A legal determination would have to be made to decide custody of a child born to a surrogate mother. Upon this decision might well hang the future of surrogate parenting. The court fight, I figured, would start in the spring of 1981, right after the baby's birth.

"Do you think she'll stick to her threat?" Lorelei wondered aloud.

"You never know," I replied. "But here's what she said in her last correspondence."

By now, the breakfast hour was long gone and the coffee-shop crowd had drifted on to their duties. I read the letter aloud to Lorelei and a lone employee, who was silently scrubbing the floor.

"Sorry, I'm returning your papers to you and I'm *not* signing. I have decided to keep my baby and the deal is off.

"I'm not having a baby for free, for strangers. No way.

"The doctor and me are out money, but you got yours, didn't you?"

Postscript: In February 1981, I filed a lawsuit in California, claiming custody for the father, John, of any child born to the surrogate mother, Rita. It was necessary to hire a private detective firm to serve the legal papers on Rita, who had fled to another small California town.

In April 1981, an eight-pound, nine-ounce baby boy was born to

Rita. She called him "Jimmy." To Lorelei and John, however, he was "A.J." or "Adam James."

The trial was set for June in Los Angeles Superior Court. A new blood test, called human leukocyte antigen, or HLA, determined within 99 percent probability that John indeed is the boy's father. However, we knew we would have to overcome the California legal presumption holding artificial insemination inadmissable as proof of paternity. We expected the case to go to the very heart of the surrogate-mother conundrum, with a judge asked to make the Solomonic decision of who should have custody of the child—the mother or the father.

Then came two new quick twists and turns. First, the news media were relentlessly following the case, and Lorelei and John became concerned that if it became known that Lorelei is a transsexual, the publicity would jeopardize not only the legal case but also her health. Thus, we settled the case, relinquishing John's claim to custody or visitation rights in return for having his name on the birth certificate as the boy's father. We were all bitterly disappointed.

Shortly afterwards, the newspapers broke the story anyway; Lorelei was reported to be a transsexual. This development prompted John and Lorelei to go public with their quest. On June 15th, the three of us appeared to "The Phil Donahue Show" describing the case. At that time, we decided that since everything is now out in the open, we would refile the lawsuit and again press for custody.

This landmark lawsuit, when finally decided, will be the first legal decision on the enforceability of the surrogate-mother arrangement.

·11·
"We just sat there and smiled at each other."

NOT ALL the news last fall, however, was bad. On the bright side was the sudden increase in requests from couples wanting surrogate mothers. Working through either my legal contacts in Kentucky or Dr. Levin's clinic, I could now legally authorize the adopting couples to pay a fee to those surrogate mothers who wanted payment. The only stipulation to the couple is that they may have to establish a legal residence in Kentucky to accomplish the adoption. These developments assured the growth of surrogate parenting.

The growth now promised to become an international phenomenon. In September 1980, I presented a paper, "Legal Problems of Surrogate Motherhood" (See appendix A), to the World Conference on Embryo Transfer and Instrumental Insemination in Kiel, West Germany. The meeting drew top physicians, reporters, and scientists from around the world, and many were intensely interested in this revolutionary new fertility option being exported from the United States. Since that time, I have received numerous requests from overseas about surrogate mothers, including requests from infertile couples and potential surrogate mothers. So far, I have limited my work to Americans, but I anticipate working in the future with international couples and surrogate mothers, who may or may not be matched with Americans.

And, finally, on Labor Day 1980, surrogate mother Sally gave birth to Raymond Alton, a strapping baby boy for adoptive parents Richard and Aralee. That birth came shortly after pregnancies were confirmed for Jeannette, the Texas midwife who volunteered as a surrogate mother for the California couple, Andy and Nancy, and for the surrogate mother selected through Dr. Levin's clinic for the Yugoslavian couple, Stefan and Nadia.

These are happy stories in which the solid bond of trust between couples and surrogate mothers enabled us to overcome intricate legal obstacles. Let me share them with you.

It was Saturday afternoon and I was interviewing prospective surrogate mothers when Martha broke the news. "Noel, Richard and Aralee just called. Sally has been in labor for several hours now and is expected to deliver any minute. They want to know if you'd like to be part of the event."

I arrived just moments before the big moment. Richard and Aralee had been holding a vigil on and off in the hospital's obstetrical waiting room for a whole day. I greeted them, and, shortly afterwards, the phone rang. It was Sally, calling us down to the delivery area. Her words were short and sweet:

"Well, here is your little boy."

Raymond Alton was still a little scrunched up from the birth process, but at six pounds, nine ounces, dark hair, and eyes of an indeterminate color, he was, in Aralee's words, "Quite a handsome young man."

We were all elated, but none more so than Richard. He is a quiet, handsome, soft-spoken man, who radiates inner confidence and peace. It was almost imperceptible, but I caught him brushing a tear from his eye.

"Richard, do you see any resemblance to yourself?" I asked. "Oh, only in every feature I see," he said smiling.

Sally tried to be offhand about it. "Well, Noel, now I can get a good Siamese cat and get on with my life. I want to get skinny and play tennis again."

"Raymond Alton," I mused aloud. "Why that name?"

Aralee responded, "Raymond after Richard's father and Alton after mine. They're both going to be pleased as punch. In fact, we better call them right now."

Later, I would talk at length to both Richard and Aralee and Sally, and be struck by the strong bond formed between them during this unique relationship. Clearly, they really cared about each other.

"It was a normal delivery," Aralee said. Thank God, Sally didn't require a Caesarian. For a while, they were worried that she might.

"Her water bag broke a few days early and she had begun very mild labor, but it was not enough to cause dilation. They had to induce labor, and the induced contractions were so painful that Sally had to have a saddle block and Demerol. I know that disappointed her because she wanted to go natural. She and a friend had attended Lamaze classes together. But it was not to be.

"The call came about seven A.M. on Friday, right before we were leaving for work. She said her water had broken, she had called her doctor, and he was going to meet her at the hospital. She hoped to deliver by the natural method at the hospital's outpatient birthing center.

"Richard and I had memorized the flight schedules to Detroit, and we were on a plane within two hours. We came right to the hospital and left our bags in the car. Sally started out in the birthing center. She was doing very well. The doctor had recommended she walk a lot to try to help herself dilate. So we spent Friday afternoon walking the hallways with her."

Richard adds, "Sally was very excited and anxious. We were anxious and worried. I tend to worry, anyway, and I was very concerned about Sally, about the baby, would it be normal. We got to the hospital about three P.M. Friday, and Sally delivered almost exactly twenty-four hours later. She was having trouble dilating, so the physician recommended she get some sleep, that Saturday would be a long day. We checked into a hotel across the street. Friday night, Sally got only about two hours sleep. She was too nervous and excited to sleep. By morning, she still hadn't begun to dilate, so they put her in the regular hospital OB unit and started induced labor."

Aralee said, "She was in the OB unit under induced labor for eight hours. And we were right there waiting. Noel, you got to the hospital just in time. Richard and I could not be in the delivery room at the time of birth because only one person was allowed in the labor room and Sally's friend from the Lamaze classes stayed with her throughout the two days. Had she delivered in the birthing center, we could have shared the moment with her. But the regular OB unit was limited to only one. But that was fine with us. The friend had been through all the classes and knew all the breathing techniques and was a big help to Sally, who was very tired after two days. When I first saw our son, all I could think was, 'A boy. A beautiful boy.' I thought he was absolutely gorgeous. And I was very pleased that he was doing so well. We would have been pleased with a little girl, too, but we wanted a boy.

"I guess it really hit me the first time I held him. I had told Richard I wanted to hold the baby first, and, believe me, I had goosebumps when I picked him up in my arms. That was a thrill of a lifetime."

Richard: "At the time of the birth, I was simply very excited and all smiles. But when I came back to the hotel room, I was very, very moved by it all. I went into the bathroom and cried. I shed a private tear or two. There are so many things that can go wrong in a situation like this. In any pregnancy, you are worried about the outcome and with all of the added complexities of this situation, I think that anyone in their right mind has to be worried throughout the entire venture. And when it all comes to a successful completion, well, it's a beautiful feeling. I feel like we have been blessed."

I was pleased to be able to tell Richard and Aralee that, legally, everything was in order. The papers were all signed. Richard had claimed paternity, Sally had relinquished custody. All that remained was for Aralee to adopt in Virginia, and that would be accomplished within a matter of months. Richard and Aralee were making plans to pick up their child and return home.

"Everything is ready back home in Virginia," said Aralee. "Both our parents have pitched in and we have two of everything. Two baby cribs, two buggies, right on down the line. We have a baby bag that is about to overflow. From here, we'll go to New Jersey, so my husband's parents can see the baby, and then we'll go back home. Our parents have been wonderfully supportive. My parents are very religious, but they knew my biological infertility and they thought the surrogate mother idea is a godsend. Richard's parents were a little more reserved at first. We explained to them what we were trying to do and they said, 'Well, that's very nice. . . . ,' but you could tell they hadn't bought the idea yet. But they came around and are very happy for us now. My father is a fireman, Richard's is a carpenter; both our mothers are housewives. I'm one of two children, he's one of three. Our parents know how important children are."

Richard adds, "Sally has asked only that we send her a photo of the boy at Christmas or sometime, just little milestones of that sort. She said she is going to stay out of our lives as much as possible. But we will play things by ear. If she wants more details about Raymond Alton, we will certainly tell her. That is certainly her right. Aralee and I have come to be very close friends with Sally. She is very easy to be friends with."

Aralee: "We will tell people back home that our son is adopted. And when he is old enough to understand, we will tell him the truth, the whole truth. If he wants to meet his birth mother and if it is OK with Sally, we will help him meet her. If Sally does not want such a meeting, then we will stop such thoughts before they begin."

Richard: "We feel that if Raymond ever meets his birth mother, he will be very impressed and very pleased. She is one in a million.

We are very happy that we came to know our surrogate mother. I think the anonymous process in which one day you donate some sperm and nine months later you are handed a baby is very eerie. You know, you have no idea what kind of woman is at the other end. My intention now is to become a physician and specialize in childhood genetics. I've been accepted to MD school and I know this experience will help me. No, we're very happy with the way we've done it."

And how about surrogate mother Sally?

"Noel," she said, "I would not have missed this experience for the world. In many ways, it was a selfish experience. I had a very easy pregnancy. The real difficulty was giving up my family and friends. My father still doesn't know what happened. My mother really doesn't understand. Most of my friends do not know what I have done. When I was five months pregnant, none of my friends knew and my tennis partners made it rough on me. Once I started to show, I avoided my friends and talked to them only on the phone. My brother's wife was delivering a baby at the same hospital at the same time I was. That meant my mother was shuttling back and forth between these two births—one natural and the other somewhat strange. My boyfriend moved out after I became pregnant.

"The toughest time, I think, came when my friends at work— the other stewardesses—wanted to give me a baby shower. If people had found out what I was doing, I suppose I would have lost my job. Everybody thought my boyfriend was the father and I begged them not to have the shower. But they said, 'It's for the baby,' so I went along with it. It was hard to try to act happy, though.

"I'm glad it's all over. I think it is much harder to raise a child than to give birth. Now I would like to get back with my boy- friend, maybe go to school. I have hopes of maybe becoming a physician. I may as well shoot for the top. I would like to hear from time to time about the baby, but I will stay out of the way of Richard and Aralee. My biggest concern is what if something happened to them. I would feel a responsibility to the baby, but I am not sure I have the right to feel a responsibility.

"To be perfectly honest, I had become obsessed with having a child. I did it as a project, and my life would not be complete without it. I view the entire experience as a solution. It has completed my life. I do not feel cheated that I do not have a child to raise. On the contrary, I feel good about it.

"I have no regrets. No, I do have one. The bias with which people judge this experience.

"Why can't people have a child this way?

"This I know. The plight of Richard and Aralee touched my inner feelings. And today, Richard and Aralee and their parents are super-happy."

That is an understatement. Richard told me, "Noel, it turned out perfect. We think of Raymond Alton as extra special. I just hope we don't spoil and make a brat out of him. That Saturday night after the baby was born, Aralee and I had dinner together in the hotel. Nothing special, but we did order champagne.

"We just sat there and smiled at each other. People were staring because we didn't say a word, just sat and smiled, as if we were a couple of fools.

"If only they knew."

Not a penny changed hands in the arrangement between Richard and Aralee and surrogate mother Sally. In this case, the surrogate mother, an airline stewardess, had ample medical insurance to cover the pregnancy and she avoided any mention of a fee because she wanted "the selfish experience of giving birth without having to be responsible for raising a child."

The other end of the surrogate mother spectrum is represented by my clients from Yugoslavia, Stefan and Nadia. Not only did they have the money—$20-$30,000—to pay a surrogate mother, but they preferred to have an anonymous arrangement. They, in short, wanted the arrangement that had been established in Kentucky by Richard Levin, M.D.

Two years had passed since I first met Dr. Levin and passed on to him my hard-earned knowledge about how to go about surrogate parenting. The issue, I believe is essentially legal, not medical. Legally, the phenomenon is virgin frontier. I was given the rare opportunity of creating a new field of law. Medically, the procedures are elementary. In the first five surrogate-mother births I represented, the artificial insemination was accomplished not by a physician, but by the surrogate mother herself and/or the adoptive mother. That's how simple this medical procedure is. But while the medical aspects of surrogate parenting are minimal, Dr. Levin did have one strong factor in his favor. Kentucky law allows the payment of a fee to a surrogate mother. With this in mind, he set up Surrogate Parenting Associates, Inc. to build a business around his obstetrical-gynecological practice. Following the trail we had blazed three years earlier, he set up a business in which surrogate mothering is just another variation of adoption.

To me, the Kentucky experience provided two new options. First, I could refer those clients of mine who either were willing to pay a fee or potential surrogate mothers who sought a fee to Dr. Levin's computerized clinic. Second, I could accomplish the same results by having adoptive couples simply establish residency in Kentucky and thus become eligible to pay a fee to their surrogate mother. In the future, I would simply require the vast majority of my clients who were able to pay a fee to establish a residency in Kentucky. Then, I could match them with those surrogate mothers who wanted to be paid. But I referred Stefan and Nadia to Dr. Levin.

This couple, I figured, had suffered enough. They were both in their forties by now and had been trying for eighteen years—their entire marriage—to have a child. This was the end of the line. They had the money to pay for a surrogate mother, Dr. Levin was prepared to provide the necessary medical care from insemination through birth, and our ad in the *Louisville Courier-Journal* had produced several potential surrogate mothers.

Stefan and Nadia had minimal requirements for the woman

who would carry their child—namely that she be tall, healthy, and white. Dr. Levin screened several women answering to that description and—for legal reasons—asked the couple to make the final choice. Once they had chosen their surrogate mother, based on studying dossiers listing applicants' vital statistics, medical records, religions, ethnic backgrounds, educational levels, and insights gained by personal interviews, Stefan and Nadia agreed to abide by the program created by Dr. Levin. Now, while the Louisville physician was a Johnny-come-lately to this new field, he did help to expand the available options for infertile couples and aspiring surrogate mothers. For that, I am grateful to him, as new efforts in this area can only help achieve our ultimate goal—state legislation and regulation.

Since my clients, Stefan and Nadia, were to be bound by the terms of Dr. Levin's program, I took it upon myself to do an intensive analysis of their contract. Simply put, the program administered by Dr. Levin allows the payment of a fee to a surrogate mother and attaches to the arrangement an elaborate legal agreement that purports to cover every eventuality. Of course, the contracts entered into at Surrogate Parenting Associates, Inc. like all the contracts enacted so far in this new field, are entirely at the mercy of the good faith of the parties involved. That is why I have kept my legal contracts relatively simple. Until we have legal precedents and/or legislative regulations, the contracts can be little more than a statement of intent.

But, for better or worse, I was advising Stefan and Nadia to cast their fate—and hard-earned dollars—with this new initiative. Since Dr. Levin's program is so new to the area, let me explain its workings. The best description, perhaps appeared last year in an issue of *American Medical News*, the official weekly newspaper of the American Medical Association.

"I thought surrogate mothering would be a reasonable alternative [to the agony of infertile couples], with the proper controls," Dr. Levin told the newspaper. The prime control implemented by Surrogate Parenting Associates is an extensive contract that calls for a surrogate mother to turn the child over to the biological father at birth, and, subsequently, be adopted by his wife. The surrogate mothers are required to be married and already have their own children.

"The child is protected," Dr. Levin said, "by making sure he's gestating in the womb of a woman who will take good care of him. We have a full physical and genetic history. She promises that during her pregnancy she won't smoke, take drugs—legal or illegal—or any alcoholic beverages."

Life insurance policies are obtained. If the biological father dies, an estate is created for the baby. If the surrogate mother dies during her pregnancy, an estate is created for her family. The contract also covers what happens to the baby if it is abnormal (the couple still must adopt it), or if twins are conceived (again, the couple must take both).

Dr. Levin conceded to the newspaper that the contract is subject to the good faith of the parties involved, but said he did not foresee any legal battles.

"All the parties involved," he said, "are evaluated psychiatrically by two psychiatrists and a psychologist." (In fact, Dr. Levin says he is trying to put together a permanent team of psychiatrists to study all parties five, ten, or twenty years down the road to determine "if we're doing a good thing." If not, he says he would alter or terminate the program.)

The typical surrogate mother in Dr. Levin's program, so far, is a married woman who has two or three children, has a minimum twelfth-grade education with some college, is from middle- to upper-class, and may have a profession.

In general, Dr. Levin's set-up is similar to the arrangements we had pioneered in Michigan. His insistence, however, on women who are already married with children and on women with advanced education seemed to me unnecessarily elitist and exclusive. His big difference from our early efforts, however, is, as I said, the legal option to pay a fee to the surrogate mother. Here's how he described to *American Medical News* how that fee is determined.

"I meet with the surrogate mother for about two hours. No money is mentioned. At the end of the conversation, just about the time when she's walking out the door, I ask [about compensation].

"They all respond, 'What's a baby worth?' I respond, 'I don't know.' It's the time and effort that eventually are priced. Basically, what we're paying for is the potential loss of income, the pain and suffering [that accompanies childbirth], and the loss of consortium.

"We're not paying for a baby. This is not baby-selling. The woman says, 'I'm returning his baby.' They do not think the baby is theirs.

"Baby-selling, or black-market baby, laws, came about to protect the public from stealing babies, or enticing teenage women into getting pregnant who did not understand the consequences of what they were doing. We're using women who understand exactly what they're doing. Also, the adoptive father has a blood tie to the baby he is adopting and this does not exist with a black-market baby.

"I am uncomfortable with women not receiving compensation. Also, I have a moral problem with paying a surrogate mother too much—as with one woman who originally wanted $100,000—or not enough. We figure it this way. The surrogate mother, counting the inseminations, the nine months of carrying the child, and the six weeks of recovery, is giving a year to a year-and-a-half of her time. So the fee we set—$10,000—comes out to be less than minimum wage. Less than I feel comfortable with.

"But we have a sliding scale so as not to make surrogate mothering an exclusive option for wealthy people. If a couple says they have only $3,000, I ask a mother to lower her price or try to find one who is willing to do it for that amount.

"The bottom line, however, is that it usually will cost $13-$30,000. I use a desk-top computer to maintain quality control and try to match adoptive couples to potential surrogate mothers. Every surrogate mother is handled by me. The personal involvement extends to routine calls to find out if she has any problems."

Turning to potential criticism from the medical profession, Dr. Levin told the AMA newspaper, "From physician colleagues, I have heard lots of inquiries but little criticism for what I am doing.

"Some say, 'I have questions and doubts.' It seems everyone knows a hole in the contract, but I say, 'This is how we deal with it.'

"I've not had one of my peers tell me this is stupid, crazy, or amoral—nor has anyone said it indirectly. They say, 'We're hopeful for you.'

"I expected some criticism from the Catholic Church, but heard none. Recently, I went to a Catholic funeral and expected the priest to later lambast me. But no, he said, 'I think this is pro-life.' "

I was gratified to hear the support for surrogate parenting from physicians, and, even more so, from a priest, and I was generally in agreement with Dr. Levin's views on how best to compensate a surrogate mother.

My main aim, however, was to find a solution for Stefan and Nadia and this we found when Dr. Levin presented them with three potential surrogate mothers, one of whom was subsequently impregnated with Stefan's sperm.

The procedures required of Stefan and Nadia by Dr. Levin's Surrogate Parenting Associates are simple, but the sacrifices great. The immigrant couple had to put $10,000 in escrow to assure payment to the surrogate mother; they also had to pay all legal, medical, and insurance costs upfront. And they had to relocate to Kentucky and establish residency. This required them to relinquish jobs in which they had considerable experience and seniority and to sell their Michigan residence, although they retained their vacation home in the Upper Peninsula.

Still, Stefan would say to me, "Noel, it is nothing but paper. That's all money is, paper, paper. We are going to use paper for flesh and blood. My flesh and blood." I could not argue with them. After their surrogate mother got pregnant, Nadia got out her yellowed clipping from *People* magazine and said, "Mr. Keane, it is a miracle. For years, I held onto that magazine, and now it has produced a miracle."

In the months after a pregnancy was confirmed for their surrogate mother, Dr. Levin's operation was to be thrust into the public spotlight. The publicity caravan that two years earlier had swept me up was now rolling through Kentucky.

As a physician, Dr. Levin claimed to prefer anonymity for his work, but one of his surrogate mothers, "Elizabeth Kane" (a pseudonym), an Illinois housewife with a husband and three children, went public in style. Suddenly, "Elizabeth Kane" and Dr. Levin were following the publicity trail we had carved out years before: *People* magazine, Phil Donahue, *The New York Times,* the network talk shows.

In a moving interview with *People* magazine, "Elizabeth Kane" said, "It's the father's child. I'm simply growing it for him." Unlike Susan, the first surrogate mother, who along with adoptive parents Debbie and George first electrified the country, Elizabeth Kane never really knew the couple for whom she was carrying a child. They stayed anonymous. But after giving birth to an eight-pound, ten-ounce boy for the couple, the thirty-seven-year-old "Elizabeth Kane" told the magazine, "I felt an overwhelming desire to help. . . . My husband finally consented but I worried whether this would hurt our marriage irrevocably. It didn't. For two months, though, we didn't tell anybody about the pregnancy. Finally, we wrote long letters to our immediate families, explaining everything. . . . My children suffered, too. It's true that I accepted a fee, but I thought of this as a pure gift of love, no strings attached. My husband, David, who had studied Lamaze, soothed me during the delivery. The adoptive parents (I hate the term— *they* are the real parents) were there. When I first saw the baby, I thought, 'He's beautiful.' During my pregnancy, I had talked to them on the telephone, and they both seemed very grateful. The father told me, 'Elizabeth, you are going to make us a complete family.' The baby was also a stranger. He didn't look like any of my other children. . . . The adoptive mother said to her husband, 'He looks just like you.' Then, she hugged me and said, 'Thank you for my baby. He's so beautiful.' I asked the new mother if it were all right if I held him, and she looked sort of surprised and said, 'Of course.' That was the last time I held him and I never nursed him.

"All of us—my husband, my children, and I—would do it again, though we won't. We fought for what we believe in, and we won. . . . To think that I could alleviate the pain and unhappiness of one woman filled me with awe. . . . My hope is that this child will be loved as I love my children, that his parents will encourage him and guide him. I don't ever want his mother to feel that she has to share him with someone else. She is his mother. My part is over."

When this story was published, Stefan and Nadia read it with a respect bordering on reverence (their baby is due in the late spring of 1981). "Noel," Stefan said, "we do not want any publicity, that is for sure. But this woman, 'Elizabeth Kane,' she makes us proud of what we are doing."

In many ways, my most remarkable case has been that of the California couple, Andy and Nancy, and their Texas surrogate mother, Jeannette. The birth is expected shortly after this book goes to press, and their story included several unusual elements.

Jeannette is married and was supported, in fact urged, by her husband Marshall to become a surrogate mother. She is a midwife and part of her motivation to become a surrogate mother is to promote the merits of midwifery. She also wants another chance at "the perfect birth," and has laid down a series of conditions to try to achieve this. She has one son and does not want the responsibility of raising another child. What she wants is another chance at giving birth. Jeannette sees surrogate motherhood from an unusual vantage point. Her background is such that she can see the controversy from every angle. She herself is adopted and is a strong believer in adoptees' rights to know their birth parents. Her two brothers are adopted and were originally offered for sale by their birth parents, who approached Jeannette's adoptive parents in a seedy coffee shop and offered to hand over the two little urchins in exchange for one hundred dollars! Jeannette's parents refused to pay, but offered to give the children a home through adoption. And that is the way it happened. Jeannette is also a strong feminist and believes "in helping my sisters, even to the extent of donating my body, if necessary. After all, the ability to have children is a gift from God and if I can use it to make others happy, why not?"

The motivation of the adoptive couple, Andy and Nancy, is more prosaic. Andy simply wants his own child; Nancy, who is barren from a hysterectomy, sees surrogate mothering as the only way it can be done. They find Jeannette's willingness to help them almost too good to be true. Their only concern, at this point, is the possible legal complications.

Which brings me into the picture. This case is, perhaps, my most difficult legally, with the possible exception of John, Lorelei, and Rita, a case that will end up in court. But I think we have found a way to assure that Andy and Nancy can take custody of the child born in Texas to Jeannette and to assure that, subsequently, they can accomplish an adoption in California.

The legal problem is this. Since Jeannette is married, her child will under Texas law be considered the child of its mother's husband. The statute requires that the birth certificate list as the father not Andy—the father in fact—but Marshall, Jeannette's husband and, thus, the father under law.

Our strategy to counteract this legal presumption is to institute a termination-adoption proceeding. Here's the way it will work.

Marshall and Jeannette will in a Texas court formally terminate their rights to the child. At the same time, Andy and Nancy will, under Texas law, be appointed as the child's managing conservators. This will give Andy and Nancy absolute rights to custody and allow them to take the child to California. Texas law allows for the parents of a child to initiate termination proceedings after the first trimester of pregnancy, although no orders may be granted until the child is at least five days old. In the parents' Affidavit of Relinquishment of Parental Rights, they are allowed to designate a qualified person as managing conservator of the child. So, we have preliminary papers filled to terminate Marshall and Jeannette's parental rights and to transfer guardianship to the adoptive couple, Andy and Nancy. If everyone continues to agree to our arrangement, Andy and Nancy will shortly after birth return to California with legal custody of the child.

Once they have returned to California, the petition of adoption can be filed. I am, of course, working with local counsel in both Texas and California to orchestrate this complex procedure. Once adoption papers are filed, the appropriate licensed county adoption agency will interview Andy and Nancy within forty-five days, with their report due to the court within 180 days of the filing of the adoption petition. Then, at a private hearing, upon the court's satisfaction that the best interest of the child will be met by the adoption, a decree of adoption for Andy and Nancy will be entered by the judge. Once the adoption is final in California, then the original Texas birth certificate—listing Jeanette's husband as the father—will be sealed. An amended certificate will be issued, showing Andy as the father and Nancy as the mother.

The entire adoption process will be completed within six months to a year after the child is born.

It has not been easy working out the legal details for this surrogate-mother story that stretches across three states. I practice in Michigan and am bound by Michigan laws; the adoptive couple live in California and are bound by California laws; and the surrogate mother lives in Texas and is bound by Texas laws. But again, it all comes down to trust and good faith. If everyone does what they say they want to do, the legal details will be swiftly accomplished. Andy and Nancy will have to pick up the fees of local counsel in Texas and California, but this will not be an undue hardship. The estimate for attorney and court fees to accomplish the termination-adoption procedure is $365 for the Texas portion and $250 for the California portion. Money well spent for a dream so long denied and once thought impossible.

So much for the legal story. The human story is even more intriguing.

Immediately after I put Andy and Nancy in touch with Jeannette, the couple boarded a bus and made the grueling trip to her home in the Texas Panhandle.

Jeannette recalls, "It was great. They walked in the door and they were in tears. They had heard women did this, but they had never met one. I go by first impressions, and my first impression of them was wonderful. And it has turned out to be true. We asked them to stay at our home that week, so that with the money they would save on a motel they could fly back to California and skip the bus trip. We had arranged the visit to coincide with my fertile period, and we hit it off so well from the start, that we decided to do the insemination right away. I did it and I hit paydirt on the first attempt. From the time I dropped my letter in the mail explaining why I wanted to be a surrogate mother to the time I became pregnant could not have taken more than two weeks. It is absolutely unbelievable.

"Here's what I was looking for in the couple for whom I would carry a child. I didn't want strong religious background as much as I wanted a strong moral background. They had to have a great deal of respect for children as individuals. Here's the question that decided me in their favor. Now, I have strong feeling about circumcision. Under no circumstances do I believe a baby boy should be circumcised. I think it is mutilation of his body. Of course, I do not press this view upon other people. But I asked Andy and Nancy, 'How do you feel about circumcision?' I tried very hard to keep my voice neutral. Andy replied, 'Well, we feel that it is his body and it should be his decision if he wants it done or not. We will not make the decision for him.' I thought, 'Fantastic, this agrees with everything I believe about respecting the child's body.' We were off and running.

"I looked for a couple that is financially stable. For a couple that will work at raising their child—who will read child care books, talk to psychologists, take child education courses. For a couple who are reasonably intelligent. Andy and Nancy are all of this and more. As for me, they had said they simply wanted a healthy mother for their baby. I had covered all my family and medical history in that first letter, and after meeting me, they were reassured that I would turn out a 'quality product.' Now, here's a coincidence. I had warned you, Noel, in the letter, that I am nearsighted, heavy-hipped, and have a receding chin. And, as you know, I have red hair. Well, when Andy walked in, he could have been my brother. Andy is near-sighted, heavy through the hips, has a red beard, and, after three days, admitted that under the beard lurks a receding chin. It is uncanny.

"It was time to discuss my 'Ten Points.' I told Andy and Nancy that there are ten conditions that must be met if I am to be a surrogate mother. They are:

'1. The child will be born at home, with the supervision of midwives.
2. The adoptive mother *must* be present for the birth.
3. If at all possible, the adoptive father and any siblings should be present.
4. The adoptive parents must be willing to have the child breast-fed for three to five days in order for the child to receive the benefit of my calostrum.
5. The child is at no time to be placed in a foster home during adoption proceedings.
6. The adoptive parents pay any medical expenses involving miscarriage or prematurity.
7. The adoptive parents demonstrate financial and emotional security and a willingness to educate themselves on all aspects of childrearing.
8. The adoptive parents be personally involved during the prenatal period, they must be willing to exchange feelings with me, and they be honest with friends and relatives about what

they are doing. The parents should feel joy and anticipation, not guilt or doubt.

9. The mother can afford to spend at least three months at home with her baby.
10. That the parents have no wish to 'forget' me after the birth. They must realize I can never forget what I've done for them'."

She continues, 'Now, I am a pretty strong-willed lady, and these conditions are nonnegotiable. But, Andy and Nancy agreed right down the line. And very soon after that, they had a surrogate mother on their hands. A pregnant surrogate mother.

"We talk on the phone about every week. At first, this baby had a strange growth pattern. He—or she—started very tiny. That worried us. Then there was a sudden spurt of growth. We thought it might be twins. But I've just had a prenatal check up and everything is normal. All signs are that there will be one normal baby. No twins. I'm having trouble getting Andy and Nancy to pick out names for the baby. I warn them, 'I'm going to call him Bozo, if you don't come up with something better.' I think they're stalling because they don't want to get their hopes up too high yet. They're still having trouble believing it's really happening."

As a midwife, Jeannette has some strong views on the merits of natural births at home, views she intends to promote through her sudden celebrity as a surrogate mother.

"With midwifery,' she said, "we do not have any hospital-induced complications or deaths. Our mothers are not on their backs. They are not fetal monitored. Their labor is neither speeded up nor slowed down with drugs. The entire family is there for support. The mother is never transported to a hospital or delivery room in the middle of labor. The entire process moves much more quickly. I have helped deliver thirty-five children, and they have all gone smoothly. Of course, we carefully screen our mothers. I turn away about half of the mothers who come to me. For everything from smoking to high blood pressure to diabetes to lack of any nutritional sense. I just turned one down because she has toxemia. All she would have to do is eat more protein, but she won't do it. So I won't work with her. I tried to have our son delivered at home, but I ended up having to go to the hospital. I was in labor twenty-four hours and never dilated beyond seven centimeters. It was a very bitter experience for Marshall and me. I will feel guilty over that all my life."

As an adoptee, feminist, mother, and housewife, Jeannette also has some strong view on surrogate mothering and mothering in general.

"About two-thirds of my motivation," she said, "is to have the experience again of giving birth. I want to have total control and do it right this time. But I also sincerely want to help Andy and Nancy. It really annoys me when people quote the Bible to say that what I am doing is wrong. I mean, you cannot commit adultery with a syringe. OK, so my body is being used. When I die, my eyes are going to be used. My kidneys will be used. It is not my body in the first place. It is just something the Lord says; if I am going to have a baby for another couple, then I guess I am.

"Now, I am not that religious. My parents are devout Southern Baptists. Dad worked as a conductor for the Santa Fe Railroad, Mom was a housewife. They gave huge sums to the church, and we three kids—all adopted—ate beans and cornbread. I am not knocking that. I just don't want that for my son. I don't want him teased at school because he has shoes from Goodwill and socks that don't match. I don't want that for him.

"My first husband is a minister, and he simply could not stand children. That's why I divorced him. It is very important to me to have a child. But I am not turning out to be Super Mom. I love my son, but I find it confining to stay at home with a toddler every day. Emotionally, I am not ready to go through it again right away. But I do want to give birth again. Being a surrogate mother is the perfect solution.

"In time, I think surrogate mothering will become a very big thing. We still have a generation of women out there who were raised not with the concept of sisterhood but with the concept of competition. That's competition against other women. My generation has more of a sharing attitude. I cannot imagine why a woman would want to be paid anything beyond medical expenses for being a surrogate mother, but I know that many do. I guess many women still view childbirth as an ordeal. But there are also many, like me, who view it as the greatest gift women have. A gift meant to be used. but it will take time for surrogate mothers to become common.

"I hope that Andy and Nancy will tell this child everything that happened. Just the way it happened. Of course, I have no control over what they do, but they tell me that is what they intend to do. I have been very active in adoptee groups. I have always known that I am adopted and I think my parents were very deceptive in keeping it from me. I accidentally found out who my real mother is, and it turns out she is a woman who has always been one of my best friends. She lives in the same town, and is sort of like an aunt to me. We even look alike, but I never dreamed of the connection. One day, I called her when I was pregnant with my son. He was growing very fast, and I wanted some information about my birth mother. I told this friend—who turned out to be my birth mother—'Look, you are very close to the family. If anyone would know who my birth mother is or who the judge is who handled the adoption it is you. Can you help me?'

"Well, she just burst into tears. The charade was over. So I hope that Andy and Nancy will not be deceptive with this child.

"I know I could trace my father, if I chose. My birth mother gave me enough information—I have a photo—and men are much easier to trace than women. At least men of his generation. But right now I still feel too vindictive toward him. When I mellow, maybe I'll try to make his acquaintance.

"My adopted brother and sister, who also know they're adopted, are not as fortunate in terms of finding their birth parents. They were adopted in strange circumstances. Mom and Dad were eating at a road side diner years ago and a woman approached with these two grubby children and offered to sell them. Just like that. Dad said, 'We'll take them and give them a good home, but we will not buy them.' Dad got an attorney and adopted them. Like I said, I was illegitimate and my birth mother simply gave me—via adoption—to her friend. My birth mother subsequently remarried and had two children, and those boys are my stepbrothers. So I am a big believer in adoptees' rights to know the facts about their birth parents.

"That's why this ridiculous Texas law really drives me crazy. That I have to lie on the birth certificate and say that the father is my husband, when the father is Andy. As a professional midwife, I will be in a lot of trouble if I ever lie on a birth certificate. Yet the state of Texas is, in effect, forcing me to lie by putting my husband's name on the birth certificate as the father of this child. I resent that. I know the woman who records the birth certificates, and she will put down whatever I tell her, but I guess I will have to go along with this complicated legal process to straighten out what is very simple. As a matter of pride for both Andy and myself, I had hoped to put his name down as the father, but I guess that will have to await the adoption in California."

Jeannette is such a believer in what she is doing that she is considering filming the actual birth in her home. She wants to use the footage as a training tool for her midwifery classes. Beyond that, she is considering letting national TV into her living room to record the event.

Now, Andy and Nancy are private people, but they are going along with Jeannette's wishes. The trio's story appeared in *Newsweek,* and they became instant curiosities, though Jeannette told me, "Noel, I may be well known throughout the country, but not in my hometown. Nobody here reads *Newsweek*, or anything else."

After the birth, Jeannette says she is looking forward to "resuming my career as a midwife, maybe going back to school and trying to get a degree in child psychology. Marshall is still going to school to get an advanced degree in computer sciences. So, we're trying to make a better life for ourselves."

Andy and Nancy are a little uncomfortable with the publicity and were especially upset when they found out that Jeannette was fired from one job she had with a nursery. But they are looking forward to the birth. Their daughter will be there, too. Nothing can stop us now, they reason.

One day, I read to Andy a portion of the letter I received from a staff attorney at the Texas Department of Human Resources, which administers the Texas Family Code. In the nasty language often typical of welfare departments, the letter concluded:

"Finally you should be aware that Department will investigate and refer for legal action appropriate cases involving baby-selling or other violations of Texas law, possibly including situations such as those described in a recent *Newsweek* article and other media reports."

I chuckled, "Don't worry, Andy, we are not buying a baby."

Andy replied, "Noel, I'm not worried. I know that what we're doing is not wrong. Every day, I put on my forest ranger's uniform and go up in the woods. I can hear the wind whistling through the tree, and it seems as if the trees are talking to me.

"They tell me that what we are doing is right."

Postscript: On February 5, 1981, Jeannette gave birth to Cody Robert, a nine-pound, fourteen-ounce boy with, in the father's words, "flaming red hair." Jeannette and her husband immediately teminated their parental rights and Andy and Nancy have returned with their son to California, where arrangements are proceeding smoothly for the adoption. Andy and Nancy tell me they are "overjoyed."

'12'

"*What we need is state legislation and state regulation.*"

I<small>T IS</small> time to sum up, to state my case for the surrogate mother and to address myself to some of the concerns and criticisms expressed by others. This chapter will summarize the legal, medical, psychological, and moral issues of the controversy.

But before we get into the polemics, I want to make some important points.

First: The solution to this controversy is very simple. We need legislation from the states to clarify the issues and we need regulation by the states to control those involved. Court decisions can only point the way. The real answer is to be found in legislation.

Second: The real experts in this field are the people who have already done it, the pioneers who have made surrogate mothering a reality. I have described my first nine cases in great detail because I think their stories illuminate the dimensions of that reality. The people who have found surrogate mothers, the women who have become surrogate mothers, and the children born to them have surpassed the most enlightened legal, medical, religious, and moral opinions. Their actions may herald a future revolution in fundamental social ethics, but the fact is that these early pioneers in surrogate parenting are simply seeking an innovative solution to some very personal problems. It is very easy for many, if not most, people to produce a pregnancy. Artificial insemination is not nearly as intimidating a procedure as it seems. There are no laws preventing a woman from being artificially inseminated with a man's sperm. You do not need an attorney, an ethicist, or a physician to engage in surrogate mothering. Add all this up and you have the story of Debbie, Sue, and George, the first people to pursue parenthood by proxy and tell the world about it. The moral dilemmas arose only after they and others like them had acted.

Third: Keep in mind an overriding reality. People want this new option to infertility. As I travel around the country doing talk shows and media interviews, one question always comes up: "Why can't surrogate parenting become widely available?" I think it can, and it should.

Fourth: The surrogate mother is an issue that has been brought to public consciousness by the news media. I chose to do it that way because I think people have a right to know what is going on and because I want everything to be above board. That is why I have written this book. But the fact is that if it were left to the "experts," surrogate parenting would never have gotten off the ground. The news media made it happen.

Fifth: Resolution of the surrogate-mother alternative requires legal and public policy determinations, not medical and moral ones. This is a brand new area of law and raises unique questions of public policy. The medical aspects are peripheral and routine. The moral dilemmas should be decided not by heated emotions and dated dogma but by public policy decisions of what is truly in the best interests of the people.

THE LEGAL ISSUES

There is one key point. There are no laws pertaining to surrogate mothers. Anywhere.

This leads to practical reality. Any and all contracts between adoptive couples and others wanting children and their surrogate mothers are unenforceable. There is no guarantee the surrogate mother will give up her child. If such agreements are to work, they will require the protection of law, and that protection can only be provided by legislation. Court decisions will precede the legislation but legislation must ultimately prevail.

Until the issue is tested in court—and it may well be soon in the case of Lorelei, John, and Rita—all agreements or contracts between the adoptive couple and the surrogate mother must be considered illegal. But it is interesting to note that when artificial insemination first became available in the 1950s, an Illinois judge ruled in a divorce and custody case that artificial insemination constituted adultery. That opinion was later reversed, and enabling legislation later paved the way for AI and sperm banks to become models of state-regulated procedures to cope with infertility. I think the same should be true of surrogate parenting.

In the legal papers attached as Appendices B and C to this book, I fully outline my legal arguments as to why the surrogate mother should legally be paid a fee. Until this issue is resolved, however, such payments will be illegal, unless either there is no adoption or the adoption is accomplished in Kentucky. The following discussion, however, is based upon the premise that a fee can legally be paid to the surrogate mother.

Currently, here are some of the dilemmas posed by the unenforceability of the surrogate mother contract or agreement:

1) If the biological father and his wife breach the contract, either by refusing to pay the agreed-upon compensation or to adopt the child, the surrogate mother can either keep the child or give the child up for adoption, and can sue the couple for compensation due. If the surrogate mother chooses not to keep the child, then the child is illegitimate and becomes the responsibility of the state. Whether she keeps or gives up the child, the surrogate mother is unlikely to be awarded damages against the married couple. Fortunately, this turn of events should be extremely rare, since couples entering into such arrangements are strongly motivated to have a child, especially one fathered by the husband.

2) Breach of contract by the surrogate mother, however, poses more difficult problems. If she refuses to submit to artificial insemination, the married couple could probably sue for recovery of any compensation already paid, but beyond that their remedies are uncertain. In any event, the real loss to the married couple is not money paid to the surrogate mother but the emotional distress and disappointment over the frustration of their parental aspirations. Damages for emotional distress are usually not recoverable in contract actions. Even if such a suit were successfully brought, it is unlikely that the surrogate mother could satisfy the judgment. Rich women, after all, are not likely to become surrogate mothers.

3) The alternative remedy to money damages in cases of breach of contract by the surrogate mother is an order that the breaching party perform as she has promised. In regard to a pre-birth breach by a surrogate mother, however, it is very unlikely that a court would order a woman to submit or resubmit to artificial insemination, to become pregnant, and to give birth to a child. Certainly, enforcement problems would be monumental. The reluctant surrogate mother might surreptitiously practice contraception, or engage in activities harmful to the health of the fetus, or even arrange to be impregnated by someone other than the husband of the adoptive couple. Since the contract could not be enforced short of taking the surrogate mother into protective custody, it is obvious that not much can be done about pre-birth breach of contract by the surrogate mother.

4) If the surrogate mother gives birth but refused to give up the child for adoption as promised, there is a new set of legal issues, issues that will be tested if Rita carries through on her threat not to give Lorelei and John the child born to her through artificial impregnation with John's sperm. Such a case boils down to a dispute between two biological parents over an illegitimate child. Since most courts look with disfavor upon prenatal releases of parental rights or consent to adoption by the expectant mother, legislative reform is imperative to accomodate the special circumstances of surrogate parenting. I think that such release and consent

by the surrogate mother, given in the context of a deliberate, pre-pregnancy decision to bear a child for another, should be not only lawful but irrevocable.

Legislation to assure binding contracts between adoptive couple and surrogate mother is absolutely essential if people pursuing surrogate parenting are to have peace of mind.

Again, I must return to the problem of John, Lorelei, and Rita. Here we have a truck driver (John) and his transsexual wife (Lorelei) pressing the biological claim of John against the biological claim of a surrogate mother (Rita) who has become a runaway. At issue is the fate of a child who will be born illegitimate. I have hired private detectives and, currently, know where to find Rita. If Rita gives birth and decides to keep the child, then we go into a California court of law and litigate the first case of surrogate parenting in the United States. Among other things, I will be arguing that Rita is an unfit mother to the three children she already has by three different men (she was married to only one of the three fathers and he committed suicide). Among the judicial precedents I will have to overcome is an apparent California presumption that AI cannot be acknowledged to help establish paternity. Such a case, of course, will make lurid headlines, and as this book goes to press, we are heading toward a showdown in court sometime in the summer of 1981.

Incredibly, there is a precedent, though the outcome is not favorable to my cause. A few years ago in London, England, a professional man and his lover, faced with the prospect of never having children of their own, paid a prostitute their life savings of 3,000 pounds (about $7,200) to have the man's child through artificial insemination. The search for the surrogate mother was conducted at London's Bow Street Magistrates' Court, where prostitutes are regularly arraigned and fined. A woman was found and she subsequently was impregnated with the man's sperm and gave birth to a son. However, she decided to keep the baby boy, despite the promises from the couple of added inducements including a car and—in desperation—their house. The Family Division of London's High Court ruled the prostitute/surrogate mother could keep her son, since the agreement is a pernicious contract for the sale and purchase of a child. This story is an astonishing one that has left nothing but worry and woe for all concerned.

The moral of this British story, as is the moral of the John-Lorelei-Rita story, is whomever you choose as a surrogate mother, choose wisely.

I have become a legal expert on surrogate parenting simply by being a maverick attorney who did on-the-job training. The legal lessons learned in the eight other cases I have described are not as dramatic as in John, Lorelei, and Rita's case, but they should be emphasized.

For one thing, paying a fee to the surrogate mother is not a prerequisite. All of my first nine cases (except for Stefan and Nadia, who were referred to Kentucky and Dr. Levin's clinic, and Joseph, the single man) did not include payment of anything other than medical expenses. So with or without a fee, surrogate parenting can continue, though its growth and prominence will require legal approval for paying the surrogate mother. The two surrogate mothers who went haywire, Diane and Rita, did so largely because others told them they were foolish not to demand money.

For another thing, more important than the contract or the money, is the trust between couple and surrogate mother and the emotional stability of the surrogate mother. Of my first four surrogate mothers to give birth—Sue, Carol, Diane, and Sally—there were problems only with Diane.

Carol gave birth to Tom, Jr. for Tom and Jane without even entering into a written agreement. She did it to feel good about herself, and to help Jane.

Sue gave birth to Elizabeth Anne for Debbie and George not only without entering an agreement but before she even heard of surrogate parenting. She did it as a gift of friendship.

Sally gave birth to Raymond Alton for Richard and Aralee with the benefit of a signed agreement, but her reason was so she would not miss out on the experience of giving birth.

I have had few problems in accomplishing adoptions for these three children.

Now, I do have a problem, however, in achieving an adoption for Bill, Jr., who lives with Bill and Bridget. This is because the surrogate mother, Diane, lives outside of Michigan. In Michigan, where the other three cases were handled, it is legal to acknowledge the paternity through AI of the man in the adoptive couple. In Tennessee, where Bill, Jr. was born, this is not legal, and at first I could not get Bill's name on the birth certificate. (The matter is greatly complicated, of course, by Diane's chaotic circumstances, her troubles with the law, and her dropping out of sight. She is not around to sign some important papers.) However, through legal proceedings initiated in Michigan, I have now accomplished that. Bill's name will be listed on the birth certificate as the father. If I can get court approval in Michigan to terminate the parental rights of Diane, then Bill's wife, Bridget, can adopt Bill, Jr. If not, then Billy cannot be adopted, though he will always be legally connected to his father. His birth certificate will simply list the surrogate mother, Diane, as his mother. Bill and Bridget intend to tell their son this circumstance anyway. But, meanwhile, I am hopeful that I can still accomplish the adoption. At worst, Bill and Bridget may not have the piece of paper they want, but they will have the son they want.

Other cases taught other lessons.

With Joseph and Kay, I learned that a single man can legally pay a fee to a surrogate mother because as the biological father he can take custody of the child without having to adopt. And because he doesn't have to adopt, there is no ban against payment to the mother. I also learned that the agreement between the person seeking a surrogate mother and the surrogate mother is neither enforceable nor constant. After originally entering into an agreement to be a surrogate mother for $10,000 for Joseph, Kay later changed her mind about several things and made demands Joseph found unreasonable. There was no legal way, of course, to make Kay stick to the original terms or to the agreement at all.

With surrogate-mother candidate Donna, I learned the bitter lesson that it is one thing to get a surrogate mother pregnant and another to keep her pregnant. I also learned that the surrogate mother can back out at any time for any reason and the adoptive couple has no recourse, except to look for another surrogate mother. Which is what Thomas and Cindy Sue are doing.

With Stefan and Nadia, I learned that if a couple has the money and the motivation, it is perfectly possible to legally pay a surrogate mother and to accomplish the adoption by establishing residency in Kentucky.

With Andy and Nancy and surrogate mother Jeannette, I am learning that married women can make excellent surrogate mothers if they have their husbands' blessing, and that I can overcome the legal presumption that the husband of a surrogate mother is by law considered the father of a child even if the child is born through AI with another man's sperm. In orchestrating this complex three-state legal adoption, I have learned that if there is a will—and trust by all involved—there is indeed a way.

So, while I have solved some of the legal questions posed by the surrogate mother, until I have obtained courtapproval to pay a fee and legislative guarantees to make contracts binding, I will not have all the legal answers.

THE MEDICAL ISSUES

Except for the psychiatric issues, which will be discussed in a subsequent section, the medical aspects of the surrogate mother story are minor. This is a legal story, not a medical story. The clinical case is ordinary. It is the social situation that is extraordinary.

For the truth is that artificial insemination, the primary medical contribution to surrogate mothering, is relatively simple. Although it may be desirable, you hardly need a doctor to accomplish AI and pregnancy.

In my first four cases—and first four births—the surrogate mothers either did the AI themselves or were inseminated. Debbie herself inseminated—and impregnated—surrogate mother Sue on the first try. She used a thirty-nine-cent drugstore syringe, a glass cup, and a description of AI from the *Reader's Digest Family Health Guide* to perform this simple medical procedure. Not only was medical advice not available for these early cases, but it also was not needed.

Subsequently, of course, I would refer my surrogate mothers to sophisticated medical facilities, including private physicians, sperm banks like Idant Corporation in New York City, and Dr. Levin's clinic in Louisville. But the medical component is essentially the routine prenatal, obstetrical, and well-baby care typical of most births. One surrogate mother, Jeannette, of course, balks even at this. She has insisted on delivery at home attended only by a midwife. This is her way of trying to achieve "the perfect birth."

The most interesting medical twist in my work, perhaps, is the emerging technology of sperm-splitting and sex-selection. Building on research in the cattle-breeding industry, scientists have found methods to separate the male-carrying Y chromosome in human sperm and achieve artificial inseminations that are up to 90 percent effective in producing males. I am working with one of the best of these scientists, the Indian fertility expert Dr. B.C. Bhattacharya of Omaha, Nebraska, in an attempt to help my client, Joseph, have a son. Joseph and surrogate mother Kay twice traveled to Omaha for the sperm-splitting and AI, but neither took Kay has subsequently backed out, but we are looking for a new surrogate mother to continue the quest. Contrary to popular belief, most people using sex-selection techniques are not doing so because they think a boy is better. Most are people who already have one or two daughters and simply want to balance their family. In any event, this technology opens new doors.

Two other medical breakthroughs are the "test-tube" baby clinic in Norfolk, Virginia, and the embryo-transfer research being done by the Seed Clinic in Chicago. Unfortunately, however, the technology in both areas is rudimentary and not likely to be of any practical help to most infertile people for the rest of this decade. Their best hope is still the surrogate mother.

Most medical organizations are very conservative and their policies tend to lag well behind the cutting edge of change. Simply put, they vote policies upon controversial issues only when the issues are forced upon them. I have sought the viewpoints of the major medical groups that can reasonably be expected to have an interest in this area and the feedback is unanimous. Not one has a policy position. The American College of Obstetricians and Gynecologists does not have a position. The American Academy of Pediatrics does not have a position, though it says its Committee on Adoption and Dependent Care plans an "in-depth" study. The American Fertility Society does not have a position, noting, "This is a very conservative organization dealing entirely with the scientific and educational side of infertility. We have not taken any stand in regard to surrogate motherhood. We are interested in any factors that influence infertility, but at the present time we are very much on the sidelines insofar as this issue is concerned." The American Medical Association does not have a position.

Some medical viewpoints have been expressed, however. Kamran S. Moghissi, M.D., professor of obstetrics and gynecology at Detroit's Wayne State University School of Medicine, replied:

"It is my belief that at the present time the procedure of surrogate motherhood is ethically objectionable, psychologically fraught with hazards, and legally on dubious grounds. We will not be willing to participate, at this time, in such a program. I hope that you will understand."

I understand, but I note that the objections are qualified to "at this time."

Dr. Moghissi and other M.D.s, I think, need to face up to the agony of the infertile. It is easy to get wrought up about exploiting a woman's body and buying and selling babies but how about the emotional distress of those who want babies and can't have them? Who speaks for them?

Andrea Shrednick, for one, She is the executive director of the

United Infertility Society, Mahopac, New York, and says, "I am totally in favor of any method that can provide an infertile couple with children. . . . No one can possibly begin to comprehend the sense of frustration, pain, and futility involved with infertility—unless they have been there. I can well understand the motivation of the couples who seek alternate methods of conception."

Ms. Shrednick offered some caveats and questions:

"In the case of a donor (surrogate) mother, does the surrogate mother already have children? If so, how is the pregnancy and subsequent lack of a baby explained? What health records are provided to the adoptive parents? How is the surrogate mother found? How is the amount of compensation agreed upon?

"I am opposed to couples who venture forth into these new frontiers without counseling as to their expectations and their feelings of not being able to produce a child through conventional means.

"As infertility counselor, I come in contact with couples who have chosen donor insemination (AI) of the wife from a sperm bank. Several years after a normal, healthy child is born, it seems the 'father' often has difficulty dealing with the circumstances surrounding the child's conception. While this does not happen all the time, it happens enough to warrant our attention. Will this same situation occur with surrogate mothers?

"I presently have one client (a couple) who are interested in a surrogate mother. The woman's sister is willing to be inseminated with the brother-in-law's sperm and later surrender the child. I have cautioned this couple to further consider the ramifications. The sister's husband, the sister's children, the grandparents, and so on.

"The legal system seems so unwilling to tackle the questions involved in alternative methods of conception. Perhaps this is due to the moral questions."

Ms. Shrednick's points are well-taken, and we are working to answer her questions to everyone's satisfaction—and safety.

What makes the work worthwhile is that women who for years

have been put through countless fertility workups at one clinic and then at another, who have been "treated like monkeys" (and all at great expense and absolutely no benefit), suddenly have their baby through the surrogate mother. Four years ago before the first birth to a surrogate mother, the *Los Angeles Times* published a poignant letter from an infertile wife. I have kept that letter because it eloquently speaks to the plight of those women who cannot have children and cannot understand why. The woman wrote:

"Today's emphasis is on contraception. Please consider the fight for conception by those who suffer in silence. My medical life has become an open book. Every part of your body is explored in the search for an answer. Your once uncomplicated sex life loses its romance due to the many pressures. In your sleep, you have your children and they're around you and everything is beautiful. I'm walking with a baby in my arms. Sometimes, I wake up and I almost feel it's real, I want it so bad. What's hard, what's really, really difficult is that everyone around you has children. I am a teacher. I think this is a world of children and I wonder, why can't I have any?

I just feel people should be more understanding. They're not. They either brush you off or they give you all these pat answers: 'See my doctor.' You don't want to break down and cry. You're sitting there and the mother is going on about what Johnny did today and you think, 'I would like this life,' but you can't make it happen. I've gone to some really good friends with children but it hurts. You get a tug. You say, 'It should be me.' Then, you think you shouldn't feel that way. Many times I'll be sitting there looking at the dumbest thing on TV. There was something on the morning show about couples going through pregnancy. I got sort of upset. My husband turned it off. He said, 'Yeah, I know.'

You have to have a strong marriage. You could tear each

other apart. You have to be able to talk about it and cry
together.

I don't think we want to adopt. We want a Jewish baby
and there are virtually none available. Legally, that is. A
reputable doctor here in Beverly Hills told a girlfriend of
mine, 'Give me $10,000 and I'll get your Jewish baby.' But
we don't want to do anything illegal.

And the infertility workups, they are painful. The first test
is basically to see if you ovulate. You take your temperature
each morning with a basal thermometer. (At ovulation there
is a dip in temperature followed by a rise.) I did it for a year
and a half. I called the thermometer my constant companion.
When you wake up, before you do anything, you stick it in
your mouth. It's funny. You get your temperature up and
you're sort of happy. Then all of a sudden it goes down and
your mood goes down. You know you're going to get your
period. You wake up and you go to work and you know it's
going to happen. You try not to get upset, but you come
home at the end of the day and cry. It's terrible, too, because
everything that was once, oh, spontaneous is in a different
perspective.

The next test was the Rubins (in which carbon dioxide is
blown through the Fallopian tubes to see if they are open),
then a hysterosalpingogram—I can't spell it. It's an X-ray
technique in which dye is inserted to see if the tubes are open.
From there, they take a biopsy of uterine tissue lining and you
go through basic blood and urine tests to check hormones and
general health. Your husband also gets tested. There's sperm
analysis and a test for compatibility because sometimes a
woman can build up antibodies against sperm. There's also a
post-coital test, after having sex and he examines a specimen
of live sperm under a microscope. He let me look at the slide.
You see these little darts going around, crashing together.
Another thing is insemination with your husband as the
donor. I've tried that and it's one of the worst. You have to

walk into the fertility clinic with a paper bag and the person there asks you what you want. The infertility clinic is right next to obstetrics and you look around and notice you're the only one there with a flat stomach. You say, 'I'm here for insemination.' You're just dying.

A laparoscopy—that was the last thing. (The surgical procedure involves a small incision in the curve of the navel in which a thin instrument is introduced for a visual examination of the peritoneal cavity.) They call it, 'Band-Aid Surgery.' Again, nothing was found.

I'm told I'm normal, but I cannot seem to have children. I want to talk to other people who've been there. I want to say, 'This is how I feel. Am I crazy?' I can't decide, well, I'm going to have children or not have children. OK, I'm going to plan a trip to the Orient. My husband and I are going to save up for a house, but there's no future. My God, my life is not mine."

If you take this moving story and multiply it by thousands, you have an idea of the kind of people I'm dealing with. They are desperate to have children and they desperately do not understand why they cannot. They are looking for hope. The surrogate mother offers them new hope. To my mind, that is the most important medical dimension of this controversy.

THE PSYCHOLOGICAL ISSUES

We do not know, and will not know for some time, what the long-range psychological consequences of the surrogate mother are.

Certainly, this is a key area. At minimum, we must, through legislation and regulation, assure adequate psychological screening protocols to make sure all the people seeking this option are mentally sound. Beyond that, we must offer ongoing psychiatric assistance for those adoptive couples and surrogate mothers who need it or who can benefit from it.

Our goal is to assure that the consent of each person participating in the surrogate-mother procedure is an *informed consent,* and that each person is *competent* to grant that consent and carry through on it.

The first nine cases that I have described in this book did not have the benefit of psychiatric counseling, and some suffered because of this lack. I am making sure this will not happen again. I now refer all potential surrogate mothers to a Detroit-area psychiatrist, Philip J. Parker, M.D., who is a specialist in pregnancy and childbirth psychology. Dr. Parker, who practices in Southfield, Michigan, minutes from my law office, interviews prospective surrogate mothers for two to five hours—at a cost to the adoptive couples of only $250—to probe their family history and background, psychological makeup, reasons for wanting to be a surrogate mother and the possible psychological advantages and disadvantages of this procedure. After the counseling, Dr. Parker submits a report to me that answers two questions: Is the potential surrogate mother likely to suffer serious adverse psychological consequences? Is she competent to decide to be a surrogate mother? If the woman is both psychologically stable and competent, I offer her name to couples who want to adopt. If she is either not psychologically stable or competent to give informed consent, I do not accept her.

Recently, Dr. Parker has been evaluating potential surrogate mothers at the rate of about three a week, and he reports that so far the candidates are "surprisingly normal. They are as competent psychologically as the women you see every day. It is just that they all have their own unique reasons for wanting to be a surrogate mother."

What Dr. Parker is isolating is the surrogate mother's motivation for wanting to do such an unusual thing. He plans to publish his findings later. If he finds that motivation consistent with the candidate's general psychological makeup and if that makeup is sufficiently stable, then I proceed. As I have found, the motivations are unique for each surrogate mother and often fascinating. It can range from money to guilt over a past abortion.

There can be no doubt but that many of my early surrogate mothers were compensating for psychological deficiencies and deprivations in their lives.

Carol had never found the right man to help raise her three boys, and she wanted to give a baby to a couple, Tom and Jane, who had both a loving marriage and a strong, stable male figure.

Sue had been raised by alcoholic parents and a stern, cold grandmother. She had never known love or genuine human closeness until she met Debbie. She wanted to repay that debt by giving her friend the gift she could never otherwise have—a baby.

Diane had enormous guilt over her alcoholism and drug addiction, her lesbian relations, and her neglect of her son. I think that in some strange way she initially may have wanted to do something good for somebody else, but her problems proved too much for her. We are very lucky that she delivered a normal, healthy baby. She should not have been allowed to be a surrogate mother and one fifty-minute psychiatric interview would have ruled her out. But that is hindsight. Bill and Bridget are disgusted with Diane, but delighted with their son.

Sally simply did not want to miss out on the experience of giving birth. All the men in her life had for one reason or another denied her this experience, which had become an obsession. To her, being a surrogate mother was a solution.

Kay wanted to make a private protest against abortion, though she never carried through.

Rita, I think, started out like Diane, wanting to do something good. Her life was otherwise a shambles. Three children by three different men, the first—her husband—a suicide, the other two long gone. She was living on welfare. Having children was something she did well, and she seemed to enjoy the experience. The problem came only when others told her about paid surrogate mothers in Dr. Levin's clinic. Then, she mistakenly felt cheated and started to raise the ante.

Donna, a rebel, was deprived of love at home and with men. Being a surrogate mother was a chance to get some gratitude and love. Her demands on the adoptive couples were not financial, but for affection.

The surrogate mother found by Stefan and Nadia at Dr. Levin's clinic was thoroughly evaluated psychiatrically and found sound. She will give birth in the spring of 1981.

And Jeannette wants to be a surrogate mother to have "a perfect birth," to promote midwifery—this birth will be to a midwife delivered by a midwife—and to help an infertile couple.

Were these first nine mothers referred to Dr. Parker, I think that only Diane and Rita would have been rejected. Neither one really understood the commitment she was making and neither one was competent to carry out her word.

The American Psychiatric Association views surrogate mothering with concern. E. James Lieberman, M.D., chairperson of the APA Task Force on Changing Family Patterns says:

"There are some extremely negative opinions about surrogate motherhood, which is thought by some to be a bizarre phenomenon with overemphasis on biological parenting. The husband is willing to pay the emotional price of the wife/surrogate mother for the privilege of having his genes in a child. The woman is placed in the role of breeding and being bought for service. The psychological part of child-rearing is much more important than the biological or animal part. Surrogate motherhood really amounts to the adoption of a child with the father's genes."

The APA medical director, Melvin Sabshin, M.D., adds:

"There are serious questions about the mother-child bonding in these kind of arrangements. There are also implications of the child seeking the 'birth mother.'" Dr. Lieberman indicates that he is opposed to such a phenomenon until such time as there really aren't enough children in the world. "While it would probably be unwise to legislate against the practice, it is to be noted that marriage suffers many strains without the additional burden of surrogate motherhood. This latter practice is substantially different from the practice of infertile couples who seek artificial insemination, using either the husband's sperm or the sperm of an anonymous donor, since in these cases the birth mother will also be the psychological mother."

Upon my referrals, Dr. Parker is counseling not only the surrogate mothers, whom I now require to have a psychiatric evaluation, but also the adoptive couples, whom I recommend seek psychiatric evalution.

The questions to be probed include:

Is the surrogate mother sure she can give up the child? Why? Is she likely to suffer adverse consequences later in life? If the surrogate mother is married (many are), is the husband likely to become jealous? (We do not proceed unless the husband signs an affidavit of agreement.)

Is the adoptive husband angry at his wife for not being able to give him a child? Will the wife envy the surrogate mother for doing what she cannot? Are both parents prepared to deal with any subsequent search by the child for his surrogate mother? If the adoptive parents divorce and there is a custody fight, who has the stronger claim—the father with his blood tie or the mother with her psychological ties?

To cope with some of these questions, of course, the surrogate mothers and adoptive parents may benefit from extended or intermittent psychiatric counseling.

Dr. Parker's approach is nonjudgmental. He does not try to second-guess the participants in the surrrogate-mother procedure. He simply tries to help them understand their motivations, make their own informed decisions, and learn to live with those decisions.

The trick is to deal honestly with real feelings. In my preliminary interviewing of couples and surrogate mothers, I try to zero in quickly on attitudes.

A major potential problem is the psychological well-being of the barren woman who is about to become an adoptive mother. One client couple, whom we'll call Michael and Rose, describe it this way.

Rose: "We discussed it last night, and Michael understands my feelings. I started feeling jealous that another woman is going to be doing my job."

Michael: "It bothered me for a while. I want Rose to feel the child is as much hers as mine. I don't want her to think that I am the real father and she is a stepmother, or something like that. I thought maybe adoption would be better, because that way we would both have an equal stake in the baby."

Rose: "The only way the surrogate-mother method would really hurt me is if Michael said something like, 'This is mine. I am the real father.' "

Michael: "I would never feel that way. I want Rose to believe that."

Rose: "If we ever divorced, and Michael thought he had a greater claim to the child, well, I am sorry, but that child is still mine. I would act like the real mother. It will be my child as well as his. I would take the child and we would have it out in court. I have three sisters and they all have children, and, yes, I feel cheated that my tubes are shot and I can't have children. But now that Michael and I have cleared the air, I am willing to proceed with finding a surrogate mother."

The question of jealousy on the part of the adoptive mother also came up with Carol and Jane, but like everything else in their story it worked out fine.

Jane told me, "Noel, Tom and I have seen Carol only a couple of times after the baby was born. During the pregnancy, we tried to make things as nice as possible for Carol and her three sons. We would take them to ballgames, out to dinner, whatever, just little things. We were like one big, happy family. But after Tom, Jr. was born, things were sort of cut-off. So, one day, I called Carol and made a date to have lunch. She picked me up and, at the last minute, I decided to bring Tom, Jr.—he is almost three years old by now—along. For me, it was a strange feeling to have them see each other. But it was my idea. I wanted her to see him. I wanted to say, 'Well, there he is and he is fine.' I love Carol that much.

"After lunch, Carol and I went out in the backyard and played with Tom, Jr. and his toys for a while. I think our son looks about 90 percent like his father, but I must admit there is something that reminds me a little of Carol. Knowing Carol so well and her gestures and her smile and knowing her three children, I do recognize something in the way Tom, Jr. smiles, in the way his mouth kind of turns up, that reminds me of Carol. But he is my baby, and everything Carol has done has been to make me feel good about things. She loves me and I love her.

"When Tom, Jr. is old enough to understand—after he has heard the story of The Stork—we plan to tell him that his Mommy couldn't have a baby, so we found a lovely woman who was willing to help us and his Dad planted a seed and it grew in this other woman and from the day he was born, he has been my son. When he gets a little older, we will take him and introduce him to Carol. I am very proud of my son and I want to share that with her. As Tom, Jr. grows into manhood, if he wants to know Carol better and wants her at his wedding or at anything else, you can count on this: She will be there. But he is my child.

"You know, they say that the greatest gift you can give is to die for your brother or sister. Well, I don't think so. I think the greatest gift is what Carol gave to us. If I were able, and if she were ever in the position I was, I know I would do it for her. This is the deepest gift anyone can possibly give. You know, for a while we were considering letting Carol give Tom, Jr. a brother or sister. But after the first insemination didn't take, we called it off. God— and Carol—had given us enough."

The strongest motivation of couples seeking surrogate mothers is to have a blood tie to the child. One of my clients, Phil, a black man, describes it this way:

"Seven years ago, we adopted a black child. I don't think we could find a better kid than mine anywhere. Now, I have been a father to him, a friend to him, but I cannot be a brother. He is at the point where he asks me, 'Where is my brother?'

"Now, when my wife first had her hysterectomy, I was a basket case. I almost went berserk. I thought the doctor was a quack, that the hysterectomy was not necessary, and so on. I went through a lot of different head trips. Then, we adopted. Now, I know I could go out and adopt another black child in a minute. There is a lockup on white babies, but a black baby you can get in a minute. But you know, just because I am black, I mean I don't just want to go and grab and hit and miss, either, OK? So, when I heard of the surrogate mother, I thought this might be for us. I want a biological connection to my next child. Instead of just shooting the dice, we'll have some shot of knowing what is happening. I don't care what other people might say about us. This is my decision and my wife's decision. We have decided we want a blood connection."

Phil's wife, Barbara, added:

"I will be jealous at first of the surrogate mother. I will be a little uneasy meeting her. But I am secure in my relationship with Phil. We have gone through a lot together. I am not worried about his getting romantically involved with the surrogate mother. And I will think of the child as mine. Giving birth is a piece of cake compared to what you have to do in raising the child."

The motivations can be mixed and strange—but still solid—as in the case of Don, Sharon, and Sari.

Don is a policeman who always hated kids because once a group of teenagers taunted him while he was trying to change a tire along the highway. Sharon, his wife, had formerly been married to a man with seven children fom a previous marriage. Sharon has had several ectopic pregnancies and figured that God was punishing her for her former drug addiction. She thought it was her duty in life to care for others' children, that she would never have her own. But, after divorcing her first husband and marrying Don, she "found out what it meant to be in love. All of a sudden, she wanted children, but the doctors told me it was impossible." Don, loving Sharon, discovered, "She has changed my mind about children. I think it would be great to raise and love kids with Sharon." Their only hope is the surrogate mother. The one they chose, Sari, wants to do it for them without payment because "I love my own son so much and because when I had him I was only sixteen and couldn't really appreciate the experience. This is a chance to relive the experience without having the responsibility. I want Sharon to be as happy as I am." Sari's boyfriend approves, though he is not readily available for consultation. He is in jail on a drunken-driving charge. Yet psychiatric reports indicate that these three people are competent to pursue surrogate parenting.

As is true of all the elements of surrogate mothering, the experts, in this case the psychiatrists, can talk only theory. The people who are doing it are talking from their hearts. Most are doing the right thing for themselves.

My psychiatric consultant, Dr. Parker, has a novel theory about the surrogate mother. He calls it "an informed speculation," and it is this.

The growth of the phenomenon will be resisted—and limited— by some irrational fantasies on the part of society. Dr. Parker has widely studied the psychology of pregnancy and child birth and has co-authored a paper in the *Journal of the American Psychoanalytic Association* called, "The Stork Fable—Some Psychodynamic Considerations." This is his hypothesis:

Strong opposition to the surrogate-mother concept will, in many cases, be due to the fact that the concept triggers unconscious fantasies of adultery and incest. Although the surrogate mother is artificially inseminated and often does not even meet the biological father, Dr. Parker explains, to many adults her very existence will trigger anxieties and guilt about sexual intercourse. He says it all goes back to Freud and Oedipal complexes. In other words, the surrogate mother may remind many people of the represessed fantasies they may have had about having sex with their parents, or others, and their guilt may make them rise up and in knee-jerk fashion, condemn the surrogate mother. Also, Dr. Parker believes that our own unacceptable anger and hostility towards children may be stirred up and expressed by an irrational condemnation of the surrogate who will give up the child she bears. Such irrational opposition, he says, should be identified and discredited.

Certainly, there are enough genuine problems presented by the surrogate mother that we do not need any that only exist in fantasy.

THE MORAL ISSUES

The question: By promoting the surrogate mother, are we doing good? Are we on the side of the angels (in promoting life) or the devils (in violating traditional moral taboos)?

I say we are doing good. But honorable and reasonable men and women can—and do—disagree.

The debate cuts into bedrock values: the varying importance this nation's people put on children and the different ways they think they should be conceived and raised.

The pastor of my church, Divine Child, in Dearborn, Michigan, tells me it is too early for the Church to have an opinion. Should the Church decide that surrogate mothering is wrong, well, that does not bother me. I follow my own conscience.

A generation ago. artificial insemination itself was considered adultery. That has changed. And a generation ago, when John Rock, M.D., a staunch Catholic, took a wild Mexican yam and turned it into a miracle contraceptive—"The Pill," or oral contraceptive—he was widely reviled within the Church. The pill, of course, has changed the world, John Rock is, at ninety-one, still at peace with himself, and the Church finally has come around to common sense. The Church will usually come around to the truth, but it can take a long time.

Today, Americans have become so good at birth control that the government may in the future have to pay people to maintain the population. Charles Westhoff, Ph.D., head of the Princeton University office of population research, predicts that in the year

2020 the U.S. population will begin to decline because of such things as birth control, abortion, and lifestyles that either preclude marriage or allow it only at later ages. He noted, "The idea of paying people to reproduce and raise children seems ironic and even ludicrous in view of our concerns only a few years ago about a population explosion." If Dr. Westhoff's views are even remotely prophetic, certainly there is no reason why infertile couples should not be able to pay surrogate mothers to have their children. The *Detroit Free Press* recently polled readers, "Would pay encourage you to have children?" Some 29 percent said yes, commenting, "Only if marriage doesn't have to follow. . . . It's OK if the government will pay child support. . . . If Aid-To-Dependent-Children mothers can do it now, why not? . . . At today's prices, you can't lose."

I am making my stand on the side of the people who want to create life. It is the greatest responsibility and the greatest privilege.

Middle-class parents will spend $85,000 to raise a child born in 1980, according to population economist Thomas J. Expenslade, a senior research associate for the Urban Institute in Washington, D.C. He said that figure would include the costs of seeing the child through birth, eighteen years at home, and four years at a public university, but warned that his calculations take into account only "direct maintenance costs—childbirth, food, housing, clothing, medical care, and education." Rebutting the Institute's figures, *Parents Magazine* said that the true cost of raising one child by middle-class standards from birth through college is more like $250,000.

I don't know what the accurate figure is, but whatever it is, it is worth it. When I buy my son a baseball bat, the transaction becomes an infinitesimal part of the Gross National Product. But when he uses that bat to hit a home run in a game I am watching, well, that is an emotional transaction that is priceless. I want to help other people be able to share similar wondrous moments with their children.

In a decision potentially important to many women, Wayne

State University in Detroit agreed last year to include single women in its artificial insemination program. The university pledged it will not consider the marital status of applicants, after a lawsuit brought by the American Civil Liberties Union on behalf of a thirty-six-year-old divorcée alleged that the university discriminated through an "unwritten policy" against single women who asked to be artificially inseminated. Mary Ann Smedes of East Detroit, who brought the suit, alleged that her rights were violated because she was excluded from the insemination program solely because she was unmarried. Ms. Smedes was divorced in 1976 after a childless, ten-year marriage and said in her lawsuit that she "desperately wants a child." The university agreed that in the future single women will have the right to artificial insemination.

On a level less relevant to most people, a plan was announced last fall to breed superior children by impregnating intelligent women with the sperm of Nobel Prize scientists. The Nobel sperm bank operates mail-order style, according to a lawyer who applied for motherhood and then described the operation to *Parents Magazine*.

Lori B. Andrews of Chicago said women are chosen after being screened by written application. They check off a blind choice of whose sperm they want, by personal characteristics but not by name, she said. Sperm is then shipped to chosen mothers-to-be by common carrier for do-it-yourself insemination. A two-inch vial of sperm, frozen in liquid nitrogen, is sent in a special two-foot-high container. The shipment is timed to arrive at the time the woman is about to ovulate. Andrews said she met the sponsor of the plan, Robert K. Graham, after presenting herself as a possible candidate for experimental motherhood.

She said she reached Graham, at his Repository for Germinal Choice in Escondido, California, by leaving a telephone message that said: "I'm a well-adjusted, childless Mensa woman and a Yale lawyer." Membership in Mensa, a club for people in the top 2 percent of measured IQ, is a requirement set by Graham for recipients of free Nobel sperm. Graham, who says he has been contacted by more than one hundred women, decides in collaboration with two San Diego physicians who will get the sperm.

Andrews described the procedure:

"They choose on the basis of application forms requesting information regarding IQ, medical background, and achievements. The women who fill out these applications are not informed why these particular doctors qualify to pass judgment on their ability to mother. If chosen, a woman receives a listing of the ostensibly inheritable characteristics, but not the names, of two or more Nobel laureate donors. On the bottom of these forms, to help the woman make her choice, are Graham's own comments [such as a 'very famous scientist—a mover and shaker—almost a superman.'] Once the woman and her husband [the plan is so far limited to couples] make their choice, they are asked to sign a witnessed agreement to 'respond fully to questionnaires regarding offspring which the Repository may submit from time to time.' "

So much for this elitist approach to obtaining artificial insemination. We have no intention to require that our surrogate mothers belong to Mensa because more than one happy couple I have worked with has told me, "Had we looked the world over, I don't believe we could have found a better woman to carry our child than the one we had."

In most dictionaries, the word "mother" is found to mean: "A female parent"; "The origin of anything"; "Characteristics of a mother; native; original"; "To be the mother or author of; to adopt as one's own"; "To cherish, as a mother her child"; "The state of being a mother"; "Having attributes of a mother."

Many women who have never given birth can call themselves "mother" much more honestly than some women who have simply delivered a lot of children. We live in a time when many mothers neglect and, in some sad cases, actually cruelly abuse their own children, children whom they may not have wanted in the first place. I find it hard to believe that anyone could actually be against bringing a wanted child into the world to be cared for my loving parents.

Many newspapers still refuse to carry our ads seeking surrogate mothers. Prominent among the holdouts are *The New York Times,* the *San Francisco Chronicle* (Ironically it was the *Chronicle* that in 1976 got me into this whole movement by, first, carrying a single man's ad for a surrogate mother and, then, by publishing a feature story about his success. I guess they've had enough.), the *Berkeley* (California) *Independent Gazette,* the *Boston Herald-American* (though the *Boston Globe* does), and the *Detroit Free Press* (though the *Detroit News* does and the *Free Press* has prominently reported its backyard story).

Most prominent among the papers that have accepted the ad is the *Washington Post,* though the list includes many others. Some papers will carry the ad one year, not the next, depending upon current management. They all continue to report on surrogate mothering, however.

In Detroit, where the story began, the newspaper reaction is mixed.

The Wayne State University campus paper, *The South End,* which carried our first ads, lashed out at the concept in a 1980 editorial entitled, " 'NO' TO SURROGATE MOTHERS." Accompanied by a cartoon of nurses in single-file carrying babies out of "The Baby Factory," the editorial said:

"WSU students should give a resounding 'no' to the advertisement currently running in *The South End* asking for surrogate mothers to bear children for infertile women. Attorney Noel P. Keane of Dearborn is soliciting a pool of young women. . . . Not only is such crass marketing in children a pure violation to the basic moral fiber, it is also a purely repressive way for the well-to-do to take advantage of those less prosperous. Today, the proposal is intended to help only infertile women. Tomorrow, it may be simply a matter of convenience, with a woman hiring someone younger, and poorer, to have her baby. . . . Shopping for surrogate mothers in the same manner as one shops for a new car is a repulsive practice, which should be put to an end before it gets any further off the ground."

In a more reasoned editorial entitled "Parents by Proxy," the *Detroit News* commended Judge Gribbs' decision disallowing payment to a surrogate mother. ["Children must be protected," the newspaper noted, "from those who would engage in an unscrupulous barter in human lives and from unregulated adoption based on money rather than the qualifications of the prospective parents."]

The newspaper added, "However, the Gribbs decision does not really deal with the deeper social and ethical questions. Artificial insemination for the purpose of adoption is already accepted. . . . How can surrogate fathers be accepted while surrogate mothers are not? Possibilities abound for abuse of proxy mother, child, and adoptive parents. One can imagine baby 'breeders' who peddle for profit the products of stables of paid or exploited surrogates. One can imagine unscrupulous surrogates who conceal genetic defects or physical problems to obtain money. . . . Current law, based as it is on traditional assumptions about biological parenthood, legitimacy, and adultery, has no clear answers. One obvious solution might be to place surrogate motherhood, like adoption, under the financing and regulation of the state. But this opens up possibilities for intentional genetic engineering because the state will be able to decide who can be a surrogate and who can use surrogates.

"The dilemmas of surrogate motherhood, like the controversies over test-tube babies and abortion, will not be solved by one or even a thousand court cases. As reproductive technology continues to sever the once-inescapable ties between sexual intercourse and procreation, society must begin to search for man-made restraints to replace those of nature. Michigan's surrogate-mother case is just one of the many omens of a future revolution in fundamental social ethics."

Detroit News columnist June Brown supported a fee for surrogate mothers. She wrote, "Equal Rights Amendment, where are you now that we need you? For years, men have fathered children by artificial insemination, giving babies to wives whose husbands were sterile. Some of these men were paid for their services. In a turnaround, women want to mother babies by AI and give those babies to married women who are sterile. There are logical reasons why they should be paid for their services—and not just expense money. The state bans payment because it wants to avoid the appearance of selling human beings. However, its attempts are not convincing, since some adoptive parents have paid agencies as much as $6,000 for a home study. No matter who got the money, these parents had to pay before they got a baby. . . . There is a world of difference between selling a child and compensating a surrogate mother for the physical stress of having a child. Whatever amount the surrogate mother receives, it is small compensation for the task she performs. . . . Surrogate Motherhood should be given a chance."

Ethicists disagree. Paul Ramsey, professor of religion at Princeton and outspoken opponent of the conception revolution, told *The New York Times,* "I'd rather every child were born illegitimate than for one to be manufactured. Already women think of themselves as machines of reproduction. Look at the ease with which young women have abortions, so sure that they can have another child any time they want. And now women are selling their bodies for nine months and people are talking about freezing fertilized eggs. Pretty soon, a woman will be able to go to the supermarket and pick out an embryo."

However, Joseph Fletcher, author of *The Ethics of Genetic Control* and chief proponent of the conception revolution, argues in the same forum, "A person begins not at conception but at birth. Artificial insemination and surrogate mothering are tasks of tenderness. Why shouldn't we share our reproductive resources, just as we share our educational and economic ones? We ought to love our neighbors, we ought to help them. That is an important part of our humaneness. Now we are able to give help of a far more intimate and personal sort."

Most church and adoption groups are opposed to surrogate mothering.

The American Lutheran Church says its Statements on Human Sexuality and Sexual Behavior "admit the relevance of the issue (surrogate mothers), but seek greater clarity based upon further study."

Bishop Thomas C. Kellogg, general secretary of the national Conference of Catholic Bishops, provided a copy of his statement on test-tube babies. "I realize that this is not the same question," he wrote, "but some of the principles are applicable." The bishop's statement on test-tube babies cautioned, "Christian morality has insisted on the importance of protecting the process by which human life is transmitted. The fact that science now has the ability to alter the process significantly does not mean that, morally speaking, it has the right to do so."

B. Robert Biscoe, executive secretary of the American Council of Christian Churches, writes, "The parties involved (in surrogate mothering) have not sought God's will in the matter. To circumvent God's law simply so that creation may come about and to say it is scientific progress, that it is better to have a little than none (of the birth process), is wrong. God may have seen fit that none was the better part. We would raise our voice to protest the 'surrogate mother,' and would pray that the Lord give understanding to couples involved in childless marriages, and that scientists and practitioners within the field of genetics be aware of the grave responsibilities of turning the events from what may prove to be God's choice for barren individuals to man's choice, to which there is no comparison."

Jean Paton, coordinator of the adoptee group, Orphan Voyage, writes, "It will be difficult for you to find among adult adoptees one voice that approves what you are doing. This is because surrogate parenting will make it difficult to avoid the problems posed by present-day adoption—secrecy, anonymity, and failure in a steady identity."

Mrs. Lee H. Campbell, president of Concerned United Birthparents, Inc., an organization that provides support and advocacy for parents who—for whatever reason—have surrendered one or more of their borne children to adoption, writes, "The findings of our organization have determined that all mothers establish a primal in-womb bond with their children, a bond that cannot be subsequently eradicated through any legal process or intellectual reasoning. It is the position of our organization that this bond shoud be valued and respected, for the sake of the mental health of both the mother and the child. It is expected that some surrogate mothers may join our organization. Surrogate mothering in which all the parties involved meet each other and maintain a form of ongoing communication would be humane and just. . . . Another concern is that the surrogate mother not be compelled to terminate parental rights before forty-eight hours after the birth, and that a minimum revocation period of fourteen days be extended her so that she can live with the loss and determine its manageability. The sperm donor would need to be aware of the primal dynamics involved. In the event of 'default' (by the surrogate mother) the sperm donor's bond with his offspring should be respected and communication established with the surrogate mother and his child, possibly to include joint custody or visitation. In sum, no party in surrogate parenting should be exploited, primal bonding should be valued, and communication between all parties should be established to ameliorate sensations of loss."

After sifting through all the learned commentary, I keep coming back to the memo my office manager, Martha Makridakis, wrote me years ago about the surrogate mother. Although she is repulsed by aspects of surrogate mothering—"Some of the girls volunteering only want a nine-month temporary job with a chance to make a little greenery; it's kind of like a Kelly Girl, or Kelly Belly."— she concluded:

"Why is it when one speaks of donor sperm, we are repulsed? We are not dealing with sex. We are dealing with medical science and technology. We are dealing with the advancement of our society. People have portrayed the scientists and interested couples and the medical profession involved in surrogate mothering as playing God. Was the medical profession playing God in the invention of the pacemaker? The iron lung? The transplanting of kidneys and other vital organs? Did anyone reject these options and say no? If life can be supported, sustained—and given—should it not? Or, as mere mortals, should we do nothing, since we are not the Supreme Being? I have no second thoughts. The zest for life is so great that we must do these things.

"Basically, we are all selfish people. It comes down to the fact that if we are the ones in need, then it's a horse of a different color. It's funny, but when our own personal needs are involved, we seem to be able to condone everything. I would never be a surrogate mother. I am much too selfish. But I will not sit in judgment. It is time we look at surrogate mothering a little closer and a little clearer."

I'm with Martha.

THE NEED FOR LEGISLATION
AND REGULATIONS

My recommendation: Each state should pass laws to *fund* and *regulate* the new surrogate-mother procedures. People want this new option, and the state should make it widely available by paying for it and by regulating it. Enabling legislation can then be enacted through existing adoption agencies. Adoptive parents and prospective surrogate mothers can register with the adoption agencies, and the agencies can determine who is competent to proceed—and how best to go about it. The system will have to be supported by statutes that irrevocably bind both the adoptive and surrogate parents to the obligations of their agreement. Otherwise, there is the potential for people to back off from their agreements, and everything to become a mess.

In the case of "surrogate fathers," we have state legislation and state regulation. This nation's sperm-banking industry is strictly controlled. The Reproductive Council of the American Association of Tissue Banks has drawn up guidelines for sperm banks to use in selecting donors. Essentially, the rules stipulate that to qualify, a man must be as perfect a male specimen as humanly possible: in prime condition; free of inheritable diseases and abnormalities; product of a family with a history of fitness and longevity; mentally alert; and emotionally stable. What's more, all this glowing good health must be reflected in his semen, which has to be of superior rank, as determined by sophisticated tests.

It will take time before guidelines for surrogate mothers can be made as effective as those for surrogate fathers, if ever. But the legislative debate must begin.

First, let's dispel the myth that we are selling babies. There is a black market in white babies, but it has nothing to do with surrogate mothers. It has to do with the shortage of healthy, white babies for adoption and the willingness of those involved—natural mothers, adoptive parents, and lawyers and doctors—to deal in the black market. Prices run as high as $25,000, authorities report, and it is the doctors and lawyers who often make the arrangements and keep most of the money. Rep. Henry J. Hyde (R., Illinois), who is trying to draft legislation to make the interstate sale of babies illegal, estimates that thousands of infants are sold annually. So, surrogate parenting may actually *prevent* the sale of babies.

I have learned my lessons about surrogate parenting on the job, not through theoretical musings. When the legislative debate begins, it will be stormy and controversial, but it must focus on the practical aspects of the surrogate-mother arrangement. Questions like those raised in the *Detroit News* editorial:

"What happens if the proxy mother gives birth to a defective child and the couple refuses to adopt it? Can the surrogate mother sue the father for damages arising from pregnancy? How can the husband be sure he is indeed the father of his 'investment,' short of isolating the surrogate from other male contacts? What if the surrogate mother refuses to part with the child and demands support? If the adopting couple divorces before the child arrives, who is responsible for the child? Is the child illegitimate under the law?"

There are many other questions. What if the surrogate mother has twins? Wants an abortion? Makes a career out of baby-bearing? Advertises her own services?

Beyond this is the *Brave New World* scenario of people shopping at frozen embryo banks for children of certain qualities, depositing the chosen embryo in an artificial womb, and eight-and-a-half months later, presto, a baby!

For now, though, I think surrogate mothering should be legalized, the surrogates should be paid a fee, the adoptive parents should be carefully screened as the surrogates, and the state should assure quality and safety for all parties.

Last year, the West Virginia University School of Social Work, urged the same thing. After an exhaustive study of surrogate parenting and other approaches to infertility, the school concluded that public policy should support the surrogate mother. Project Administrator LeRoy G. Schultz wrote:

"In short, society has surrounded the childless couple with a battery of interferences, illegalities based on outdated facts and values, and red tape, most of which is based on vague, ill-defined definitions of the 'child's best interest.' This is an excuse to hold back innovation.

"In fact, society protects itself first, the child next, and the couple last.

"The state has felt no obligation to help infertile couples per se, unless that helping effort proved useful to itself in meeting other state interests.

"In America, such conditions are fertile ground for individual innovative efforts. Surrogate parenting is one such individual solution. Society should not continue to refuse to recognize this innovative solution to childlessness and allow it to go unregulated.

"It is time for society to acknowledge that surrogate mothering does exist and is already being used, both visibly and underground, and that *all parties involved need state sanction, support, regulation, and funding.*

"Our recommendations are sound and defensible and warrant the serious attention by those state agencies most likely to assist in implementing the research experimentation, and, ultimately, the policy and practice of surrogate parenting."

I could not agree more.

The best news is this. There is now support in both houses of the Michigan Legislature to draft bills on surrogate parenting. I have been sought out by State Senator George S. Hart (Dearborn) and State Representative Richard Fitzpatrick (Battle Creek), as well as the Family Law Section of the Michigan State Bar Association, to help draft proposed legislation.

Rep. Fitzpatrick notes, "We know that passage of such a law will be controversial, but it is time to begin."

I hope this book will be read by everyone involved in the legislative process so that those making the decision on where we are headed should know where we have been.

It is time to either prohibit surrogate mothering entirely or permit it with the proper controls. I am excited to be an important part of that decision-making process.

How nice it would be if Michigan, where this option was created five years ago, should now take the lead in enacting a comprehensive law that guarantees new hope to the infertile.

·13·

The Surrogate-Mother Alternative—Is It For You?

AT THE time this book goes to press, every step in the surrogate-mother scenario remains a risk. By now, the terrain is familiar to me, but it is still hazardous. This chapter will tell you what to expect if you choose the surrogate-mother alternative, and you'll read the detailed agreements, forms, and procedures required for participation. But remember this: They are only paper, only a means of getting what you want—a baby born to a surrogate mother. Until we have clarifying litigation and legislation, the legal status of the surrogate mother will remain unclear.

So much for the bad news. The good news is this: The first children born to surrogate mothers will very shortly be starting school! They represent dreams fulfilled. And the steps I outline in this chapter, though supported by neither clarifying litigation nor enabling legislation, are legal.

Infertile couples can now find and pay a surrogate mother to have their child. And surrogate mothers can now accept a fee for carrying the children of others. Here's the way it works.

FOR ADOPTIVE PARENTS

I am now representing two kinds of couples: those who can afford to pay a fee to a surrogate mother and those who cannot. Of the women volunteering to be a surrogate mother, some want to be paid and some do not. Most, however, do, so your chances of quickly finding your surrogate mother are better if you can afford to pay a fee. The fee I have set for the surrogate mother is $10,000, no more, no less. Couples paying a fee can expect a total cost of about $20,000. Those who cannot afford a fee and who are lucky enough to find a surrogate motther who does not want one can expect a total cost of anywhere from $5,000 to $7,500.

The first interview will cost $100 and will take forty-five to ninety minutes. I ask the couple to come to my office in Dearborn, Michigan, for this first appointment. We zero in on one overriding concern. Namely, that whether or not we are paying her, there is always the possibility that the surrogate mother will not give the child up. We talk about this over and over and from every possible angle because I want the couple to understand that I cannot guarantee they will get the child they want. Until the couple has adopted the child or until a single man has taken custody of the child, there is always the worry that the surrogate mother can change her mind. So that's the Number One topic of concern.

Of course, many of these couples will say, "Well, we don't have children now, so if we find a surrogate mother and she later backs out, so what? We're not out any more than when we started." Not so. You're out not only money, but, more importantly, you're out emotionally. It can be a big crash from the ecstasy of thinking you're about to have a baby to the agony of having him or her snatched away from you.

Now, contractually, we will have an agreement that says the surrogate mother must return all monies and expenses paid if she does not surrender the child, but if she breaks her word on the essence of her promise there is little reason to think that she will keep it on the extraneous. In any event, getting one's money back is apt to be scant consolation. So we confront this possibility head on. The other major question I ask in this first interview is whether or not the couple is prepared to pay a fee of $10,000 to the surrogate mother in related cases. If so, we will look for paid surrogates. If not, we will look for surrogates volunteering strictly for medical expenses.

I then ask the couple to return home, think things over, and give me their answer in a week or so. I also ask them to complete a questionnaire designed by a psychiatrist. If we decide to proceed, my fee is $3,000 for either a volunteer surrogate or a paid surrogate. In either case, the legal fee is for work that cannot be guaranteed and the fee is absolutely nonrefundable. If things work out, the fee will cover all legal work right through adoption; if things do not work out, the fee will have covered the attempt.

CONFIDENTIAL PARENTAL
INTAKE FORM FOR
SURROGATE MOTHER PROCEDURE

Please fill out this form as truthfully and completely as possible. Feel free to use more spaces if you need it. Each applicant of a marital couple must fill out a separate form, as all questions may not apply to you.

Name: _____

Address: _____

Home Phone: _____ Birthdate: _____ Religion: _____

Social Security Number: _____ Race: _____

Occupation: _____ Business Phone: _____

Marital and Fertility History
Please give your past marital history including previous marriages and present marital status.

If you are a woman, give a history of all previous pregnancies, if any. How did they end (e.g. miscarriage, abortion, etc.)

Please describe your fertility problem.

What doctors did you see for it?

Has there been any other fertility problems in your family?

Have there been any adoptions in your family?

Psycho-Social History
How do you feel about your (your spouse's) fertility problem?

How has the problem affected your relationship with your spouse?

Have you ever spoken to a mental health professional about your fertility problem or about anything else? Please give details.

Have you or anyone else in your family ever been a patient in a psychiatric hospital? Give details.

How much and how often do you drink liquor or use drugs?

Have you ever had any problems with the law? Please list any arrests, convictions, sentences, etc.

Attitude About Surrogate Mother Procedure
Why do you want to have a child using the surrogate mother procedure?

Have you already tried ADOPTION, ARTIFICIAL INSEMINATION, or IN VITRO FERTILIZATION? If not, why not? If you did try any of them, what was the result of each?

Do you foresee any possible emotional reactions or problems to you or your spouse with the surrogate mother procedure? (For example: anger, resentment, envy, depression)

Which would be most likely to happen? Why?

How will you feel having a child who is biologically related to one of you but not to the other?

Do you think these feelings will interfere with your ability or desire to care for this child?

Attitude About the Surrogate
Please rate the following characteristics of a surrogate in order of importance to you. (Use a scale of one to six with number one being the most important to you)

Married or single _____

Educational background _____

Medical history _____

Physical characteristics _____

Family history of physical and mental illness _____

Personality characteristics and habits _____

Do you think the surrogate will have any emotional reactions or problems?

How do you think she will react to giving up the child?

I, the undersigned, hereby swear and affirm that the above statements are true and correct to the best of my knowledge.

Signature _____ Date _____

Let me explain why married couples can legally pay a fee to the surrogate mother and then adopt the child.

At first, we thought that this was possible only in Kentucky, through a quirk in that state's law (now under challenge) that does not disallow a surrogate mother to be paid and still to terminate her parental rights, thus clearing the way for a possible adoption.

However, as my experience in the field has widened and as my understanding of the law has deepened, I have learned that, for a different reason, payment is also legal in eight other states—Alaska, Arizona, California, Florida, Iowa, Nevada, North Dakota, and Oklahoma.

These eight states allow the payment of a fee in connection with a "stepchild" adoption. Their laws specifically exclude the need to report any payment made in connection with a stepchild adoption. My understanding of the laws in the forty-one other states, including Michigan, is that they specifically require the reporting of all payments connected with adoption and, thus prohibit payments to surrogate mothers. Kentucky's law simply does not cover this eventuality, thus allowing it. So, in nine states— Kentucky, plus the eight with stepchild adoption laws, a married couple can legally pay a surrogate mother. Here's how it works:

If the surrogate mother is single, it is very simple. The natural father can, at the time of birth, file an Acknowledgment of Paternity to place his name on the birth certificate. Next, the surrogate mother relinquishes custodial rights. At this point, the natural father's wife can obtain a stepchild adoption to establish her legal connection to the child.

If the surrogate mother is married, then things get a little more tricky. In most states, the law presumes that the husband is the father of any child born to his wife. Thus, legal procedures would have to be instituted to terminate the presumed parental rights by the surrogate mother's husband and to establish the actual paternity of the man who fathered the child by artificial insemination. This is not that difficult, as we have seen in the case of surrogate mother Jeannette and her husband Marshall, and the adoptive couple, Andy and Nancy. After this procedure, we proceed as before—the surrogate mother relinquishes custody, the natural father assumes custody, and his wife accomplishes the stepchild adoption.

These paid adoptions will require the establishment of residency (though often without actual relocation) in the nine states that currently allow them. We are researching the laws of the other forty-one states to see if they, too, might, through some new understanding, allow payments. Beyond that, we are considering the possibility of paid adoptions in foreign cuntries that would be honored in the United States.

Finally, keep in mind that the single man can, without known exceptions, legally pay a surrogate mother because as the natural father, he is automatically on the birth certificate and he does not need to establish a further legal connection. And, of course, couples both married and unmarried can legally pay a surrogate mother if they choose to forego adoption and raise the child in legal limbo. We hope, however, that the possibility will never have to be seriously considered.

Once my clients understand the legal procedures, we move on to the important thing—selecting a surrogate mother. I require that the adoptive parents select their own surrogate mother. I stay out of it entirely. However, before the names of potential surrogates are turned over to the adoptive parents, they will have already been screened by comprehensive medical and psychiatric tests. This assures that they are healthy, both physically and emotionally. Once I have been assured of that, I let the couples make the choice. I turn over to them the complete dossier on each potential surrogate mother, including family background, personal photos, and information about her children, if any. Then, I wish the adoptive parents well.

There is one other major choice the adoptive parents must make—whether or not they want to deal directly or anonymously with their surrogate mother. Of course, we also give the same choice to the surrogate mothers. If either party prefers anonymity, then that is the way it must be. If both prefer to get to know each other well, then so be it.

Once the adoptive parents have chosen a surrogate mother, it is time to talk costs and contracts. Actually, "contract" is too strong a term. Since the surrogate-mother arrangement does not yet have the force of law, it is best to refer to it as an "agreement." It is also important to remember that I represent the adoptive parents only, not the surrogate mother. However, I do require that the adoptive parents pay $200–$500 for independent legal representation to the surrogate mothers. This is to assure that the surrogate mothers do not rashly enter into a legal agreement without benefit of expert counsel. The adoptive parents have a choice of two basic agreements with me (agreements between couples and surrogates will be discussed later):

If the surrogate mother is an unpaid volunteer, then the adoptive couple must sign an "agreement of understanding," which releases me from all liability in the event of an untoward or unsuccessful result. We simply promise to do our best for a fee of $3,000. Only court-approved medical expenses can be paid.

The agreement between legal counsel and the adoptive couple in cases involving a volunteer (unpaid) surrogate mother reads as follows:

AGREEMENT OF UNDERSTANDING

Mr. and Mrs. _____ of _____ , have contacted Noel P. Keane and requested that he assist them in attempting to locate a "surrogate mother" to be artificially inseminated with the semen of Mr. _____ , and who will deliver a child and then return the child to Mr. and Mrs. _____ by means of adoption.

Mr. and Mrs. _____ have agreed to pay to Noel P. Keane, the sum of $3,000.00 as attorney fees.

It is expressly understood that Mr. Keane *has not* guaranteed any of the following:

a) That in fact a surrogate mother will be found;
b) That Mr. and Mrs. _____ will in fact receive a child;
c) That the surrogate mother, if found, is artificially inseminated and does deliver a child, that she in fact will give up the child to Mr. and Mrs. _____ .

It is further understood that no portion of the attorney fee paid to Noel P. Keane is refundable, regardless of the amount of time expended in this matter, and that the said fee shall include all matters pertinent hereto, up to and including the adoption proceedings, if same take place in the State of Michigan.

It is further understood that the undersigned will be responsible for any and all charges and/or bills related to advertising, et cetera, regarding this matter, and that the fee heretofore mentioned does not include these charges for advertising.

It is further understood and agreed that the undersigned shall be solely responsible for the final selection and determination of the surrogate mother. That the undersigned will hold Noel P. Keane harmless from any and all problems which may be encountered with the surrogate mother or from any actions on the surrogate mother's part. Noel P. Keane's only participation as to the surrogate is to furnish information, recommend and give advice as requested by Mr. and Mrs. _____ , but in no way, will he be responsible for the selection of the surrogate.

It is further understood and agreed by the undersigned that they shall be responsible for any and all expenses related to this undertaking, including but not limited to, medical, transportation, advertising, et cetera.

It is further understood that any and all expenses paid to the surrogate mother *must be approved* by the court that has jurisdiction over this matter.

It is further understood that Mr. and Mrs. _____ will hold Noel P. Keane harmless from any and all liability associated with this undertaking.

Mr. and Mrs. _____ have expressly agreed and understand THERE IS ABSOLUTELY NO REFUND ON ATTORNEY FEES IN THIS MATTER.

_____
MR.

_____
MRS.

Dated: _____

If the surrogate mother is paid a $10,000 fee, then I enter into a more elaborate agreement with the "natural father," who, of course, will be legally bound by any untoward or unsuccessful results.

The agreement between legal counsel and the natural father in cases involving payment of the $10,000 fee to a surrogate mother reads as follows:

AGREEMENT

Mr. _____ , (hereinafter referred to as "natural father") hereby retains Noel P. Keane to assist him in drafting an appropriate agreement between himself and a prospective surrogate mother and her husband if said surrogate is married, wherein the surrogate will be artificially inseminated with the semen of Mr. _____ , the natural father. During the pregnancy and upon birth of said child*, Noel P. Keane will institute and represent the natural father in the necessary and allowable proceedings contemplated by all parties as evidenced in the aforementioned surrogate contractual agreement. In the event the first surrogate selected by _____ , does not become pregnant or miscarries, Noel P. Keane shall be under a further obligation to negotiate with additional prospective surrogate mothers on behalf of Mr. _____ .

(1) Mr. _____ hereby pays to Noel P. Keane compensation for his services hereunder the sum of $_____ plus expenses. Said expenses are to be itemized periodically and billed to Mr. _____ .

(2) It is expressly understood that Noel P. Keane does not guarantee or warrant that the surrogate will in fact conceive a child fathered by Mr. _____ . Nor does Noel P. Keane guarantee or warrant that if said child is conceived, it will be a healthy child, free of all defects; nor that the surrogate and her husband will comply with the terms and

---

*Child is defined as all children born simultaneously as a result of the insemination contemplated herein.

provisions of the contract entered into between Mr. _____
and the surrogate and her husband. Subsequent to drafting the appropriate
agreement for Mr. _____ and the surrogate and her
husband, Noel P. Keane agrees to negotiate said contract on behalf of Mr.
_____ with the surrogate and her husband and their legal
representative.

(3) Noel P. Keane agrees to report to Mr. _____ on the
progress of the insemination and pregnancy and oversee, by reviewing
medical records, the surrogates's compliance with the terms and conditions
of the contract. Noel P. Keane shall be under no obligation to disclose the
identity of the surrogate to Mr. _____ or any member of his
family.

(4) Noel P. Keane agrees to advise Mr. _____ on
applicable law only as it relates to all matters relevant to the surrogate
proceedings. Noel P. Keane further agrees to institute and represent Mr.
_____ in all proceedings necessary to have Mr.
_____ 's name placed on the child's birth certificate.

(5) Mr. _____ recognizes and assumes the risk that the
surrogate procedure has never been legally tested and that as such this
procedure is a case of first impression. Mr. _____
understands Noel P. Keane cannot guarantee his name will be placed on
the birth certificate or that the surrogate's rights to the child can or will be
terminated. However, Noel P. Keane agrees to use his best efforts and
conduct all necessary and allowable procedures in order to do so.
Therefore, Mr. _____ accepts the fact that Noel P. Keane
cannot advise him of all the legal procedures and implications which may
occur incident to said surrogate procedure, but, he nevertheless, assumes
all possible legal risks.

(6) It is further understood that no portion of the fee paid to Noel P.
Keane is refundable regardless of whether Mr. _____ ever
receives a child pursuant to the contract entered into between Mr.
_____ and the surrogate, assuming Noel P. Keane complies
with his duties and obligations hereunder.

(7) Mr. _____ further agrees that he will hold Noel P.
Keane harmless from any and all liabilities associated with the surrogate
mother procedure.

(8) Mr. _____ hereby agrees to assume the legal and

medical risks incident to the surrogate procedure, both known and unknown.

(9) In the event of litigation between Mr. _____ and/or his family or estate, and the surrogate and/or her husband and/or any state, nation, governing body or party, Noel P. Keane will not be required to represent Mr. _____ .

(10) Prior to signing this Agreement, each party consulted with an attorney of his own choice and the terms and legal significance of the Agreement and the affect which it has upon an interest of each party. Each party acknowledges that he fully understands the Agreement and its legal affect which it has upon any interest of each party. Each party acknowledges that he fully understands the Agreement and its legal affect, and that he is signing the same freely and voluntarily and that neither party has any reason to believe that the other did not understand fully the terms and effects of the Agreement or that he did not freely and voluntarily execute said Agreement.

(11) No provision in this Agreement is to be interpreted for or against any party because that party drafted the provision.

(12) In the event that any of the provisions of this Agreement are deemed to be invalid or unenforceable, the same shall be deemed severable from the remainder of this Agreement and shall not cause the invalidity or unenforceability of the remainder of this Agreement. If such provisions shall be deemed invalid due to its scope or breadth, then said provision shall be deemed valid to the extent of the scope or breadth permitted by law.

_____   _____

Natural Father   Date

State of _____   )
) SS
County of _____   )

    The foregoing instrument was acknowledged before me this _____
day of _____ , 19_____ , by
_____ .

_____

NOTARY PUBLIC

My commission expires: _____

_____   _____

NOEL P. KEANE, Attorney at Law   Date

State of Michigan)
) SS
County of Wayne)

The foregoing instrument was acknowledged before me this _____
day of _____ , 19_____ , by NOEL P. KEANE,
Attorney at Law.

_____

NOTARY PUBLIC
Wayne County, Michigan

My commission expires: _____

FOR SURROGATE MOTHERS

The women currently volunteering as surrogate mothers—
either paid or unpaid—are responding either to our advertisements
or to news reports. The news stories are varied, but the ads come
in two basic types—those for volunteers and those for paid surrogates.

The ad for volunteer surrogates, which is currently running in
several major newspapers across the country, reads as follows:

INFERTILE MARRIED COUPLE LOOKING FOR
WOMAN TO BEAR CHILD FOR THEM.
CONCEPTION TO BE ACHIEVED THROUGH
ARTIFICIAL INSEMINATION SUPERVISED BY
MEDICAL DOCTOR. CHILD TO BE GIVEN TO
COUPLE THROUGH ADOPTION. ALL EXPENSES
PAID. ALL RESPONSES CONFIDENTIAL. RESPOND
TO: NOEL P. KEANE, ATTORNEY, 1129 PARKLANE
TOWERS EAST, DEARBORN, MICHIGAN. 48126. (313)
336-9290.

The ad for paid surrogates, which also is running in several major newspapers across the country, reads as follows:

COUPLE UNABLE TO HAVE CHILD. WILLING TO
PAY $10,000.00 FEE AND EXPENSES TO WOMAN TO
CARRY THEIR CHILD. CONCEPTION TO BE BY
ARTIFICIAL INSEMINATION. PLEASE CONTACT
NOEL P. KEANE, ATTORNEY, 1129 PARKLANE
TOWERS EAST, DEARBORN, MICHIGAN 48126. (313)
336-9290. ALL RESPONSES CONFIDENTIAL.

In either case, the ads will prompt calls or letters to my office.

Initially, I am looking hard at four basic questions—the woman's age, marital status, height and weight, and if she has children or not. Ideal answers would be twenty-fiveish, single or divorced, five-foot-five to five-foot-eight with proportional weight, and two children. The idea, of course, is to find a woman who will deliver—and relinquish—a healthy baby. It is believed that women who already have children can more easily relinquish a surrogate child. With single or divorced women, of course, we do not have to worry about a husband complicating the surrogate-mother agreement.

If the potential surrogate mother measures up on these basic four questions, I then ask her to complete a detailed "Surrogate Mother

Questionnaire," and return it with photos of herself and her children, if any.

The questionnaire reads as follows:

SURROGATE MOTHER APPLICATION
Please type or print clearly

Date of Application ____/____/____   Married ☐ Single ☐ Widow
          month   day   year   Separated ☐ Divorc

Name _____
      last   first   middle

Address _____
      street   city   state   zip

Home Phone No. _____ Age _____ Date of Birth ____/____/_
           area code   number   month   day

Social Security No. _____ Drivers License No. _____
                                    state   numbe

Occupation _____ Business Phone No. _____
                                    area code   num

Employer _____ Employer's Phone No. _____
                                    area code   num

Employer's Address _____
          street   city   state   zip

Husband's Name (if applicable) _____
                             last   first   middle

Husband's Occupation _____ Business Phone No. _____
                                   area code   num

Husband's Employer _____

Employer's Address _____
          street   city   state   zip

Dates of all marriages _____

Dates of divorces _____

Other _____

City, County & State of all marriages _____

ımber of Pregnancies _____ Date of each pregnancy _____

ımber of Miscarriages _____ Date of each miscarriage _____

ımber of Abortions _____ Date of each abortion _____

ımber of Stillbirths _____ Date of each stillbirth _____

sent Obstetrician/Gynecologist _____ Phone _____
                                                              area code   number

dress _____
        street   city   state   zip

ımber of children at home _____ List names, ages, birthdates & addresses of all

ldren: _____

_____

_____

_____

sent Pediatrician _____ Phone No. _____
                                                        area code   number

dress _____
        street   city   state   zip

:e _____ Blood Type _____ Allergies _____

ight _____ Weight _____ Hobbies _____

ınic _____ Education _____

ır color _____ Eye color _____ Complexion _____ Religion _____

> you smoke cigarettes? _____ How often? _____

> you drink alcohol? _____ How often? _____

e you presently using marijuana? _____ How often? _____

ve you ever used marijuana? _____ How often? _____

Have you ever used illegal or unprescribed drugs? _____ What drugs & how of

_____

Are you presently using illegal or unprescribed drugs? _____ If so,

drugs and how often? _____

Please list all medications you are presently taking and the reason(s) for each: ____

_____

What birth control method do you use? _____

Do you have any congenital diseases in your family? _____

_____

Medical Insurance: Yes ☐ No ☐ Maternity Benefit Coverage _____

_____

Surgery: Yes ☐ No ☐ Reasons and results of surgeries _____

_____

Reasons for applying for surrogate procedure _____

_____

_____

SURROGATE MOTHER INTAKE FORM

Please fill out this form as truthfully and completely as possible. Feel free to use an extra sheet if you need it. Also please enclose a recent picture of yourself.

NAME

ADDRESS

PHONE NUMBER   BIRTHDATE   RACE   RELIGION

Personal History

What is your marital history and what is your present marital status including children?

Give your history of *all* previous pregnancies including physical and mental problems during and after the pregnancy.

How did each pregnancy end (e.g. delivery, miscarriage, abortion, etc.) and how did you react to each emotionally?

List all serious illnesses, hospitalizations and surgery. Are you presently taking medication? If so, why?

Have you had any previous therapy with a psychiatrist or any other mental health professional? When and why? Please specify in detail. Were there any previous psychiatric hospitalizations? Please give details.

Have you ever had any problem with drug or alcohol abuse? Please explain.

How far did you go in school?

Please give a brief employment history.

Have you ever had any problems with the law? Please list any arrests, convictions, sentences, etc.

Family History
Are your parents still living? If so, what is their age and health? Do they have any serious illnesses either physical or mental? If they are not living, when and how did they die? How old were they?

Please answer the same questions for your children.

Do any illnesses (physical or mental) run in the family? If so, which ones and to whom?

Why do you want to be a surrogate mother? (Why do you want to get artificially inseminated, carry the child, and then after delivery give the child to the biological father?)

To what extent is payment for services a necessary requirement for you?

Of all the possible ways of satisfying the above needs, wants, and desires you listed, why do you want to satisfy them in *this* particular way?

Would you participate in this procedure *only* for a *married* couple who could not have a child of their own? Why or why not?

Do you foresee any possible emotional reaction or problems to the surrogate mother procedure? Which would be *most likely* to happen to you? Why?

Who would you have to help you with getting any emotional support during the entire procedure (e.g. spouse, other relative, friend, etc.)?

If married, how does your husband feel about your participation?

Please attach recent photograph of applicant and all children. These photographs cannot be returned.

Please include a family medical and genetic history tracing back as far as possible.

I, the undersigned, hereby swear and affirm that the above statements are true and correct to the best of my knowledge.

Signature _____   Date _____

I carefully check these questionnaires to see if the woman responding to our ads is a suitable candidate to be a surrogate mother. If so, I ask her to come to Detroit for comprehensive medical and psychiatric exams. The physicians conducting these evaluations will simply report back to me as to whether or not the candidate is physically and emotionally qualified to be a surrogate mother. If she passes these tests, I then turn her name and records over to the prospective adoptive parents, who must make the final choice.

I require all potential surrogate mothers to sign a "Release & Hold Harmless Agreement." This agreement, like the ones with the adoptive parents, simply releases legal counsel from any and all liability associated with an untoward or unsuccessful result. A key part of this agreement is the waiver by the surrogate mother's husband—if she is married—of any and all claims in the event of a mishap. As I have stressed before, I prefer to deal with single surrogates.

The agreement with the surrogate mothers and, if married, their husbands, reads as follows:

RELEASE AND HOLD HARMLESS AGREEMENT

I, _____ , (hereinafter referred to as "Surrogate"), and _____ her Husband, if married (hereinafter collectively referred to as "Surrogate"), have applied to NOEL P. KEANE, Attorney at Law, to be considered as a surrogate mother of a child for an unknown male individual. It is my desire to enter into a fee paid contract whereby I will be artificially inseminated by a doctor for the purpose of becoming pregnant. Upon birth, I (We) will subsequently surrender my (our) custody rights to said child in favor of the child's natural father (whom we will never meet or know the identity of) and where necessary and permitted by law terminate all parental rights to said child.

I, _____ , Surrogate Mother, represent that I am healthy (both physically and mentally) and am capable to the best of my knowledge of conceiving and carrying a fetus to term.

We, as Surrogate and Husband, if married, represent that we were
married at _____ , on _____ , 19_____ ,
and that we have cohabited together as man and wife since that date.

I (We) undersstand that several attempts at artificial insemination may
be necessary, and that NOEL P. KEANE, Attorney at Law, does not
guarantee that pregnancy or full term pregnancy will result from artificial
insemination. I (We) have been advised as to the potential psychological
implications that the birth of a child or children through the Surrogate
Parent Program via artificial insemination may have on our marital
relationship and our family.

I (We) agree with and will comply with the following policies:

1. Under no circumstances shall I (We) require that the name of the
donor of the semen be divulged to us or to anyone else, and accordingly,
forever waive all rights, if any, that I (We) may have as to the name,
identity, or any information of any kind concerning the donor.

2. I (We) recognize that surrogate parenting is a new procedure, that
the laws relevant thereto are unclear in many areas. I (We) have therefore
retained our own independent legal advisor.

3. I (We) release NOEL P. KEANE, Attorney at Law, from any and
all liability and responsibility of any nature whatsoever which may result
from the complications of childbirth or delivery or from the birth of an
infant or infants abnormal in any respect, or from the hereditary
tendencies of such issue, or from any adverse consequences which may
arise in connection with, or as a result of the artificial insemination herein
authorized. However, nothing in this agreement shall be construed as an
attempt by NOEL P. KEANE to exonerate himself or limit his liability in
the event of personal malpractice.

4. It is acknowledged by all parties hereto that the persons referred to in
the contract herein are entering into this contract for the benefit of
themselves and as a good will gesture and effort for the prospective born
child and the person referred to in this contract as the "natural father".

_____   _____

Surrogate   Husband, if married

Having completed these preliminary forms, we are ready for the
basic agreement—the "contract" between adoptive parents (only

the husband, or "natural father," signs the contract with a paid surrogate) and the surrogate mother.

I explain to all parties that the artificial insemination will be accomplished by a licensed physician—unless otherwise preferred—and that the surrogate mother is expected to obtain during her pregnancy and childbirth medical and obstetrical care of the highest quality.

Basically, the agreements break down as follows:

If the surrogate mother is a volunteer (unpaid), then *the couple* agrees to pay all court-approved medical expenses during the pregnancy and six weeks postpartum period; to pay for all paternity testing; and to accept responsibility for the child regardless of its health. If the surrogate mother is paid, *the couple* further agrees to pay $10,000 to the surrogate mother for her loss of time from otherwise gainful employment; to purchase term life insurance policy on the life of the surrogate mother to be effective for one year from the date of conception; and to compensate the surrogate mother at a reduced rate in the event of miscarriage.

In all cases, *the surrogate mother* agrees to submit to complete physical and genetic examinations; to submit to psychiatric examinations; to comply with all medical instructions of the inseminating physician and/or her private physician; to terminate her parental rights and allow adoption by the couple; and to submit to paternity testing. If paid a fee, the *surrogate mother* further agrees to reimburse the couple for all payment, expenses, and legal fees in the event custody is awarded to the surrogate mother and legal action ensues.

Presently, the overwhelming majority of our agreements are between adoptive couples who can afford a fee and paid surrogate mothers. However, we also represent couples who cannot afford to pay a surrogate mother—I am not going to let the poor people who started this phenomenon be squeezed out—and surrogate mothers who want nothing but medical expenses. Three other unusual developments deserve notice:

Single men are increasingly seeking surrogate mothers as a solution to having children without romantic entanglements;

Likewise, some single women are seeking surrogate mothers for the same reason as single men. Unlike the males, however, the women will have to take an extra step and find a sperm bank or anonymous donor willing to provide the semen for artificial insemination;

Finally, although right now I require that the wife of an adoptive couple and all single women provide proof of infertility, this in the future may not be a prerequisite. If a woman is fertile but chooses nonetheless to have children by a surrogate mother, I am willing to represent her and her husband, provided a big "if" is met. Namely, that we have enough surrogate mothers to first meet the demand from the infertile. Only time will tell if this is the case.

Following are copies of, first, my early streamlined agreement between adoptive couple and the volunteer (unpaid) surrogate mother, and, then, the latest elaborate agreement between the husband of the adoptive couple and the paid surrogate:

STATEMENT OF UNDERSTANDING

That Mr. and Mrs. _____ of _____ are unable to bear their own child.

That _____ of _____ , has consented to carry a child for them.

That as a result of that consent and agreement, _____ will be artificially inseminated with the semen of _____ .

It is the understanding of all the parties concerned that actual and legal custody of the child will be given to Mr. and Mrs. _____ and _____ will cooperate in whatever manner necessary so that this agreement and undefstanding can be brought to a conclusion.

_____
MR.

_____
MRS.

_____
SURROGATE

Dated: _____

AGREEMENT

THIS AGREEMENT is made this _____ day of _____ ,
19_____ , by and between _____ (hereinafter referred
to as "Surrogate"), and her husband, if married, _____
(hereinafter referred to as "Husband") and _____
(hereinafter referred to as "Natural Father").

Recitals

THIS AGREEMENT is made with reference to the following facts:

(1) The Natural Father is an individual over the age of eighteen (18)
years who is desirous of entering into the following agreement.

(2) The Natural Father desires to have a child who is biologically
related to him.

(3) The Surrogate, and her Husband, if married, are over the age of
eighteen (18) years and desirous of entering into the following agreements
in consideration of the following:

Now therefore, in consideration to the mutual promises contained
herein and the intentions of being legally bound, hereby the parties agree
as follows:

I. The Surrogate represents that she is capable of conceiving
children, but agrees that she will not form or attempt to form a parent-
child relationship with any child she may conceive pursuant to the
provisions of this contract and shall freely surrender custody to the
Natural Father immediately upon birth of the child, and where necessary
and permitted by law terminate all parental rights to said child pursuant to
this Agreement.

II. The Surrogate, and her Husband, if applicable, have been
married since _____ and the Husband is in agreement with
the purposes, intents and provisions of this agreement and agrees that his
wife, the Surrogate, shall be artificially inseminated pursuant to the
provisions of this agreement. The Husband will not form a parent-child
relationship with any child the Surrogate may conceive by artificial
insemination as described herein and agrees to freely and readily surrender
immediate custody to the child and where permitted terminate his
parental rights, and further acknowledges he will do all acts necessary to
rebut the presumption of paternity as provided by law including blood
testing.

III. The Natural Father is hereby entering into a written contractual agreement with the Surrogate, whereby the Surrogate shall be artificially inseminated, with the semen of the Natural Father, by a physician. The Surrogate, upon becoming pregnant, shall carry said embryo/fetus(s) (hereinafter referred to as "child") until delivery. The Surrogate and her Husband, if married, agree that they will, surrender custody of the child to the Natural Father immediately upon birth and where necessary and permitted by law institute proceedings to terminate their respective parental rights to said child, and sign any and all necessary affidavits, documents, etc., in order to further the intent and purposes of this agreement. The Surrogate, and her Husband, if married, agree to sign all necessary affidavits prior to the birth of the child and voluntarily participate in any paternity proceedings necessary to have the Natural Father's name placed on said child's birth certificate as the biological father.

IV. The Natural Father and the Surrogate recognize and acknowledge that the attorney(s) for the Natural Father, Noel P. Keane, shall act as agent for the Natural Father in all matters pertaining to this agreement in order to maintain complete confidentiality.

V. The consideration for this Agreement, in addition to other provisions contained herein, whall be as follows:

a. $_____ shall be paid to the Surrogate upon surrender of custody to the Natural Father of the child born pursuant to the provisions of this contract.

b. The consideration to be paid said Surrogate shall be deposited with the attorney for the Natural Father at the time of the signing of this agreement and held in escrow until completion of the duties and obligations of the Surrogate as herein described.

c. The Natural Father shall pay the expenses incurred by the Surrogate pursuant to her pregnancy, more specifically defined as follows:

1. All medical, hospitalization, and pharmaceutical, laboratory and therapy expenses incurred in the Surrogate's pregnancy, not covered or allowed by her present health and major medical insurance, including all extraordinary medical expenses, but excluding any expenses for emotional/mental conditions/problems related to said pregnancy, lost wages, or other incidentals.

2. The Natural Father shall not be responsible for any latent

medical expenses occurring six (6) weeks subsequent to the birth of the child unless the medical problem/abnormality incident thereto was known prior to the expiration of said six (6) week period.

    3. The total costs of all paternity testing.

    4. The Surrogate's travel expenses incurred pursuant to this Agreement.

    5. The Natural Father shall not be responsible for any lost wages of the Surrogate, child care expenses of the Surrogate's children or any other expense not specifically enumerated herein. (See Exhibit "A")

VI. The Natural Father shall pay the cost of a term life insurance policy on the Surrogate's life payable to a named beneficiary of the Surrogate with a policy amount of $_____ and said policy shall remain in effect for six (6) weeks subsequent to the birth of the child.

VII. The Surrogate and her Husband, if married, understand and agree to assume all risks including the risk of death which are incidental to conception, pregnancy, childbirth and postpartum complications. A copy of said possible risks and/or complications is attached hereto and made a part hereof. (See attached Exhibit "B")

VIII. The Surrogate, and her Husband, if married, hereby agree to undergo psychiatric evaluation by _____ psychiatrist(s), designated by the Natural Father or an agent thereof. The Natural Father shall pay for the cost of said psychiatric reviews. The evaluations of said psychiatrist shall be submitted to the Natural Father, absent any information which would tend to identify or allow identification of the Surrogate or her Husband. The Surrogate and her Husband, if married, shall sign prior to their evaluations, a medical release of said psychiatric evaluations.

IX. "Child" as referred to in this Agreement shall include all children born simultaneously pursuant to the inseminations.

X. In the event that the child is miscarried prior to the fifth (5th) month of pregnancy, no compensation, as enumerated in Paragraph V (a), shall be paid to the Surrogate. However, the expenses enumerated in Paragraph V (c) shall be paid or reimbursed to the Surrogate. In the event the child is miscarried, dies or is stillborn subsequent to the fourth (4th) month of pregnancy and said child does not survive, the Surrogate shall receive $_____ in lieu of the compensation enumerated in Paragraph V (a). In the event of a miscarriage or stillbirth as described above, this Agreement shall terminate and neither the Surrogate nor the Natural Father shall be under any further obligation under this Agreement.

XI. The Surrogate and the Natural Father, shall undergo a complete physical and genetic evaluation, under the direction and supervison of a licensed physician, to determine whether the physical health and well being of each is satisfactory. Said physical examination shall include testing for venereal diseases, specifically including syphilis and gonorrhea. Said venereal disease testing shall be done prior to each insemination.

XII. In the event that pregnancy has not occurred within a reasonable time, in the opinion of the Natural Father, this agreement shall terminate by written notice from the attorney for the Natural Father to the Surrogate.

XIII. The Surrogate agrees that she will not abort the child once conceived except, if in the opinion of the inseminating physician, such action is necessary for the physical health of the Surrogate or the child has been determined by said physician to be physiologically abnormal. In the event of either of those two (2) contingencies, the Surrogate desires and agrees to have said abortion. (See Exhibit "C")

XIV. The Natural Father assumes the legal responsibility for any child who may possess congential abnormalities and they have been previously advised of the risk of such abnormalities. (See attached Exhibits "D" & "E")

XV. The Surrogate further agrees to adhere to all medical instructions given to her by the inseminating physician as well as her independent obstetrician(s). The Surrogate also agrees not smoke cigarettes, drink any alcoholic beverages, use any illegal drugs, non-prescription medications or prescribed medications without written consent from her physician. The Surrogate agrees to follow a pre-natal medical examination schedule to consist of no fewer visits than: One visit per month during the first seven months of pregnancy, two visits (each to occur at two week intervals) during the ninth month of pregnancy.

XVI. Each party acknowledges that he or she fully understands this Agreement and its legal affect and that he or she is signing the same freely and voluntarily and that neither party has any reason to believe that the other(s) did not freely and voluntarily execute said Agreement.

XVII. In the event any of the provisions of this Agreement are deemed to be invalid or unenforceable, the same shall be deemed severable from the remainder of this Agreement and shall not cause the invalidity or unenforceability of the remainder of this Agreement, if such provision shall be deemed valid to the extent of the scope or breadth permitted by law.

XVIII. This Agreement may be executed in two (2) or more counterparts, each of which shall be an original but, all of which shall constitute one and the same instrument.

Prepared By:

_____

NOEL P. KEANE
Attorney at Law
1129 Parklane Towers East
Dearborn, Michigan 48126
Phone: (313) 336-8833

I, _____ recognize that there is a signature line on the attached page for signatures by the Surrogate and her Husband, if married, and that in order to maintain confidentiality, I will never see any signatures of said Surrogate and her Husband, if married, although it is our collective intention to enter into a binding legal obligation.

_____   _____
Natural Father   Date

_____   _____
Attorney for Natural Father   Date

_____   _____
Attorney for Surrogate and her   Date
Husband, if married

STATE OF MICHIGAN)
) SS
COUNTY OF WAYNE)

The foregoing instrument was acknowledged before me this _____
day of _____ , 19_____ , by _____ ,
_____ , and _____ .

_____
NOTARY PUBLIC
Wayne County, Michigan

My commission expires: _____

I, _____ and _____
_____ , her Husband, if married, recognize that there is a signature
line on the attached page for signatures by the Natural Father and that in
order to maintain confidentiality, I will never see any signature of said
Natural Father, although it is my collective intention to enter into a
binding legal obligation.

_____   _____
Surrogate   Date

_____   _____
Surrogate's Husband, if married   Date

_____   _____
Attorney for Surrogate and her   Date
Husband, if married

_____   _____
Attorney for Natural Father   Date

STATE OF MICHIGAN)
) SS
COUNTY OF WAYNE)

The foregoing instument was acknowledged before me this _____
day of _____ , 19_____ , by _____ ,
_____ , _____ , and _____ .

_____
NOTARY PUBLIC
Wayne County, Michigan

My commission expires: _____

CONTRACT ATTACHMENT A
STATEMENT OF CONDITIONS
INCIDENT TO THE SURROGATE SERVICE

Pregnancy is by no means a condition to be taken lightly. It is not without risks both from conditions caused by the pregnancy itself as well as from its effects on other non-pregnancy related diseases and conditions. All known disease processes can affect the course of pregnancy and should be taken into account.

Maternal Mortality: Definition of direct maternal death:

> Death of the mother resulting from obstetric complications of the pregnancy state, labor, or puerperium, and from interventions, omissions, incorrect treatment, or a chain of events resulting from any of the above is considered a direct maternal death. (Example—exsanguination from rupture of the uterus).

Maternal deaths per 100,000 live births have decreased remarkably in the past quarter century. In 1959, the maternal mortality rate was 83.3, or one per 1,200 live births; in 1960, 37.1; in 1970, 21.5; and in 1974, 20.8, or one in 4,800 births. There were only 462 *direct* maternal deaths reported in 1974, or one in 6,900 births. (taken from Williams-Obstetrics edited by Pritchard & MacDonald)

For a complete accounting of the complications of pregnancy or the effects pregnancy may have on a given disease state, it is important that you discuss this with your own independent obstetrician. On the following two pages is a partial list of some of the diseases commonly seen during pregnancy, commonly complicating pregnancy or caused by the pregnancy state. It is by no means complete, as all disease states known to man can be seen during pregnancy or complicated by pregnancy. If you have any doubts about these states or how they may relate to you as an individual it is your responsibility to consult with your own independent obstetrician. Only when you are satisfied that the risks of pregnancy are small enough for you should you then sign the contract.

Urinary System: cystitis, pyelonephritis (acute & chronic), renal insufficiency, urinary calculi, acute and chronic glomerulenephritis, nephrosis, polycystic disease of the kidney, acute tubular necrosis, curtical necrosis and postpartum acute renal failure.

Hematologic: anemia from blood loss, inadequate uptake of iron, folic acid & other blood precursors. Hemolysis, hemaglobinopathics Sickle cell anemia, sickle cell hemoglobin C disease, sickle cell thalassemia disease, hemoglobin C and C-thalassemia disease, sickle cell trait, hemoglobin C trait, B-thalassemia, A-thalassemia, polycythemia, thrombocytopenia purpura, thrombotic thrombecytepenic purpura, Von Willebrand's disease, hemophilia A & B, leukemia and Hodgkin's disease.

Cardiac System: Rheumatic heart disease, congenital heart disease, hypertensive heart disease, coarctation of the aorta, coronary thrombosis and ischemic heart disease, postpartum heart disease, kyphoscoliotic heart disease and bacterial endocarditis.

Respiratory System: Pneumonia, thromboembolism and pulmonary infarction, asthma, tuberculosis and sarcoidosis.

Endocrine System: Diabetes mellitus, diabetes insipidus, adrenae hypofunction, Cushing's syndrome, Addison's syndrome, primary aldes terenism, acromegally, pheochromocytoma, porphyria, hyperthyroidism, hypothyroidism, hyperparathyroidism, hypoparathyroidism and obesity.

Venereal Diseases: Syphilis, gonorrhea, granuloma ingainale, lymphopathia venereum and chancroid.

Liver & Alimintary Tract: Viral hepatitis A & B & C, cirrhosis of the liver, acute yellow atrophy of the liver, obstetric hepatosis, cholelithiasis, cholecysititis, hyperemesis gravidarum, appendicitis, peptic ulcer, pancreatitis, intestinal obstruction, careinoma of the bowel, ulcerative colitis, regional enteritis and gingivitis.

Other Viral Infections: Rubella (German measles), cytomegalovirus disease, herpesvirus Hominis infections type 1 & 2, varieella, coxsackie virus disease, mumps, measles (rubeola), influenza, common cold and poliomyelitis.

Bacterial Infections: Scarlet fever, crysipelas and typhoid fever.

Protozoal, Parasitic and Fungal Infections: Toxoplasmosis, malaria amebiasis and coccidiaidomycosis.

Collagen Diseases: Systemic lupus erythematusus, rheumatoid arthritis, dermatomyositis, scleroderma, polyarteritis nodosa, Marfan's syndrome and rheumatic fever.

Diseases of the Skin: Herpes gestationis, melanoma, pruritis and abnormalities of pigmentation.

Diseases of the Nervous System: Carcinoma of the breast, diaphragmatic hernia, rupture of the spleen, otosclerosis, retinitis gestationis and separation of the symphysis pubis.

Obstetric Disorders: Obstetric hemorrhage, acquired coagulatien defects, placental abruption, placenta previa, amnionic fluid embolism, hemorrhage with abortion, ectopic pregnancy (tubal, abdominal, ovarian and cervical), hydatidiform mole, choriocarcinema invasive mole, tumors of the placenta, diseases of the amnion and amnionic fluid, varices, inflammation of Bartholin's glands, condylomas, relaxation of the vaginal outlet, vaginal tumors (Gartus or mullerian), cervicitis, carcinema of the cervix, sacculation of the uterus, acute edema of the cervix, hypertrophy of the cervix, salpingitis and tubo-ovarian abseess, ovarian and uterine tumors, endometriosis preeclampsia-eclampsia, chronic hypertension, uterine dystocia, cephalopelvic disproportion, traumatic injuries to the birth canal, uterine rupture, genital tract fistulas from parturition, postpartum hemorrhage, retention of the placenta, placenta accreta, invension of the uterus, puerperal infection, superficial thrombophlebitis, deep venous thrombosis, pelvic thrombphlebitis, antepartum thrombophlebitis, pulmonary embolism, subinvolution of the uterus, postpartum cervical cerosions, prolapse of the uterus, puerperal hematomas, urinary incontinence, engorgement of the breasts, mastitis, galactocele, enlargement of supernumerary breasts, complete hysterectomy and Caesarean section.

Amniocentesis is a test used by doctors to detect congenital defects of the fetus, usually performed between the sixteenth and twentieth week of pregnancy. Besides Amniocentesis, there are other tests that may presently be employed or that will be available to the physician rather soon, to detect genetic defects of the fetus. They are: Ultrasonography, Radiography, Setoscopy, Maternal Endocervical Sampling, and Maternal Blood and Urine Sampling. The Amniocentesis was first used in the 1930s, but, it was not until about 1970 that the test was "commonly accepted in medical practice." The test is performed by removing a sample of amniotic fluid surrounding the fetus of the mother's placenta with a needle and syringe, and testing the fluid for chromosomal abnormalities. The test is useful in detecting a number of hereditary diseases, for example, Tay-Sachs Disease and Down's Syndrome, but will not detect Sickle-Cell Anemia, which is carried by 7% to 9% of the United States Black population or cystic fibrosis.

Amniocentesis is elective treatent and costs anywhere from $400.00 to $500.00. A doctor should recommend an Amniocentesis only for certain circumstances, specifically if the mother developed Rubella during pregnancy. The mother's age at the time of conception may also require an Amniocentesis. For an expectant mother between the age of 35 and 40 years, the chance of her child being born with Down's Syndrome is one in two hundred and eighty. For the ages of 40 and above, the risk jumps to one in fifty.

Based on these statistics, most physicians in the United States offer Amniocentesis to patients over 35 years of age. Many doctors consider the risks inherent in the test are not justified by the likelihood of detecting defects, especially for women under 40 years of age for whom the incident of defects is only one in two hundred and fifty to three hundred. Statistics also indicate that in less than 1% of the cases, miscarriage may result because of the test.

All Surrogates have been questioned in detail about their family medical history. Part of the reason for doing this was to elicit any genetically related diseases or congenital (birth defects) anomalies. It has been estimated that 3% to 5% of all live births carry some type of genetic defect. These defects are demonstrated as either dominant traits or recessive traits. In a person who possesses a dominant genetic defect there is a 50% to 100% chance of passing this defect. For the offspring to be affected, however, the child must have two parents with a dominant trait. Only one parent need carry the defect in order to have an affected child. Birth defects can occur as either major or minor abnormalities. An example of a major genetic defect would be Tay-Sachs Disease. In this disease the affected child has severe neurologic impairment eventuating in spasticity, paralysis and death within the first two to three years of life. An example of a minor genetic defect would be low setting of the ears. This obviously presents only minor cosmetic problems.

As a result of this high incidence of genetic defects in all live births (3% to 5%) producing both major and minor abnormalities in the child, it would be impossible for anyone to warrant a child to be free from genetic defect. Just as in the case of pregnancy occurring naturally between you and your spouse, a genetic defect could occur as a result of the forthcoming pregnancy with your chosen surrogate. With the information supplied by the surrogate (to the best of her knowledge of her family's medical history) an appropriate genetic tree has been made with information about the state of health of each individual.

CONTRACT ATTACHMENT B
STATEMENT OF NATURAL FATHER
INCIDENT TO SURROGATE SERVICE

I, as prospective Natural Father pursuant to a Surrogate agreement, which I am hereby entering into, realize that there are certain genetic conditions which contraindicate the use of a person's sperm for artificial insemination, and that a Court may find a physician negligent if he allows such fertilization. I therefore state and affirm, that to the best of my knowledge, I do not possess, nor does anyone in my family possess defects, or diseases, genetic in nature, of the following type:

1. Tay-Sachs Disease: A disease primarily found in Jewish East Europeans, which is characterized by failure to thrive, hypertoxicity, progressive spastic paralysis, loss of vision and occurence of blindness, usually with muscular degeneration and optic atrophy, convulsions, and mental deterioration.

2. Sickle-Cell Anemia: It affects 79% of the U.S. Black population. Homozygous carriers of the sickle-cell gene are characterized by the presence of a crescent-shaped or sickle-shaped erythrocytes and peripheral blood. Symptoms include those of leg ulcers, arthritic manifestations and acute attacks of pain.

3. Neurofibromatosis: A familial condition, characterized by developmental changes in the nervous system, muscles, bone and skin and marked superficially by the formation of multiple pedunculated soft tumors (neurofibromatomas) distributed over the entire body associated with areas of pigmentation.

4. Down's Syndrome (Also known as mongolism and tri-somy 21 syndrome): A syndrome of mental retardation associate with a variable constellation of abnormalities caused by representation of at least a critical portion of chromosome 21, three times, instead of twice, in some or all cells; the abnormalities include retarded growth, hypoplastic face with short nose, prominent epicanthic skin folds, protruding lower lip, small rounded ears with prominent antihelix, fissured and thickened tongue, laxness of joint ligaments, pelvic dysplasia, broad hands and feet, stubby fingers, dry, rough skin in older patients and abundent, slack neck skin in newborns.

5. Polycystic Kidney Disease: Characterized by numerous cysts of varying sizes, scattered diffusely throughout the kidneys, sometimes resulting in organs that tend to resemble grape-like clusters of cysts. This disease is congential and may be transmitted by either parent, and probably represents the result of a dominant gene.

DATE

CONTRACT AGREEMENT C
STATEMENT OF CHARGES
INCIDENT TO THE SURROGATE
SERVICE

While all expenses incidental to a pregnancy vary from case to case, the following is a list of *known* expenses which should be considered only as a minimal estimate of the total expenses.

Medical Expenses

The Natural Father agrees to pay the medical expenses incident to the Surrogate's pregnancy. Many of the Surrogates have medical insurance which includes maternity benefits. The policy for the Surrogate only if she did not have the insurance herself. The medical insurance generally covers almost all of the Surrogate's delivery expenses and a good deal of the office visits involved. These expenses are billed monthly.

Transportation Expenses

If it is necessary for the surrogate or Noel P. Keane to travel the cost of same will be billed to the client monthly.

Paternity Testing

A set of highly reliable blood tests is available to determine after the child is born that the child is the biological child of the Natural

Father. This test costs approximately $550.00. If elected, this expense is payable after the child is born.

Surrogate's Fee

This fee is determined by the Surrogate and the Natural Father with Noel P. Keane acting as intermediate. The Surrogate's fee is due prior to the first insemination. This fee is placed in an escrow account at this time. The fee is not paid to the Surrogate until she delivers the child and surrenders custody to the child.

Psychiatric and Psychological Expenses

Each Surrogate must be evaluated by an independent psychiatrist. I generally recommend two (2) evaluations. The average cost is approximately $250.00. Psychological aptitude testing is optional and costs an average of $125.00.

Initial Medical Evaluation

Each Surrogate must be evaluated by a medical doctor. The cost in approximately $250.00, but could be higher depending on the need for testing and further examination.

Surrogate's Attorney's Fees

It is very important for the Surrogate to receive independent legal counseling relevant to the surrogate procedure so that she is aware of any and all legal problems incident to the procedure. The general cost is approximately $200.00 to $300.00.

Court Costs, Xerox and Postage Fees

1. Court Costs—due after the child is born and approximately $100.00.
2. Xerox and postage—approximately $40.00 for contracts, etc.

Legal Fees

This fee covers all legal contract negotiations and representations for the Natural Father. The procedure will include legal proceedings to amend the child's birth certificate naming him as natural father.

Advertising Fee

This fee covers a pro rata share of advertising costs for surrogate. $300.00.

A fourth and final agreement is an escrow arrangement between myself and the adoptive parents. The $10,000 fee for the surrogate mother is placed in escrow—where it earns interest payable to the adoptive parents—until the surrogate mother has given birth and given up the child for adoption. At that time, the surrogate mother is paid $10,000.

As you can see, my initial agreement between the adoptive couple and the volunteer surrogate mother is a model of simplicity compared to the detailed recitals of the agreement between the natural father and the paid surrogate mother.

In point of fact, however, it all gets down to trust. The fifteen-page detailed "contract" for the paid surrogate is no more valid than the fifteen-paragraph agreement signed by the volunteer surrogate. Although the former is admirable in the scope and precision of its intent, there remains that hovering doubt. Neither surrogate nor natural father is bound by the terms. The surrogate may be paid $10,000, but there is nothing to stop her from later demanding $100,000. The couple may promise to take the child rain or shine, but there is nothing to stop him from backing out on a defective child.

Answers to these basic questions await legislation. Which is why I have written this book. So, if you believe that the surrogate-mother alternative should be made widely—and safely—available, please put down this book, take up paper and pencil, and write your local state legislator.

Laws are made for people, and people want the surrogate mother as a revolutionary new option for the infertile. Ultimately, the surrogate mother means hope.

APPENDIX A
Legal Problems of Surrogate Motherhood

Noel P. Keane*

I. INTRODUCTION

THE development of new reproductive technologies, such as artificial insemination, poses a variety of legal questions which often cannot be readily resolved in terms of traditional legal doctrines and categories. Those who employ technically feasible but legally unrecognized solutions to marital or reproductive difficulties often must act without being certain of the legal consequences. Such a state of affairs cannot be reconciled with the recent recognition of a constitutional right of privacy which protects personal decisions with respect to marriage and reproduction.

This article concerns the legal issues raised by the practice of surrogate

*B.S., 1964, Eastern Michigan University; J.D., 1969, University of Detroit. Partner, Keane & Fellrath, P.C., Dearborn, Michigan. The author wishes to acknowledge and express appreciation to Robert C. Black for his efforts and assistance toward completion of this paper.

motherhood by means of artificial insemination. This refers to an arrangement between a married couple who is unable to have a child because of the wife's infertility and a fertile woman who agrees to conceive the husband's child through artificial insemination, carry it to term, then surrender all parental rights in the child. Often, the surrogate mother receives compensation for her services. The final step in the process is typically the father's acknowledgement of paternity and adoption, with his wife, of the child. Through surrogate motherhood, a couple desiring a child need not wait an indefinite number of years for an adoptable baby, as generally happens at the present time. The married couple obtains a child who is the husband's biological offspring—a child for whose existence both husband and wife can feel responsible.

Despite the arrangement's simplicity and advantages for all concerned, surrogate motherhood is fraught with legal difficulties. In most, perhaps all states, a contract providing for surrogate motherhood is probably void. In some states, payment for parental consent to the adoption of a child is a crime. Moreover, the child itself may be considered illegitimate, and some courts have even taken the view that artificial insemination, except between husband and wife, is adultery. The applicable law, whether statutory or decisional, was not fashioned with surrogate motherhood in mind.

If the surrogate mother is married, additional difficulties arise at the adoption stage. In some states, adoption by the donor and his wife may be blocked by an irrebuttable presumption that a child born to a married couple is the legitimate offspring of that couple. The donor-husband and his wife would be unable to adopt the child in such a state, unless direct private adoption is available. Other states regard this presumption as rebuttable, thereby offering a friendlier forum for the adoption proceedings

Use of surrogate mothers is increasing. It may become as well established as its counterpart, artificial insemination by a donor (AID), the procedure by which the fertile wives of sterile husbands are artificially inseminated, usually by an anonymous donor. Between 6,000 and 10,000 children are born annually in the United States as a result of artificial insemination. It has been estimated that at least 250,000 Americans now living were conceived in this way. The circumstances of their birth have already occasioned legislative and judicial action, much of which has implications for surrogate motherhood as well as AID. Overall, however, the law is at best awkwardly adapted, and at worst, hostile to the surrogate motherhood arrangement.

II. ADULTERY AND ILLEGITIMACY

One problem posed by the surrogate motherhood arrangement is the possibility that the relationship between the husband/father and the surrogate mother will be considered adulterous. In some states adultery is a crime, and in many states it furnishes grounds for divorce. An early Canadian decision suggested that the artificial insemination by a donor of a married woman constituted adultery, and a New York decision reached a similar result. Presumably, surrogate motherhood stands on the same footing as AID with respect to adultery since both situations involve impregnation of a woman by a man to whom she is not married and one of the biological parents of the resulting offspring is married to someone else.

In addition to the direct adverse legal consequences, an adjudication of adultery would render any surrogate motherhood contract illegal on the basis that its object was the commission of a crime or that the contract was against public policy.

Even if surrogate motherhood were adultery, insofar as it is relied upon as grounds for divorce, it may be defeated in most jurisdictions by involving the recognized defenses of "connivance," whereby a spouse consents to his spouse's adultery, and "condonation," whereby the aggrieved spouse resumes marital relations after discovering the adultery, and in effect, excuses it.

In AID cases the issue of adultery is closely related to, and seemingly confused with, the issue of the child's legitimacy. A few decisions hold that the child of a married woman artificially inseminated by a man other than her husband is illegitimate. However, because the child of a single surrogate mother is born out of wedlock, he is definitely illegitimate. Traditionally such a status carried numerous legal disabilities, especially with respect to inheritance, although constitutional limitations recently have been placed upon discrimination against the illegitimate.

Recent decisions have maintained that a child conceived by means of AID is legitimate, not the product of an adulterous relationship, at least where AID was with the husband's consent. A 1948 New York decision was the first reported case to hold that such a child is legitimate. In 1968, the California Supreme Court held that a husband who consented to the artificial insemination of his wife by an anonymous donor is deemed the "father" of the resulting child for purposes of the duty of child support. As the court put it, "[c]ategorizing the child as either legitimate or illegitimate does not resolve the issue of the legal consequences flowing from the defendant's participation in the child's existence." Treating the husband as the father serves the statutory objective of assuring support to all children, and "no valid public purpose is served by stigmatizing an artificially conceived child as illegitimate."

Such a child is not the product of an adulterous relationship since there has been no sexual intercourse between a married and unmarried person. The court ridiculed the suggestion that the donor who administered the artificial insemination process had committed adultery with the wife:

> Since the doctor may be a woman, or the husband himself may administer the insemination by a syringe, this is patently absurd; to consider it an act of adultery with the donor, who at the time of insemination may be a thousand miles away or may even be dead, is equally absurd. Nor are we persuaded that the concept of legitimacy demands that the child be the actual offspring of the husband of the mother and if the semen of some other male is utilized the resulting child is illegitimate.

A recent New York decision likewise held that a wife does not commmit adultery with the sperm donor and that the resulting child is legitimate. A number of states have enacted statutes legitimizing children conceived through AID with the husband's consent.

Recent decisions holding that AID is not adultery have corrected legally unjustifiable conclusions to the contrary. Adultery has been defined as "the voluntary sexual intercourse of a married person with a person other than the offender's husband or wife," and as "the sexual intercourse of 2 persons, either of whom is married to a third person." Since AID does not involve sexual intercourse, it cannot be adultery. Contrary decisions apparently adopted the view that adultery can be considered the voluntary relinquishment of one's reproductive capacities to an illicit partner. However, this "is quite inconsistent with the usual definition of adultery, and is really theological rather than legal." Adultery does not depend upon the possibility of conception. Surrogate motherhood, like AID, involves no sexual intercourse. Where the wife consents to a surrogate motherhood arrangement, as where a husband consents to AID, there is no basis for treating the fertilization technique as an act of adultery.

The stigmatization of the child of a surrogate mother as illegitimate is probably unaffected by recent statutory and decisional developments relating to AID. It has been persuasively argued that distinguishing legitimate from illegitimate children for many legal purposes is a denial of equal protection. Many states provide for the legitimation of illegitimate children, or confer the same rights legitimate children enjoy, through acknowledgment of paternity by the father, acknowledgment coupled with reception of the child into the family or in other ways. The terms of any surrogate motherhood contract should provide for acknowledgment of paternity by the husband/father and for the adoption of the child by the biological father and his wife. The offspring of a surrogate mother may be born illegitimate—but he need not remain that way for long.

III. STATUTORY AND PUBLIC POLICY IMPEDIMENTS TO COMPENSATING THE SURROGATE MOTHER

Among the most serious impediments to surrogate motherhood arrangements are statutes in effect in some states which make it a crime to make payments to a (biological) parent in connection with the adoption of his child. Although the evident purpose of these statutes is to prevent the "sale" of infants as if they were property, their language is sufficiently broad—or overbroad—to forbid compensation for a surrogate mother. Thus a California statute makes it a misdemeanor to pay or offer to pay a parent in return for the placement of his child for adoption, or his consent to, or cooperation with the child's adoption. A Michigan statute forbids payment of any money or other consideration in connection with placing a child for adoption or the release of parental rights, except as approved by a court. Parties are required to file an accounting of all fees and expenses which are subject to court approval.

A respected Michigan judge with considerable experience in the domestic relations area has expressed his informal opinion that only the direct medical expenses of the surrogate mother—not the value of her services in carrying the child or even her foregone income—could be approved by the court.

Although such statutes are rarely enforced, their very existence deters surrogate motherhood arrangements. Apart from the possibility of criminal prosecution, such statutes render surrogate motherhood contracts void and unenforceable under the doctrine that contracts requiring an illegal act are unenforceable by any party.

A contract is deemed unenforceable if it contravenes the law or a known public policy. Even without a statute, a court may hold, as did the Georgia Supreme Court, that a contract calling for payment to a mother in return for placing her child for adoption is unenforceable on public policy grounds. If a surrogate motherhood contract is unenforceable, the married couple would be without recourse if the surrogate mother aborted the husband/father's child or decided to keep it, and the surrogate mother would likewise be unable to enforce payment if the married couple failed to pay her.

Unless surrogate mothers can be offered meaningful compensation for their services, very few children will be brought legally into the world in this manner. Pregnancy and childbirth are hazardous, time-consuming, painful conditions which few women can be expected to experience for the sake of someone else unless they receive meaningful compensation. The irony is that the masculine counterpart to surrogate motherhood—the "surrogate fatherhood" of a sperm donor in the AID situation—is apparently lawful in all jurisdictions, enjoying explicit legislative recognition in some, despite the fact that the semen is usually paid for and the sperm donor assumes none of the risk and burdens with an "ovum donor" does.

A. Public Policy—The Child's Best Interest

Statutes like those in Michigan and California serve a legitimate purpose insofar as they forbid the sale of infants as if they were chattels. Children are not the property of their parents and cannot be made the subject of barter. Due to the scarcity of adoptable babies—a scarcity aggravated by the increased availability of abortion and contraceptives as well as other circumstances—the baby black market is flourishing. Prohibitory legislation may well be justified although it is often difficult to enforce. Surrogate motherhood, though, is radically different from baby-buying and presents a situation which was never envisaged by the legislatures who enacted the penal statutes now in force. As applied in such situations, their impact is harmful and as discussed below, their constitutionality is questionable.

Policy reasons underlying the antipathy to payment for adoption are largely inapplicable to the surrogate situation. The principal reason for this policy is undoubtedly a desire to protect and promote the family, which the courts have often identified as the foundation of society. An Illinois decision, *Willey v. Lawton*, held that an agreement between the natural parent and the adopting parents, whereby the latter agreed to pay the natural parent for adoption of the child, was unenforceable as contrary to public policy. The court reasoned that the bartering away of children for a property return "tends to the destruction of one of the finest relations of human life," the parent/child relation. There is merit in the court's decision considering the particular facts of the case. The former husband of a woman who had remarried was in arrears in paying child support, and the couple contracted with the delinquent husband to forego the arrearages and pay $5,000 in return for his consent to their adoption of the child born to the divorced parties during their marriage. Thus an established parent/child relationship between the biological and custodial father and his legitimate child would have been disrupted, and the father's motive in consenting to adoption could only have been economic duress overbearing his desire to keep the child.

In the typical baby-buying situation, an involuntarily pregnant unwed mother gives birth to an illegitimate child whose biological father usually takes no interest in it. Even if the mother desires to keep the child, she is often financially unable to do so. An intermediary whose motives are strictly mercenary brings "buyer" and "seller" together on the basis of the buyers' urgent desire for a child and the seller's financial exigency. Both "adoptive" parents are biologically unrelated to the child, which is removed from the single mother who, despite her perhaps difficult circumstances, may well represent a rudimentary but real "family" for the child. The "adoptive" parents' fitness is not ascertained by anyone, and the biological mother may well experience guilt and pain over reliquishing her child, especially in these circumstances. At least in some cases, a potential parent/child relationship is precluded for reasons unrelated to the child's well-being or the true desires of its biological mother.

Surrogate motherhood is different. A married couple desiring a child which the wife is incapable of bearing herself enters into the arrangement, not to "buy" a biologically unrelated baby, but to bring a child into existence by conscious prearrangement which is, as far as biologically possible, their "own." Without entering into an adulterous sexual relationship which might impair the marriage, the husband arranges to become the child's biological father. The surrogate mother, on her part, consciously chooses to bear a child for another couple with the understanding that she will consent to their adoption of it. The decision to give up the child for adoption is not the product of the adverse circumstances of an unplanned pregnancy. When the child is born, there is already a home prepared for it with its biological father and his wife. The potential for feelings of guilt or loss on the biological mother's part is minimized, though not eliminated.

Realistically, the only true "family" whose future is at stake is the one the child is predestined to enter—that of the childless married couple— not the nominal, intentionally temporary "family" represented by the surrogate mother. Clearly, surrogate mothehood, like AID, *strengthens* the family insofar as it offers a solution for couples whose marriage may well be endangered by a desire for children which is frustrated by one spouse's reproductive incapacity. Whatever implications surrogate motherhood has for the family in the abstract, it means joy and fulfillment for certain real, flesh-and-blood families approaching despair over their inability to realize their parental aspirations.

B. Commercializing Aspect and Black Market Statutes

Ringing denunciations of baby-buying and declarations that children are not property may make stirring reading, but it is difficult to specify precisely why the "commercialization" of a surrogate motherhood arrangement is inconsistent with public policy. In a commercial society, "commercialization" is the usual way in which many individual needs are satisfied. There is no doubt that the financial return may motivate the surrogate mother to make her reproductive capacity available to others. Any broker or intemediary who brings the interested parties together could also act from motives of pecuniary gain, although he may also be acting incidental to a role such as attorney or physician, serving his client's best interests as he sees them. What is important, however, is that the adoptive parents are no more acting upon economic considerations than are married couples who elect to have children. The involvement of third parties whose actions are influenced by the profit motive may well justify regulation of surrogate motherhood agreements, but not their prohibition.

The application of the anti-black market statutes to surrogate motherhood contracts poses a number of problems on the issue of what, if anything, may be paid to the surrogate mother without contravening the statutes. Under the Michigan statute, medical and other "expenses" may apparently be paid, but nothing beyond that. One authority is of the opinion that the surrogate's foregone wages cannot be paid, but this is not clear from the statutory language. If the object of the statute is to prevent anyone from "profiting" from an adoption, it should not be necessary to proscribe payments which merely compensate the surrogate mother's income loss. In a Nevada decison, the issue arose as to whether a newspaper had libelled an attorney by referring to his arrangement of an adoption in which the biological mother was paid for foregone wages as a "black-market" sale of the child. The court stated: "Under any reasonable construction of the term, 'black-market sale' contemplates a sale contrary to regulations with a profit calculated either to compensate for the risk for apprehension or to match the buyer demand which has created the market." The court held that a jury could properly decide, as it did, that compensation for lost wages did not turn the transaction into a sale, stating:

> Appellants contend that the compensation paid for loss of wages amounted to a profit and constituted the transaction a sale. In absence of statute the determination of whether such compensation was proper rested in the first instance with the jury. We shall not disturb their determination, implicit in their verdict, that such compensation did not constitute the transaction a sale. There is nothing to indicate that the payment permitted to the mother to profit from childbirth. To the contrary, it would seem to have been intended simply to prevent her confinement from resulting in pecuniary loss.

One difficulty in applying these statutes to surrogate motherhood contracts is that they relate only to the final phase—the adoption—of a contract which has other important provisions. The surrogate mother is not paid primarily for consenting to the adoption of the child. The services performed which justify substantial compensation consist rather of pregnancy and parturition, together with the risks and limitations which these experiences entail. The statutes do not purport to make it a crime to pay someone for becoming pregnant or having a baby. This omission, of course, confirms that surrogate motherhood was never the intended target of the anti-black market statutes. What the surrogate mother has to offer is what the sterile wife of the biological father unfortunately lacks: the biological capacity to reproduce. The essence of the surrogate motherhood contract is to redress the injustice of nature in conferring this capacity on certain individuals who are able but unwilling to assume parental responsibilities while denying it to others who are willing but unable to do so. Thanks to artificial insemination, the solution of the biological problem is technically simple. What complicates the situation is the legal significance that the state has placed on the fact of biological parenthood. Because the custody of and parental responsibility for the child of an unmarried mother is automatically assigned to her upon the child's birth, it is necessary to terminate the parental rights and bestow them on the biological father and his wife through adoption of the child by the latter. Yet this final stage of the surrogate arrangement is apparently interdicted by the anti-black market statutes.

Because "the statutes prohibiting black-market transactions are normally couched in terms of a prohibition against receiving compensation for child placement," surrogate motherhood contracts appear to be proscribed by the statutory language if it is read literally. But it is certain that surrogate motherhood was not within the contemplation of the legislators who enacted these statutes, and surrogate motherhood contracts present few of the evils of baby-buying. Where statutory language is of doubtful meaning, a reasonable construction must be given to effect the purpose of the statute; the spirit of the statute should prevail over the strict letter to avoid unjust applications and absurd consequences. Additionally, as these statutes carry criminal sanctions, they should be narrowly interpreted. Ambiguities with respect to the ambit of criminal statutes should be resolved in favor of lenity. Finally, even if such statutes render surrogate motherhood contracts technically illegal, it may not follow that they are invariably unenforceable. The rule that contracts requiring an illegal act are unenforceable is not inflexible, and courts must look to the legislative intent before invalidating such agreements. No specific legislative intent to invalidate surrogate motherhood contracts can be shown, since such arrangements have only recently come to the attention of the public, and courts should await explicit legislative direction before invalidating these voluntary agreements among adults.

C. *Common Law Examples*

Several decisions suggest that there is not necessarily a public policy objection to paying compensation incident to an adoption agreement, at least within the family context. A Kansas decision involved an oral agreement between the grandmother and the mother of a child whereby the mother consented to the grandmother's adoption of the child, in return for which both daughter and the child would share in the grandmother's estate upon her death. The grandmother had already taken the child into her home because the mother was financially unable to provide adequate care. Later, all parties concerned consented to the readoption of the child by her own mother and her husband after she remarried and her circumstances improved. In resolving the claims of the mother and child against the grandmother's estate, the Kansas Supreme Court considered whether the contract was against good morals and public policy. For the court it was "fundamental that parents may not barter or sell their children nor may they demand pecuniary gain as the price of consent to adoptions. In this case, though, the motivation for both parties was the desire to provide the best home possible for the child. Under the circumstances, this "family compact" was in the best interests of the child and, accordingly, was not against public policy:

> [A] contract of a parent by which he bargains away for his pecuniary gain the custody of the child to a stranger and attempts to relieve himself from all parental obligation, placing the burden on another who assumes it, without natural affection or moral obligation, but only because of the bargain, is void as against public policy. Such a contract would be the mere sale of the child for money. But the instant case involves a family compact. The proposal for adoption upon which the contract was based came from the grandmother. It was not prompted by self-seeking on the part of the

mother. Implicit in it is the favorable inference that the controlling consideration was the welfare of the two-year-old child. That fact permeates all the circumstances alleged. While the mother received the promise of the grandmother that she would receive one-third of her estate we cannot say that, under all the circumstances alleged and the favorable inferences to which they are entitled, the mother's consent to the adoption falls within the rule that a parent may not transfer his parental rights and duties to another in an attempt to sell or barter his child for his own financial gain.

Although there are differences, in many respects the *Shirk* situation is analogous to the surrogate motherhood situation. The adopting party took the initiative unprompted by maternal "self-seeking." If the "controlling consideration" is the welfare of the child, it obviously serves the best interests of the child, in all but the most extraordinary circumstances, to be adopted by his biological father and his wife rather than remain the surrogate mother's responsibility. Custody of the child is not given to a stranger "who assumes it, without natural affection or moral obligation, because of the bargain"; custody is granted to the child's own biological father—and his wife.

Since both the biological father and the biological mother at the outset have parental obligations toward the child, it is possible to view their contract as a sort of "family compact," although of course it is the compact which gives rise to the family relationship and also provides for its supersession by a different one. The most important difference, in terms of the factors which concerned the *Shirk* court, is the fact that both parties in *Shirk* were found to have acted out of affection rather than pecuniary motives, whereas in surrogate motherhood, pecuniary motivation may be important to the mother, but not the father. Yet this did not prevent the *Shirk* court from approving payment from the grandmother's estate to the *mother* as well as the child. Presumably the best interests of the child could have been served by making the child the sole beneficiary and framing the agreement as a third-party beneficiary contract. If nothing else, *Shirk* suggests that it is going too far to lay down a general rule that payment of compensation for consent to adoption is immoral and invariably adverse to the child's own interests. In surrogate motherhood, as in *Shirk*, the rule should not apply when the adopting

party feels "natural affection" for his own offspring and "moral obligation" for a child he has brought into being.

In 1975 a federal court sustained an agreement similar to the one in
Shirk in terms which suggest that the best interests of the child is the
determinant of whether an adoption contract is against public policy:

> [I]t is not against public policy to enforce an agreement to provide
> for the mother of an illegitimate child in the putative father's will,
> incidental to an agreement to permit the adoption of the child by its
> father, where the adoption was in the best interests of the child and
> pecuniary gain was not the motivating factor on the mother's part.

As in *Shirk,* the court distiguished such a case from baby-buying because
the agreement was between family members: "The fears that approval
of such a policy would lead to the bartering or sale of children are not
borne out where we deal only with agreements between parents or close
family members." Surrogate motherhood contracts, of course, are also
agreements "between parents," or at any rate prospective parents. Cases
like these suggest some judicial willingness to depart from old doctrines
in novel circumstances when the rationales of the old rules may have
limited relevance. The states where these cases were decided, though,
had no statutes outlawing adoption contracts. Absent repeal or revision
of prohibitory statutes in the states where they are in effect, those interested in surrogate motherhood contracts may have to challenge the
constitutionality of those statutes in order to assure their right to form a
family on this basis.

IV. SURROGATE MOTHERHOOD AS A
CONSTITUTIONAL RIGHT

Domestic relations had long been regarded as the virtually exclusive
province of state law; however, in recent years state action in this area
has been increasingly subject to federal constitutional limitations. The
most important of these involves the constitutional right of privacy. A
private realm of family life exists which the state cannot enter and which
as been accorded both substantive and procedural protection. Among

the decisions which an individual may make without unjustified interference are personal decisions relating to marriage, contraception, family relationships, and child rearing and education. The right of privacy means the right of an individual, married or single, to be free from unwarranted governmental intrusion into matters which fundamentally affect a person, such as the decision whether to bear or beget a child. Insofar as they invalidate surrogate motherhood contracts by which individuals effectuate their rights of procreation and familial self-determination, the anti-black market statutes and equivalent judicial decisions appear to invade the protected realm of privacy in the most direct and devastating way.

The statutes are not invalid merely because they affect decision-making relative to procreation and the family. But "where a decision as fundamental as that whether to bear or beget a child is involved, regulations imposing a burden on it may be justified only by compelling state interests, and must be narrowly drawn to express only those interests." The means must be no more restrictive than necessary to accomplish the purpose.

Several possible purposes of the anti-black statutes—namely, the promotion of the family and the prevention of "commercialization" of adoption decisions—have already been examined. The statutes are not narrowly drawn to accomplish either of these purposes. As applied to the compensation of a surrogate mother by a childless married couple, the statutes actually prevent a family from alleviating the childlessness which may endanger its viability. It is not just the traditional nuclear family which can claim the protection of the right of privacy.

As to "commercialization," the issues are somewhat more cloudy. Generally, however, otherwise constitutionally protected activity cannot be deprived of protection simply because it is the subject of commerce. Statutes which make it a crime to *pay* a physician for delivering a baby or performing an abortion would unquestionably be held unconstitutional. Yet to say that a surrogate mother has the right to conceive and bear a child but not be compensated is to make essentially the same argument. What the state cannot overtly prohibit, it cannot indirectly outlaw either. A state-created obstacle need not be absolute to be impermissible. Thus requirements which unduly burden the right to abortion are unconstitutional.

The Supreme Court's decision in *Carey v. Population Services Interna-*

tional furnishes an instructive analogy. Prior decisions of the court had invalidated laws forbidding the use of contraceptives whether by married or unmarried persons. In *Carey*, the Court was faced with a state law forbidding the *distribution* of nonmedical contraceptives to adults except through a licensed pharmacist. The Court held that the distinction between use and distribution was not constitutionally significant; what the Constitution protects is the individual decision in matters of childbearing. By way of example, the Court suggested that a prohibition against the *sale* of contraceptives would be just as repressive as a prohibition against their use:

> Restrictions on the distribution of contraceptives clearly burden the freedom to make such decisions. A total prohibition against sale of contraceptives, for example, would intrude upon individual decisions in matters of procreation and contraception as harshly as a direct ban on their use. Indeed, in practice, a prohibition against all sales, since more easily and less offensively enforced, might have an even more devastating effect upon the freedom to choose contraception.

Because limiting the distribution of nonprescription contraceptives "clearly imposes a significant burden on the right of individuals to use contraceptives if they choose to do so, the restriction was invalid. The *Carey* argument is, if anything, even more compelling as applied to surrogate motherhood than when applied in the contraception context, since the services of a surrogate mother are far too onerous to be provided gratuitously in all but the most unusual situations. Just as a prohibition on the sale of contraceptives would be tantamount to a prohibition on their use, so a prohibition on compensation for surrogate motherhood is equivalent to a prohibition of the practice.

Any state concern over "commercialization," then, must be addressed to the particular abuses to which payments in connection with adoption may lend themselves. The underlying danger is that "the welfare of the baby and the natural mother, as well as the fitness of the adoptive parents, are subordinated to the profit motive of the black marketeer." But some adoption contracts are in the best interests of the child, and the evils of the black market are attenuated or absent in the surrogate mother situation where, as in the ordinary family situation, the would-be parents decide upon and arrange for the birth of the child they desire.

The argument has been made that reliance on the right of privacy to justify surrogate motherhood contracts is misplaced because there is no fundamental right to adopt a child; prospective adoptive parents cannot invoke the state's machinery for adoption while rejecting some of the conditions which the state imposes on adoption. It was apparently an argument along these lines which a Michigan judge found persuasive when he rejected privacy objections to the Michigan anti-black market statute as applied to surrogate motherhood contracts.

It is true that adoption, which was unknown at common law, is purely statutory. Ordinarily, adoption statutes must be strictly complied with in order to consummate a valid adoption. Nonetheless, the argument misses the point that, whether or not the state is obliged to authorize adoption, once it has done so, its activity in that area is subject to constitutional limitations. Thus a state is not constitutionally compelled to provide for appeals in criminal cases, but if it does so, due process and equal protection forbid the state from requiring indigent appellants to pay for transcripts if they cannot afford to do so. A state need not maintain public schools and may allow them to be closed, but not if the object is to circumvent a racial desegregation order. A city may prohibit the posting of flyers on utility poles, but if it opens the forum by allowing any such use of utility poles it cannot condition such use on the prior permission of city officials unguided by explicit and nondiscriminatory standards.

Where the state monopolizes the means of implementing certain fundamental decisions protected by the right of privacy, it may not impose conditions which effectively exclude some individuals from resorting to the only means provided. In *Boddie v. Connecticut* the Supreme Court held that as a matter of due process a state cannot constitutionally impose court fees and costs on indigents which restrict their access to the courts for the purpose of seeking a divorce. Due process is implicated because resort to state courts is the only avenue to dissolution of a marriage. A statute may be held constitutionally invalid as applied when it operates to deprive an individual of a protected right, even if its general validity as a legitimate exercise of state power is beyond question.

The right to go to court "is the exclusive precondition to the adjudication of a fundamental human relationship. The requirement that these appellants resort to the judicial process is entirely a state-created matter." The holding in *Boddie* with respect to divorce is equally valid with respect to adoption. Once a state provides for divorce or adoption, the procedures to be followed and the conditions to be complied with are subject to constitutional limitations. Adoption, like divorce, is a method of effectuating basic decisions about family affiliation—a method monopolized by the state. The state's general authority to impose fees on divorce petitioners or prohibit payment for consent to adoption may be well established, but if the *application* of these conditions effectively prevents particular classes of people from exercising their familial privacy rights, then as to those classes the requirements are unconstitutional. It is irrelevant that the state is not to blame for the sterility of certain married women who desire children, just as it is irrelevant that the state is not to blame for the poverty of certain married persons who desire a divorce. The point is that the state has provided the only means to implement their respective marital decisions. Consequently the state cannot enforce requirements which in practice prevent access to a state-created and state-monopolized procedure.

The right of privacy is the constitutionally protected interest most obviously implicated by anti-black market legislation, but other constitutional questions may also be raised. The disparate treatment accorded payment of "surrogate fathers" involved in AID, as opposed to surrogate mothers, is a type of discrimination by sex which may violate the equal protection clause. The uncertainty as to whether, in fact, payments to a surrogate mother for various purposes—the use of her reproductive capacity, foregone income, medical expenses, consent to adoption, *etc.*— are forbidden, may also render such statutes void for vagueness as applied to surrogate motherhood. Enactments, like the Michigan statute, which prohibit paying consideration in connection with adoption except for charges and fees approved by the court—without specifying the criteria for approval or disapproval—may well constitute a denial of due process in that no standards are provided to guide the decision-maker's discretion. Insofar as surrogate motherhood arrangements among consenting and competent adults represent an exercise of personal liberty which is not detrimental to third parties or society, state interference with these arrangements on moralistic grounds may be unconstitutional simply because it exceeds the scope and proper purposes of state action under our constitutional system. As surrogate motherhood becomes more common, inevitably these and other constitutional questions will have to be litigated unless the statutory and decisional law is modified to accommodate the undue features of the surrogate motherhood situation.

V. ENFORCING THE SURROGATE MOTHERHOOD CONTRACT

Even if surrogate motherhood contracts were lawful and enforceable, the unique features of the arrangement would still present difficulties in the event of a breach. If the biological father and his wife breached the contract, as by refusing to pay the agreed-upon compensation or adopt the child, the surrogate mother could simply give the child up for adoption and sue the married couple for the compensation due. Such a turn of events should be rare, since couples entering into such arrangements are likely to be motivated by a strong desire for a child, especially if it is the offspring of the husband. In any event, their breach presents no novel legal problems.

Breach by the surrogate mother, in contrast, poses a difficult problem in finding an appropriate remedy. If she breaches by refusing to submit to artificial insemination, the married couple could probably sue for recovery of any compensation already advanced to her, but beyond that their remedies are uncertain. Money damages (apart from restitution of money advanced) would almost certainly be inadequate: the couple's out-of-pocket pecuniary losses should be recoverable but are likely to be small. The real loss suffered is the distress and disappointment of the frustration of their parental aspirations, but damages for emotional distress are usually not recoverable in contract actions. An alternative possibility is an action in tort for intentional or negligent infliction of mental or emotional distress. However, even if such a suit is successfully brought, it may well be that the defendant cannot satisfy a substantial money judgment: rich women are unlikely to contract to become surrogate mothers.

The alternative remedy, available where money damages are not an adequate remedy, is specific performance, *i.e.,* an order that the breaching party perform as she has promised. As regards a pre-birth breach, however, it is very unlikely that court would order a woman to submit or resubmit to artificial insemination, to become pregnant and to give birth to a child. The general rule is that courts will not order specific performance of contracts for personal services because of the impracticality of assuring satisfactory performance. In this situation, enforcement problems would be monumental. The reluctant surrogate might surreptitiously practice contraception, or engage in activities detrimental to the health of the fetus, or even arrange to be impregnated by someone other than the husband of the sterile wife. Clearly the contract could not be enforced short of taking the surrogate into custody. In case of pre-birth breach by the surrogate mother there is, unfortunately, little that can be done.

The situation is not necessarily the same where the surrogate mother, having given birth, decides to keep the child and refuses or retracts her consent to its adoption. Such cases have already occurred. In these circumstances specific performance should be feasible, since all that is needed is to order the surrogate to consent to the adoption and deliver the child into the custody of its other biological parent. If the controversy arises without regard to a contract, it reduces to a dispute between the two biological parents of an illegitimate child. Currently most courts look with disfavor upon prenatal releases of parental rights or consent to adoption by the expectant mother, one area where reform is imperative to accommodate the special circumstances of surrogate motherhood. Such a release and consent, given in the context of a deliberate pre-pregnancy decision to bear a child for another, should be not only lawful but irrevocable. Present law regarding revocation of consent varies widely from state to state, but the tendency in most jurisdictions "is to hold that the natural parent may not withdraw his consent to the adoption without careful scrutiny by the courts." Because of the infant's tendency to form psychological ties with the parent who has custody, prompt resolution of the custody dispute is a matter of urgency. It would be desirable if, upon a prima facie showing of a surrogate motherhood contract containing consent to adoption, custody of the child were transferred to the biological father pending a final custody decision made on an expedited basis.

Since apparently no surrogate motherhood contract has ever been litigated, a discussion of enforcement problems can only be tentative and to some extent speculative. But it does appear that surrogate motherhood, like AID, calls for comprehensive legislation which treats the arrangement as a totality. Focusing on isolated facets of the contract tends to distort its real nature and obscure its human dimensions. The illegality of surrogate motherhood contracts does not reflect any conscious policy decision to outlaw the practice: the illegality is the unintended consequence of decisions made in dealing with altogether different situations.

VI. CONCLUSION

Surrogate motherhood is growing in popularity because it meets the urgently felt needs of those who resort to it better than any of the alternatives as they see them. As a consensual arrangement it is as worthy of legal protection as many others which, formerly suspect, are now taken for granted. Subject to reasonable regulation, it deserves to take a place among the growing array of methods available to individuals for the ordering of their own marital and reproductive lives. Doctrines fitted to other circumstances should not be allowed to bar the legality or enforcement of surrogate motherhood agreements.

For a copy of "Legal Problems of Surrogate Motherhood," complete with all footnotes and sources, please contact:

Mr. Noel P. Keane
Attorney at Law
1129 Parklane Towers East
Dearborn, Michigan   48126

APPENDIX B

JANE DOE, JOHN DOE and MARY ROE,
JANE X., JOHN X., JANE Y., JOHN Y.,
JANE Z., and JOHN Z., pseudonyms for
actual persons,

Plaintiffs,

-vs-   C.A. #78 815 531 CZ

FRANK J. KELLEY, Attorney General
for the State of Michigan, and
WILLIAM L. CAHALAN, Wayne County
Prosecutor,

Defendants.

AMENDED COMPLAINT FOR DECLARATORY JUDGMENT
ADDING PARTY—PLAINTIFFS

NOW COME the above named Plaintiffs by and through their attorneys, NOEL P. KEANE and ROBERT S. HARRISON, and file their Amended Complaint for Declaratory Judgment herein as granted by Stipulation and Order of this Court, and state as follows:

1. That this is an action for declaratory relief under Michigan General Court Rule 521, and is brought for the purpose of determining a question of actual controversy between the respective parties.

2. That Plaintiffs, JANE DOE and JOHN DOE, are pseudonyms for actual persons, who are husband and wife and who reside in the County of Wayne, State of Michigan.

3. That Plaintiff, MARY ROE, is a pseudonym for an actual person, who resides in the County of Wayne, State of Michigan.

4. That Plaintiffs, JANE X. and JOHN X. are pseudonyms for actual persons, who are husband and wife and who reside in the County of Washtenaw, State of Michigan.

5. That Plaintiffs, JANE Y. and JOHN Y. are pseudonyms for actual persons, who are husband and wife and who reside in the County of Wayne, State of Michigan.

6. That Plaintiffs, JANE Z. and JOHN Z. are pseudonyms for actual persons, who are husband and wife and who reside in the County of Genesee, State of Michigan.

7. That Plaintiffs desire to maintain their privacy in this matter and disclosure of their identity is not necessary for the adjudication of this action.

8. That Defendant, FRANK J. KELLEY, is the Attorney General for the State of Michigan and is charged with the duty and responsibility of enforcing the laws of the State of Michigan.

10. That JANE DOE and JOHN DOE are both desirous of having children.

11. That JANE DOE is biologically incapable of bearing children.

12. That JANE DOE and JOHN DOE wish to have a child biologically related to JOHN DOE.

13. That in furtherance of the aforesaid desire, JANE DOE and JOHN DOE have contemplated and do intend to enter into the following

arrangement with Plaintiff, MARY ROE, provided this Honorable Court declare same to be lawful:

(a) That JANE DOE and JOHN DOE will pay MARY ROE a sum of money in consideration for her promise to bear and deliver JOHN DOE's child by means of artificial insemination;

(b) That a licensed physician will conduct the artificial insemination process;

(c) That prior to the delivery of said child, JOHN DOE will file a Notice of Intent to Claim Paternity;

(d) That at the time the child is born, JOHN DOE will formally acknowledge the paternity of said child;

(e) That MARY ROE will acknowledge that JOHN DOE is the father of said child;

(f) That MARY ROE will consent to the adoption of said child by JOHN DOE and JANE DOE.

14. That JANE X. and JOHN X. are both desirous of having children.

15. That JANE X. is biologically prevented from having children due to medical reasons.

16. That JANE X. and JOHN X. wish to have a child biologically related to JOHN X.

17. That in furtherance of the aforesaid desire, JANE X. and JOHN X. have contemplated and do intend to enter into the following arrangement with a woman suitable to Plaintiffs, JANE X. and JOHN X., for conceiving, carrying and delivering a child, provided this Honorable Court declares same to be lawful:

(a) That JANE X. and JOHN X. will pay a suitable woman a sum of money in consideration for her promise to bear and deliver JOHN X's child by means of artificial insemination;

(b) That a licensed physician will conduct the artificial insemination process;

(c) That prior to the delivery of said child, JOHN X. will file a Notice of Intent to Claim Paternity;

(d) That at the time the child is born, JOHN X. will formally acknowledge the paternity of said child;

(e) That the woman with whom the agreement is reached will acknowledge that JOHN X. is the father of said child;

(f) That the woman with whom the agreement is reached will consent to the adoption of said chid by JOHN X. and JANE X.

18. That JANE Y. and JOHN Y. are both desirous of having children.

19. That JANE Y. is biologically prevented from having children due to medical reasons.

20. That JANE Y. and JOHN Y. wish to have a child biologically related to JOHN Y.

21. That, provided this Honorable Court declares same to be lawful, JANE Y. and JOHN Y. would enter into an arrangement with a suitable woman and would follow the same procedures outlined in Paragraph Seventeen (17) (a) through (f).

22. That JANE Z. and JOHN Z. are both desirous of having children.

23. That JANE Z. is biologically prevented from having children due to medical reasons.

24. That JANE Z. and JOHN Z. wish to have a child biologically related to JOHN Z.

25. That, provided this Honorable Court declares same to be lawful, JANE Z. and JOHN Z. would enter into an arrangement with a suitable woman and would follow the same procedure outlined in Paragraph Seventeen (17) (a) through (f).

26. That the State of Michigan has enacted a law, being MCLA 710.54, which purports to make it unlawful to offer, give, or receive any money or other consideration or thing of value in connection with the placing of a child for adoption or a release or consent regarding same.

27. That the first violation of the aforesaid statute is punishable as a misdemeanor, and any succeeding violation is a felony by virtue of MCLA 710.69.

28. That as against the provisions of said statute, Plaintiff, MARY ROE, here asserts a constitutional right as secured and protected by the Fourteenth Amendment to the United States Constitution to be free from unwarranted governmental intrusion into matters so fundamentally affecting her person as the decision whether to bear or beget a child.

29. That Plaintiffs, JANE DOE, JOHN DOE, JANE X., JOHN X., JANE Y., JOHN Y., JANE Z., and JOHN Z., have a constitutionally protected right of privacy associated with their family lives as secured by

the First and Fourteenth Amendments to the United States Constitution and the Michigan Constitution of 1963.

30. That against the aforesaid statute your Plaintiffs further assert the right to freely enter into agreements to further their rights to privacy and autonomy in their family lives in the absence of a compelling State interest.

31. That there exists no State interest sufficiently compelling for the State to prohibit the giving, offering, or receiving of any money or other consideration regarding the aforesaid arrangement.

32. That MCLA 710.54 by its terms has a chilling effect upon Plaintiffs exercise of their constitutional rights and causes them to act at their peril under threat of criminal punishment by the State of Michigan.

33. That in view of the aforesaid statute, Counsel for Plaintiffs requested the Honorable James H. Lincoln, Judge of the Wayne County Juvenile Court, to respond to the following questions:

(a) Whether a child born as a result of the aforementioned contractual arrangement would be so related to the adopting parents that they could file with the Court for adoption without going to an adoption agency?

(b) Whether the adopting parents could pay the woman for having the child, or for consenting to its adoption?

(c) Whether the adopting parents could pay the following expenses: pregnancy, delivery, medical costs, hospital costs, doctor fees, transportation fees, and attorney fees?

34. That by letter dated March 2, 1977, said Order being attached hereto as Exhibit "A", the Honorable James H. Lincoln responded to Plaintiffs' request in pertinent part, as follows:

(a) That because it makes no difference what means is used to impregnate a woman, and the adopting father is the person that produced the sperm that impregnated the woman, the adopting parents could file with the Court for adoption without going to an adoption agency;

(b) That the law "clearly forbids" the adopting parents from paying the woman (surrogate mother), for having the child, or for consenting to its adoption. (See MCLA 710.54 supra);

(c) That the law permits the adopting aprents to pay for the expenses of pregnancy, delivery, medical costs, hospital costs, doctor fees, transportation costs to the hospital and attorney fees, and that, Judge Lincoln "personally" would not object to expenses actually incurred such as transportation to hospital, etc., but that he would not approve the giving of gifts, or the payment of lost wages.

35. That because of the existence of the aforesaid statute, and its interpretation by the Honorable James H. Lincoln, there presently exists an actual case or controversy between the Plaintiffs and the State of Michigan, to-wit: The State of Michigan purports to prohibit under threat of punishment the giving, offering or receiving of any thing of value in connection with the placing of a child for adoption cr release or consent regarding same, and Plaintiffs are asserting a fundamental right to do so free from State interference and seek to adjudicate their rights as against the State of Michigan in order to guide their future conduct before said conduct ripens into violations of the law.

36. That Plaintiffs are uncertain of the legal consequences of their proposed agreements and are fearful that the consummation of same will subject them to criminal liability under the laws of the State of Michigan.

WHEREFORE, Plaintiffs pray this Honorable Court enter its Order declaring:

(A) That the private family matters involved herein are *fundamental rights* protected and secured by the United States Constitution and the Michigan Constitution of 1963;

(B) That MCLA 710.54 infringes upon the Plaintiffs exercise of these fundamental rights and is, therefore, *unconstitutionally overbroad* on its face;

(C) That the Defendants be permanently enjoined from enforcing MCLA 710.54 as it infringes upon the Plaintiffs exercise of their constitutional rights.

/s/ Noel P. Keane
——————————————————
NOEL P. KEANE (P15776)
Attorney for Plaintiffs
1129 Parklane Towers East
Dearborn, MI 48126
336-9290

/s/ Robert S. Harrison
——————————————————
ROBERT S. HARRISON (P14691)
Attorney for Plaintiffs
18860 West Ten Mile Road
Suite #200
Southfield, MI 48075
424-8000

Affidavit

STATE OF MICHIGAN)
)   SS
COUNTY OF WAYNE)

NOEL P. KEANE, being first duly sworn, deposes and says that he is one of the attorneys representing the Plaintiffs named in the within cause and knows and understands the contents of the Amended Complaint for Declaratory Judgment and that same is true of matters within his own knowledge, excepting as to those matters as are therein stated upon information and belief, and as to those matters, he believes them to be true.

/s/ Noel P. Keane
——————————————————
NOEL P. KEANE

Subscribed and sworn to before me,
this *26th day of October, 1978.*

/s/ L. Michael Renfro
_____
L. MICHAEL RENFRO, Notary Public,
Wayne Co. Michigan
My commission expires: 8/03/82

Affidavit

STATE OF MICHIGAN)
) SS
COUNTY OF WAYNE)

ROBERT S. HARRISON, being first duly sworn, deposes and says that he is one of the attorneys representing the plaintiffs named in the within cause and knows and understands the contents of the Amended Complaint for Declaratory Judgment and that same is true of matters within his own knowledge, excepting as to those matters as are therein stated upon information and belief, and as to those matters, he believes them to be true.

                 /s/ Robert S. Harrison
               _____
               ROBERT S. HARRISON

Subscribed and sworn to before me,
this 26th day of October, 1978.

/s/ L. Michael Renfro
_____
L. MICHAEL RENFRO
Notary Public, Wayne County, Michigan
My commission expires: 8/03/82

March 2, 1977

To: Miss Margaret Pfeiffer

From: Judge James H. Lincoln

Re: Artificial insemination case.
Mr. Noel Keane, attorney.

Here is the situation.

We were requested by Mr. Keane to respond to the following
questions:

First: A married couple suitable for adoptive parents wish to adopt
a child. The wife cannot have a child. The husband would be
used to artificially inseminate a non-related woman.

Would the child born as a result of this arrangement be
considered as related to the adopting parents so that the
adopting parents could file with the Court for adoption
without going to an adoption agency?

Answer: My answer is yes! After considerable study and consultation I
would hold that it makes no difference what means is used to
impregnate a woman. The father is the person who produced
the sperm that impregnated the woman. He could even be
held liable for support.

Second: Could the adopting parents pay the woman for having the
child or consenting to its adoption?

Answer: No! The law clearly forbids this.

Third: Could the adopting parents pay the expenses of the
pregnancy delivery—medical—hospital—doctor—
transportation to hospital—attorney fees, etc.?

Answer: Yes! The law permits this and it has been the custom of all
Michigan Probate Court to allow the payment of such
expenditures.

I personally would not be concerned with permitting payment of reasonable costs of transportation to hospital, etc., etc. I do not care about the manner of transportation as long as the expense was actually incurred.

Of course I would not approve giving a car, etc. That could be regarded as paying the woman. Nor would I permit payment of lost wages.

Mr. Keane wants me to approve expenditures as they arise.

Comment:

I will probably not be the Judge who handles this adoption. The petition may not be filed until after the child is born—this will be early in 1978.

The Judge who handles the case will make all the rulings and will determine what expenses to approve or disapprove.

All that I can do is to give my opinion on all of these matters.

My opinion is not binding on the Judge who will hear the petition.

I appreciate the fact that Mr. Keane wishes to clear all matters for his clients prior to proceeding and I wish I were in a position to give him something other than what I would do if I were handling the petition.

JAMES H. LINCOLN
EXECUTIVE JUDGE
JUVENILE DIVISION

JHL:gm

APPENDIX C

JANE DOE, JOHN DOE, and MARY ROE,
JANE X., JOHN X., JANE Y., JOHN Y.,
JANE Z., and JOHN Z., pseudonyms
for actual persons,

HONORABLE ROMAN S.
GRIBBS   P-14369

Plaintiffs

CIVIL ACTION
-vs-   NO. 78 815 531 CZ

FRANK J. KELLEY, Attorney General
for the State of Michigan, and
WILLIAM L. CAHALAN, Wayne County
Prosecutor,

Defendants.

_____

OPINION DENYING PLAINTIFFS' MOTION
FOR SUMMARY JUDGMENT AND GRANTING
DEFENDANTS' MOTION FOR SUMMARY JUDGMENT

STATE OF MICHIGAN
IN THE CIRCUIT COURT
FOR THE COUNTY OF WAYNE

JANE DOE, JOHN DOE, and MARY ROE,
JANE X., JOHN X., JANE Y., JOHN Y.,
JANE Z., and JOHN Z., pseudonyms
for actual persons,   HONORABLE ROMAN S.
                                             GRIBBS   P-14369
                       Plaintiffs,
                                             CIVIL ACTION
        -vs-   NO. 78 815 531 CZ

FRANK J. KELLEY, Attorney General
for the State of Michigan, and
WILLIAM L. CAHALAN, Wayne County
Prosecutor,

                       Defendants.

_____

OPINION DENYING PLAINTIFFS' MOTION FOR
SUMMARY JUDGMENT AND GRANTING DEFENDANTS'
MOTION FOR SUMMARY JUDGMENT

On May 15, 1978, plaintiffs filed a Complaint for Declaratory Judgment in the Wayne County Circuit Court. Motions for summary judgment are brought by plaintiffs and defendants pursuant to GCR 1963, 117.2(3).

Facts

The facts in this case are not in dispute. Plaintiffs, Jane and John Doe, are husband and wife. Jane Doe is biologically incapable of bearing children. The Does are joined in their complaint by Mary Roe.

The Does propose to have Mary Roe conceive a child with John Doe through artificial insemination administered by a physician. After birth, the Does would take custody of the child once he or she leaves the hospital; and, Mary Roe would consent to the adoption of the child by the Does. Mary Roe would receive $5,000, plus medical expenses, from the Does for surrendering custody of her child to the Does and for consenting to the adoption. In addition, Mary Roe will be covered by sick leave, pregnancy disability insurance, and medical insurance from her employment while she is off work having the child and recuperating from the delivery.

The statutes whose constitutionality is involved in this matter are MCLA 710.54 and MCLA 710.69. The former provides, as follows

"Sec. 54. (1) Except for charges and fees approved by the court, a person shall not offer, give, or receive any money or other consideration or thing of value in connection with any of the following:
"(a) The placing of a child for adoption.
"(b) The registration recording or communication of the existence of a child available for adoption or the existence of a person interested in adopting a child.
"(c) A release.
"(d) A consent.
"(e) A petition.
"2. Before the entry of the final order of adoption the petitioner shall file with the court a sworn statement describing money or other consideration or thing of value paid to or exchanged by any party in the adoption proceeding, including anyone consenting to the adoption or adopting the adoptee, any relative of a party or of the adoptee, any physician, attorney, social worker or member of the clergy, and any other person, corporation, association, or other organization. The court shall approve or disapprove fees and expenses. Acceptance or retention of amounts in excess of those approved by the court constitutes a violation of this section.
"(3). To assure compliance with limitations imposed by this section, by section 14 of Act No. 116 or the Public Acts of 1973, being section 722.124 of the Michigan Compiled Laws, and by section 4 of Act No. 263 of the Public Acts of 1913, as amended, being section 331.404 of the Michigan Compiled Laws, the court may require sworn testimony

from persons who were involved in any way in informing, notifying, exchanging information, identifying, locating, assisting, or in any other way participating in the contracts or arrangements which, directly or indirectly, led to placement of the person for adoption."

MCLA 71069 provides:

"Sec. 69. A person who violates any of the provisions of sections 41 and 54 of this chapter shall, upon conviction, be guilty of a misdemeanor, and upon any subsequent conviction shall be guilty of a felony."

Plaintiffs' suit seeks to have these statutes declared unconstitutional by this Court and to enjoin defendants from prosecuting plaintiffs for proceeding with the plan outlined above.

Discussion

Plaintiffs' constitutional challenge is basically two-pronged. Plaintiffs first urge that MCLA 710.54 is void for vagueness. Second, that the arrangement proposed by plaintiffs is within the constitutional "right of privacy." Contained within that second contention are the propositions that the government does not have a compelling interest to invade that area of privacy and that the statute as drawn is not sufficiently narrow.

I.

This Court does not agree with plaintiffs' first contention that MCLA 710.54 is void for vagueness. Plaintiffs are correct in asserting that a statute is violative of due process if it proscribes conduct in terms so vague that a person of common intelligence must guess at the statute's meaning. *Connally v. General Construction Co.*, 269 US 385, 70 L Ed 322, 46 S Ct 126 (1926).

The dangers involved in the existence and enforcement of a vague statute are set forth by Mr. Justice Marshall in *Grayned v City of Rockford*, 408 US 104, 33 L Ed 2d 222, 92 S Ct 2294 (1972) as follows:

"It is a basic principle of due process that an enactment is void for vagueness if its prohibitions are not clearly defined. Vague laws offend several important values. First, because we assume that man is free to steer between lawful and unlawful conduct, we insist that laws give the person of ordinary intelligence a reasonable opportunity to know what is prohibited, so that he may act accordingly. Vague laws may trap the innocent by not providing fair warning. Second, if arbitrary and discriminatory enforcement is to be prevented, laws must provide explicit standards for those who apply them. A vague law impermissibly delegates basic policy matters to policemen, judges, and juries for resolution on an ad hoc and subjective basis, with the attendant dangers of arbitrary and discriminatory application. Third, but related, where a vague statute abuts upon sensitive areas of basic first amendment freedoms, it operates to inhibit the exercise of those freedoms. Uncertain meanings inevitably lead citizens to steer far wider of the unlawful zone ... than if the boundaries of the forbidden areas were clearly marked."

In *Grayned*, Justice Marshall also enunciated a problem involved in all statutes, even those not void for vagueness. "Condemned to the use of words, we can never expect mathematical certainty from our language."

In a footnote to *Grayned*, the Court cited *American Communications Assoc. v Doreds*, 39 US 382, 94 L Ed 925, 70 S Ct 674 (1950), in which the Court stated:

"There is little doubt that imagination can conjure up hypothetical cases in which the meaning of these terms will be in nice question. The applicable standard, however, is not one of wholly consistent academic definition of abstract terms. It is, rather, the practical criterion of fair notice to those to whom the statute is directed. The particular context is all important."

The statute in the instant case is as specific is as necessary to give fair notice to those to whom the statute is directed.

Plaintiffs question the explicitness of the phrase "or other consideration or thing of value" used in the statute. Even standing alone, this phrase is sufficiently specific to give fair notice to persons of reasonable intelligence what things may not be given in connection with the acts or items listed in (a)-(e) of MCLA 710.54(1). The meaning of that phrase i even more specifically defined when it follows the only specific item listed, money. The well-established principle of *ejusdem generis* is pertinent to plaintiffs' contention of statutory vagueness. As the Court stated in *diLeo v. Greenfield*, 541 F 2d 949 (1976):

"Where general terms in a statute follow an enumeration of terms with specific meaning, the general terms can be expected to apply to matters similar to those specified." (Citations omitted)

It is not necessary that the statute list all conceivable items of value to be constitutionally specific.

II.

Plaintiffs' second basis for urging the constitutional infirmity of the statutes is that they invade plaintiffs' constitutional right of privacy and further that the statutes do not comply with the requirements of compelling state interest and the narrow drafting required of statutes regulating an act within the right of privacy. Before addressing the later two points, it must first be determined that plantiffs' proposed agreement is within the constitutional right of privacy.

That there exists a fundamental right of privacy is well established. The origins of this right were set forth in *Roe v. Wade,* 410 US 113, 35 L Ed 2d 147, 93 S Ct 705 (1973), as follows:

"The Constitution does not explicitly mention any right of privacy. In a line of decisions, however, going back perhaps as far as *Union Pacific R. Co. v. Botsford,* 141 US 250, 251, 35 L Ed 734, 11 S Ct 1000 (1891), the Court has recognized that a right of personal privacy, or a guarantee of certain areas or zones of privacy, does exist under the Constitution. In varying contexts, the Court or individual Justices have, indeed, found at least the roots of that right in the First Amendment; in the Fourth and Fifth Amendments, in the penumbras of the Bill of Rights; or in the concept of liberty guaranteed by the first section of the Fourteenth Amendment." (Citations omitted)

In stating that only "fundamental" rights are included within the right of privacy, *Roe* acknowledged that activities relating to marriage, procreation, contraception, family relationships and child rearing and education are included in the guarantee of personal privacy.

The right which plaintiffs assert is specific, narrow and is not of the same personal nature that the constitutional right of privacy protects. Plaintiffs only attack the sections of the Michigan Adoption Code that prohibits the exchange of money or other valuable consideration. Although plaintiffs seek to exclude governmental interference with reference to a portion of the adoption statutes, they do not want to exclude the government altogether. They wish to avail themselves of other portions of the Michigan Adoption Code in order to effect a legal adoption. Plaintiffs intend to utilize other protective provisions of the adoption law; i.e., total control of the child's welfare as legal parents, preserving the rights of inheritance of the child, etc. The right to adopt a child based upon the payment of $5,000 is not a fundamental personal right and reasonable regulations controlling adoption proceedings that prohibit the exchange of money (other than charges and fees approved by the Court) are not consitutionally infirm.

It is this Court's opinion that a contract to use the statutory authority of the Probate Court to effect the *adoption* of a child wherein such contract provides for valuable compensation, is not deserving of, nor is it within the constitutional protection of the right of privacy as defined by the many cases of the United States Supreme Court.

III.

Although the foregoing makes further discussion unnecessary, this Court will assume, *arguendo,* that the constitutional right of privacy does apply to the plaintiffs and proceed to the ancillary issues.

First, even if the constitutional right of privacy is applicable, such right is not absolute. It must be considered against important state interests in regulation. *Roe v. Wade,* supra. In determining the constitutionality of regulations, the *Roe* Court set forth the following test:

"Where certain 'fundamental rights' are involved, the Court has held that regulation limiting these rights may be justified only by a 'compelling state interest,' and that legislative enactments must be narrowly drawn to express only the legitimate state interests at stake."(Citations omitted)

The State's interest expressed in the statutes at issue here is to prevent commercialism from affecting a mother's decision to execute a consent to the adoption of her child. Although the case is distinguishable on the facts from the present case, the statement of the general rule by the Supreme Court of Kansas in *In re Shirk's Estate,* 350 P 2d 1 (1960), is applicable here.

"Consequently, this controversy resolves itself down to the question whether the contract with respect to the mother's rights violated public policy. It is fundamental that parents may not barter or sell their children nor may they demand pecuniary gain as the price of consent to adoptions. This is so inherent in the fabric of American law that citation of authority is unnecessary."

"Baby bartering" is against the public policy of this State and the State's interest in preventing such conduct is sufficiently compelling and meets the test set forth in *Roe.*

Mercenary considerations used to create a parent-child relationship and its impact upon the family unit strikes at the very foundation of human society and is patently and necessarily injurious to the community.

It is a fundamental principle that children should not and cannot be bought and sold. The sale of children is illegal in all states. The brief of the Attorney General cites this elementary rule in 67A CJS *Parent and Child,* §16, p 201-202, as follows:

"Parents have no property rights, in the ordinary sense of that term, in or to their minor children, and, accordingly, a parent's right of control or custody of a minor child is not a property right which may be bargained, sold or otherwise disposed of."(Footnotes omitted)

The leading and recognized authority on Contracts, Professor Samuel Williston, writes that bartering for a child is and has been against public policy. He states in 15 *Williston on Contracts,* 3rd Edition, Section 1744A, p 88:

> "The sovereign has an interest in a minor child held superior even to that of the parent: hence, there is a public policy against the custody of such a child becoming a subject of barter." (Footnote omitted)

The Attorney General cogently argues that contracts for "surrogate gestation" are against public policy. He quotes the Executive Director of the Program in Law, Science and Medicine in Yale Law School, who stated:

> "In any case, the sale of children is illegal in all states; therefore, any contract by which a host-mother is paid a fee in excess of expenses to gestate the unborn child is likely to be held unenforceable as against public policy. That being the case, the 'foster' or gestating mother would presumably be considered by most courts the natural mother of the child since she and not the donor-mother was willing to go through the inconvenience, discomfort, and dangers of pregnancy and childbirth.

> "It is highly unlikely that a judge, faced with a conflict between two women, one of whom has delivered the child and the other of whom 'should' have done so by normal means but who was too busy or disinterested, would resolve the issue of which is the true mother in any way other than by awarding parental status to the host-mother, contracts to the contrary notwithstanding.

> "Second, by statute in many states any adoption release executed by the natural mother *before* the birth of a child is invalid. Even in those states that do not declare prenatal surrenders to be absolutely void, courts appear to take a dim view of the validity of an adoption release signed prior to the birth of the child." Holder, *Legal Issues in Pediatrics and Adolescent Medicine* (John Wiley & Sons, 1977) pp 7, 8.

The evils attendant to the mix of lucre and the adoption process are self-evident and the temptations of dealing in "money market babies" exist whether the parties be strangers or friends. The statute seeks to prevent a money market for the adoption of babies. The defendant prosecuting attorney concedes that the plaintiff natural mother (Roe) and the plaintiff couple (Doe) are free to "conceive a child, bear it, and raise it as they agree among themselves because these acts are guaranteed by the right to privacy." The defendant prosecuting attorney argues perceptively when he asks: How much money will it take for a particular mother's will to be overborne, and when does her decision turn from "voluntary" to "involuntary."

In their brief and in oral argument plaintiffs vigorously argue that they are in this Court motivated by good will and with the best of intentions seek the Court's approval of their proposed course of action. The prosecuting attorney pointedly responds as follows:

"Plaintiffs seek to convince this court that the 'surrogate' mother would [act] out of altruistic rather than pecuniary motives. If that were so, no monetary payment would be necessary because under MCLA 710.54 she can still be reimbursed for fees and expenses. What plaintiffs seek is to provide her with a sum of money ($5,000) over and above the reasonable expenses she has incurred. Even if some of this money goes for legitimate expenses unrecognized by MCLA 710.54, the fact remains that the primary purpose of this money is to encourage women to volunteer to be 'surrogate' mothers. Plaintiffs have initiated this lawsuit because few women would be willing to volunteer the use of their bodies for nine months if the only thing they gained was the joy of making someone else happy by letting that couple adopt and raise her child. Thus, contrary to plaintiffs' exhortations, in all but the rarest of situations, the money plaintiffs seek to pay the 'surrogate' mother is intended as an inducement for her to conceive a child she would not normally want to conceive, carry for nine months a child she would not normally want to carry, give birth to a child she would normally not want to give birth to and then, because of this monetary reward, relinquish her parental rights to a child that she bore."

The personal desires and intentions of plaintiffs are not in question, and their good faith is conceded. Nonetheless, public policy is established to guide all of the people of this State, of whatever intent.

A desire to change the established stated public policy that meets constitutional muster is properly addressed to the legislature and not to the courts.

IV.

As to the second part of the *Roe* test, it is the opinion of this Court that the statutes here in question are drawn sufficiently narrow so as to comply with the test. The statute must be drawn so as to express only the legitimate interest of the State and no other. If other interests, as well as the State's compelling interest, are regulated by the statute, then the statute must fall. Here the statute is aimed at preventing compensation as consideration involving an adoption proceeding.

Plaintiffs urge that their arrangement is not the type of action which the statute contemplated or intended to proscribe. The fact that this is not a contract among strangers, or that one of the adoptive parents would also be a natural parent, does not alter the fact that the action prohibited interjects compensation in an adoption proceeding; that money, beyond court-approved charges and fees, *must* be paid to the biological mother before the parties will strike an agreement.

The statute is clear in expressing the public policy of this State that *all* persons involved in offering, giving or receiving anything of value in connection with an adoption are controlled by the statutes proscriptions. Neither the relationship of persons involved nor the arrangements between the parties are an exception but clearly *all* such actions are proscribed.

Conclusion

For the above-stated reasons, it is the conclusion of this Court that MCLA 710.54 and 710.69 do not violate the provisions of the Constitution. In addition, it is clear that there exists no genuine issue as to any material fact. Accordingly, pursuant to GCR 1963, 117.2(3), plaintiffs' Motion for Summary Judgment must be DENIED and defendants' Motion for Summary Judgment must be GRANTED as a matter of law.

Pursuant to the provisions of GCR 1963, 522, counsel are to present a proposed judgment consistent with this opinion within ten days of this date.

ROMAN S. GRIBBS
Circuit Judge

A TRUE COPY
JAMES R. KILLEEN

BY _____
DEPUTY CLERK

DATED: January 28, 1980
Detroit, Michigan

Index